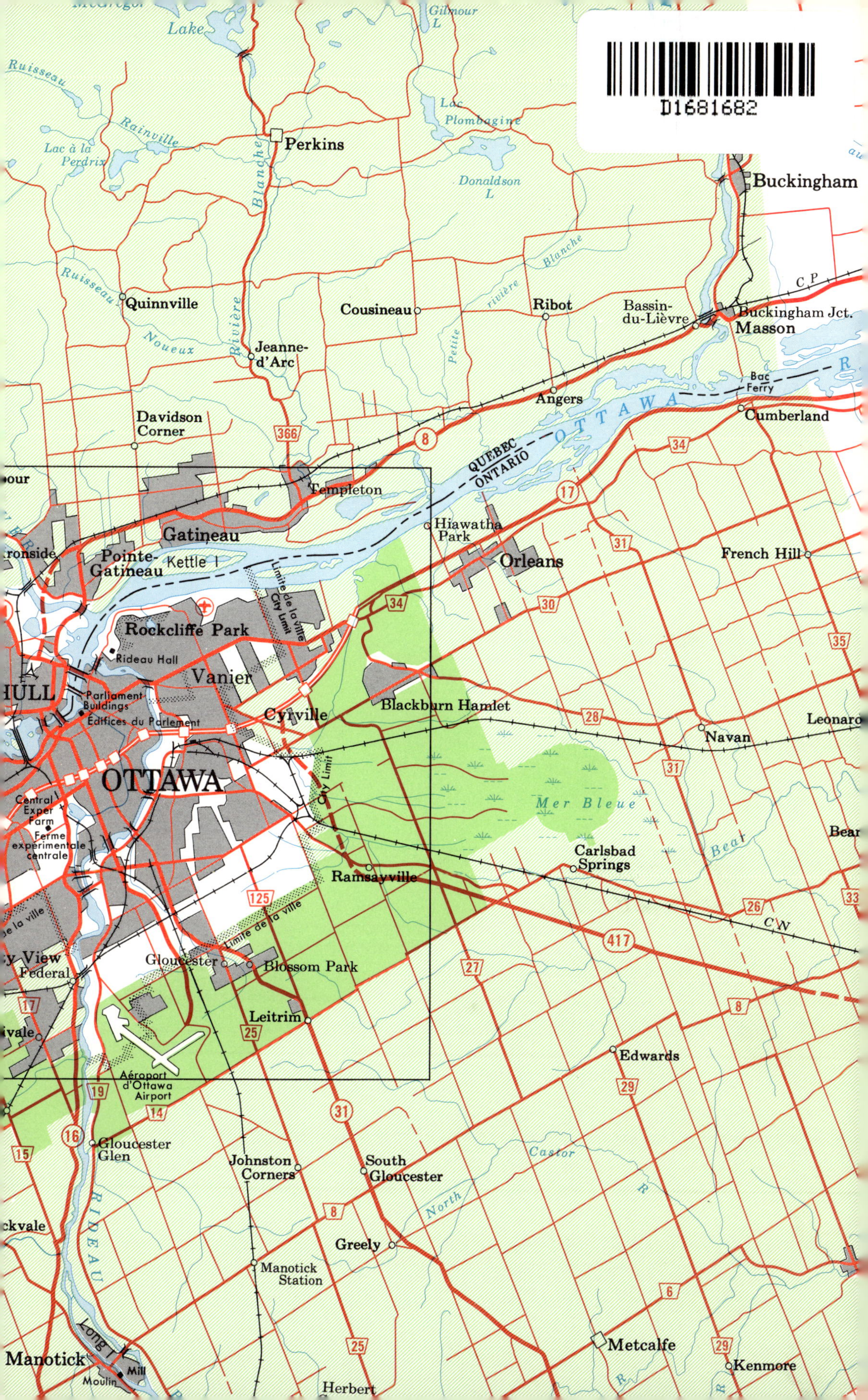

Lake
Ruisseau
Rainville
Lac à la Perdrix
Gilmour L
Lac Plombagine
Perkins
Blanche
Donaldson L
Buckingham
Ruisseau
Quinnville
Noueux
Rivière
Jeanne-d'Arc
Cousineau
Petite rivière Blanche
Ribot
Bassin-du-Lièvre
Buckingham Jct.
Masson
C P
Angers
Bac Ferry
Cumberland
OTTAWA R
Davidson Corner
366
8
34
QUEBEC
ONTARIO
Templeton
17
Gatineau
Hiawatha Park
Pointe-Gatineau
Kettle I
Orleans
31
French Hill
Limite de la ville
City Limit
34
30
Rockcliffe Park
35
Rideau Hall
Vanier
HULL
Parliament Buildings
Édifices du Parlement
Cyrville
Blackburn Hamlet
28
Navan
Leonard
OTTAWA
31
City Limit
Central Exper Farm
Ferme expérimentale centrale
Mer Bleue
Bear
Carlsbad Springs
Beat
Ramsayville
125
26
33
Limite de la ville
C N
417
Federal
Gloucester
Blossom Park
27
17
8
Leitrim
25
Edwards
Aéroport d'Ottawa Airport
19
29
14
31
16
Gloucester Glen
15
Castor
Johnston Corners
South Gloucester
R
North
8
RIDEAU
Greely
Manotick Station
6
25
Long I
Metcalfe
29
Manotick
Mill
Moulin
Kenmore
Herbert
R

THE CAPITAL OF CANADA:
HOW SHOULD IT BE GOVERNED?

A Special Study on the National Capital

by

Douglas H. Fullerton

VOLUME II

Ottawa, Canada
May, 1974

MINISTRY OF EDUCATION, ONTARIO
COMMUNICATION SERVICES BRANCH
13TH FLOOR, MOWAT BLOCK
TORONTO, ONTARIO M7A 1L3

© Crown Copyrights reserved

Available by mail from Information Canada, Ottawa,
and at the following Information Canada bookshops:

HALIFAX
1683 Barrington Street

MONTREAL
640 St. Catherine Street West

OTTAWA
171 Slater Street

TORONTO
221 Yonge Street

WINNIPEG
393 Portage Avenue

VANCOUVER
800 Granville Street

or through your bookseller

A deposit copy of this publication is also available
for reference in public libraries across Canada

Price $6.50   Catalogue No. CP 22-874/2

Price subject to change without notice

Information Canada
Ottawa, 1974

In this Volume II of the Special Study on the National Capital will be found documents, reports and special research papers which accompany and supplement the text of the Special Study.

Appendices

Appendix A—Documentation.. 227
Appendix B—Research Papers and Studies.. 287
Appendix C—"The Proposal for a Federal Territory for Canada's Capital", D.C. Rowat.. 387

Appendix A

Documentation

A-1—The National Capital Act, 1958, R.S.C. 1970 C. N-3 229

A-2—An Act Respecting the City of Ottawa, 1899, 62–63 Victoria, Chapter 10 (Creating the Ottawa Improvement Commission) 242

A-3—Harold Munro v. National Capital Commission. The Supreme Court of Canada, Judgement of Cartwright J. 247

A-4—The Commission on the Integrity of the Territory of Québec (Dorion Report). A summary of the postulates and the recommendations 255

A-5—Report of Royal Commission on Bilingualism and Biculturalism—Appendix III to Book V, The Federal Capital 260

A-6—The Special Joint Committee of the Senate and the House of Commons on the Constitution of Canada, Final Report—Chapter 16—The National Capital Area 279

A-7—Press Release of May 17th, 1973, announcing the Special Study on the National Capital, and public advertisements 282

Appendix A-1

The National Capital Act, 1958

CHAPTER N-3

An Act respecting the development and improvement of the National Capital Region

SHORT TITLE

1. This Act may be cited as the *National Capital Act*, 1958, c. 37, s. 1. `Short title`

INTERPRETATION

2. In this Act `Definitions`

"Chairman" means the Chairman of the Commission; `"Chairman" «président»`

"Commission" means the National Capital Commission referred to in section 3; `"Commission" «Commission»`

"department" means a department, division or branch of the Government of Canada, and includes any board, commission, corporation or other body being an agent of Her Majesty; `"department" «ministère»`

"Fund" means the National Capital Fund established by this Act; `"Fund" «Caisse»`

"Her Majesty" means Her Majesty in right of Canada; `"Her Majesty" «Sa Majesté»`

"highway" includes any street, road, lane, thoroughfare or driveway; `"highway" «voie...»`

"local municipality" means a municipality wholly or partly within the National Capital Region; `"local municipality" «municipalité...»`

"member" means a member of the Commission; `"member" «membre»`

229

"Minister"
«*Ministre*»
"Minister" means the Prime Minister of Canada or such other member of the Queen's Privy Council for Canada as is designated by the Governor in Council;

"National Capital Region"
«*région...*»
"National Capital Region" means the seat of the Government of Canada and its surrounding area, more particularly described in the schedule;

"property"
«*biens*»
"property" means real or personal property or any interest therein;

"property of the Commission"
«*biens de...*»
"property of the Commission" means property under the control and management of, or vested in the name of, the Commission;

"public lands"
«*terrains...*»
"public lands" means real property or any interest therein, under the control and management of a department;

"Vice-Chairman"
«*vice-...*»
"Vice-Chairman" means the Vice-Chairman of the Commission;

"work"
«*ouvrage*»
"work" means any work, structure or undertaking. 1958, c. 37, s. 2

CONSTITUTION OF COMMISSION

National Capital Commission

3. (1) There shall be a corporation, to be called the National Capital Commission, consisting of twenty members, each of whom shall be appointed by the Governor in Council to hold office during pleasure for a term not exceeding four years.

Chairman and Vice-Chairman

(2) The Governor in Council shall designate one of the members to be Chairman and one of the members to be Vice-Chairman.

Members

(3) The members, other than the Chairman and Vice-Chairman, shall be appointed as follows:

(*a*) at least one member from each of the ten provinces;

(*b*) at least two members from the city of Ottawa;

(*c*) at least one member from the city of Hull;

(*d*) at least one member from a local municipality in Ontario other than the city of Ottawa; and

(*e*) at least one member from a local municipality in Quebec other than the city of Hull.

Eligibility

(4) A member is eligible to be appointed from a province or municipality if, at the time of his appointment, he normally resides therein.

Re-appointment

(5) A person who has served two consecutive terms as a member, other than Chairman, is not, during the twelve months following the

completion of his second term, eligible to be re-appointed to the Commission in the capacity in which he so served.

(6) A vacancy in the membership of the Commission does not impair the right of the remainder to act. Vacancy

(7) The *Public Service Superannuation Act* does not apply to a member unless the Governor in Council otherwise directs. Members not contributors for super-annuation

(8) A member who is present at a meeting at which is discussed any matter in which he has, directly or indirectly, a pecuniary interest, shall declare his interest and shall refrain from casting a vote in respect of such matter. 1958, c. 37, s. 3. Interest of member

4. (1) The Commission is, for all purposes of this Act, an agent of Her Majesty, and its powers under this Act may be exercised only as an agent of Her Majesty. Commission agent of Her Majesty

(2) The Commission may, on behalf of Her Majesty, enter into contracts in the name of Her Majesty or in the name of the Commission. Contracts

(3) Property acquired by the Commission is the property of Her Majesty and title thereto may be vested in the name of Her Majesty or in the name of the Commission. Property

(4) Actions, suits or other legal proceedings in respect of any right or obligation acquired or incurred by the Commission on behalf of Her Majesty, whether in its name or in the name of Her Majesty, may be brought or taken by or against the Commission in the name of the Commission in any court that would have jurisdiction if the Commission were not an agent of Her Majesty, 1958. c. 37, s. 4. Proceedings

5. (1) The head office of the Commission shall be at the city of Ottawa. Head office

(2) The Commission shall meet at least three times a year in the city of Ottawa, and it may meet at such other times in the National Capital Region as the Commission deems necessary. 1958, c. 37, s. 5. Meetings

6. (1) The Chairman is the chief executive officer of the Commission. Chairman chief officer

(2) If the Chairman is absent or unable to act or the office is vacant, the Vice-Chairman has and may exercise all the powers and functions of the Chairman. Vice-Chairman to act

|Acting Chairman| (3) The Commission may authorize one of its members to act as Chairman for the time being in the event that the Chairman and Vice-Chairman are absent or unable to act or the offices are vacant. 1958. c, 37, s. 6.

|Salaries and remuneration| **7.** (1) The Chairman shall be paid a salary to be fixed by the Governor in Council, and the Governor in Council may authorize the payment of allowances or other remuneration to the Vice-Chairman and to any other member having special duties.

|Expenses| (2) Each member is entitled to be paid reasonable travelling and other expenses incurred by him in the performance of his duties. 1958, c. 37, s. 7.

OFFICERS AND EMPLOYEES

|General Manager| **8.** (1) The Governor in Council may appoint a General Manager to hold office during pleasure who shall be paid a salary to be fixed by the Governor in Council.

|Staff| (2) Subject to the plan of organization and terms and conditions of employment approved under subsection (3), the Commission may employ such officers and employees and such consultants and advisers as it deems necessary for the purpose of this Act and may fix their remuneration and terms and conditions of employment.

|Plan of organization| (3) The Governor in Council may approve a plan of organization for the establishment and classification of the continuing positions necessary for the proper functioning of the Commission and the establishment of rates of compensation for each class of position, and such other terms and conditions of employment as are considered desirable. 1958, c. 37, s. 8.

COMMITTEES

|Executive Committee| **9.** (1) There shall be an Executive Committee of the Commission consisting of the Chairman, the Vice-Chairman and three other members to be appointed by the Commission, of whom one at least shall be from the Province of Quebec.

|Powers| (2) The Executive Committee shall exercise such of the powers and functions of the Commission as are delegated to it by the Commission and shall submit at each meeting of the Commission minutes of its proceedings since the last preceding meeting of the Commission.

|Other committees| (3) The Commission may appoint a National Capital Planning Committee and such other committees as it considers necessary or desirable for the administration of this Act.

(4) Each member of the Executive Committee or other committee established under this section is entitled to be paid reasonable travelling and other expenses incurred by him in the performance of his duties. 1958, c. 37, s. 9.

<small>Expenses of committee members</small>

OBJECTS, PURPOSES AND POWERS

10. (1) The objects and purposes of the Commission are to prepare plans for and assist in the development, conservation and improvement of the National Capital Region in order that the nature and character of the seat of the Government of Canada may be in accordance with its national significance.

<small>Objects and purposes of Commission</small>

(2) The Commission may for the purposes of this Act,

<small>Powers</small>

(*a*) acquire, hold, administer or develop property;

(*b*) sell, grant, convey, lease or otherwise dispose of or make available to any person any property, subject to such conditions and limitations as it considers necessary or desirable;

(*c*) construct, maintain and operate parks, squares, highways, parkways, bridges, buildings and any other works;

(*d*) maintain and improve any property of the Commission, or any other property under the control and management of a department, at the request of the authority or Minister in charge thereof;

(*e*) cooperate or engage in joint projects with, or make grants to, local municipalities or other authorities for the improvement, development or maintenance of property;

(*f*) construct, maintain and operate, or grant concessions for the operation of, places of entertainment, amusement, recreation, refreshment, or other places of public interest or accommodation upon any property of the Commission;

(*g*) administer, preserve and maintain any historic place or historic museum;

(*h*) conduct investigations and researches in connection with the planning of the National Capital Region; and

(*i*) generally, do and authorize such things as are incidental or conducive to the attainment of the objects and purposes of the Commission and the exercise of its powers. 1958, c. 37, s. 10.

11. (1) The Commission shall, in accordance with general plans prepared under this Act, coordinate the development of public lands in the National Capital Region.

<small>Coordination of development</small>

Proposals submitted to Commission	(2) Proposals for the location, erection, alteration or extension of a building or other work by any person on public lands, or by or on behalf of a department, in the National Capital Region shall be referred to the Commission prior to the commencement of the work.
Approval of site, plans, etc.	(3) No building or other work shall be erected, altered or extended by or on behalf of a department in the National Capital Region unless the site, location and plans thereof have first been approved by the Commission.
Idem	(4) No person shall erect, alter or extend a building or other work on public lands in the National Capital Region unless the site, location and plans thereof have first been approved by the Commission.
Governor in Council may approve	(5) In any case where the Commission does not give its approval under this section the Governor in Council may give such approval.
Terms and conditions of approval	(6) Any approval given under this section may be subject to such terms and conditions as are considered desirable by the Commission or the Governor in Council, as the case may be, respecting the erection, alteration, extension or maintenance of the building or other work in relation to which the approval was given.
Interior alterations	(7) This section does not apply to interior alterations in a work or building. 1958, c. 37, s. 11.
Power to construct railway	**12.** (1) The Commission may construct in the National Capital Region, in accordance with plans prepared under this Act, a railway and related facilities.
Sale, lease, etc.	(2) The Commission may sell, convey or lease the railway and related facilities, or any portion thereof, to any railway company or enter into agreements with any railway company for the sole, joint or several use of such railway or facilities or portion thereof and for the maintenance by such company of such railway or facilities or portion thereof and the operation thereof.
Application of *Railway Act*	(3) The provisions of the *Railway Act*, with such modifications as circumstances require, are applicable to and in respect of the exercise of the powers conferred by this section, but nothing in this section shall be deemed to constitute the Commission a railway company except for the purpose of carrying out subsection (2). 1958, c. 37, s. 12.

EXPROPRIATION

National Capital Act 1958, s. 37	Section 13 is repealed and the following substituted therefor:
7 July 1970	"**13.** (1) Where in the opinion of the Commission the taking or acquisition of any land or interest therein by the Commission with-

out the consent of the owner is required for the purposes of this Act, the Commission shall so advise the appropriate Minister in relation to Part I of the *Expropriation Act*.

(2) For the purposes of the *Expropriation Act*, any land or interest therein that, in the opinion of the Minister mentioned in subsection (1), is required for the purposes of this Act shall be deemed to be land or an interest therein that, in his opinion, is required for a public work or other public purpose, and, in relation thereto, a reference to the Crown in that Act shall be construed as a reference to the Commission."

PROPERTY

14. Except with the approval of the Governor in Council, the Commission shall not {Restrictions on transactions}

(*a*) dispose of any real property for a consideration in excess of a value of ten thousand dollars;

(*b*) acquire any real property for a consideration in excess of a value of twenty-five thousand dollars; or

(*c*) enter into an agreement or lease enduring for a period in excess of five years. 1958, c. 37, s. 14.

15. (1) The Commission may pay grants to a local municipality not exceeding the taxes that might be levied by the municipality in respect of any real property of the Commission if the Commission were not an agent of Her Majesty. {Payments in lieu of taxes}

(2) Subsection (1) does not apply to parks or to squares, highways or parkways or to bridges or similar structures. {Exception}

(3) The Commission may pay grants to the appropriate authorities in respect of real property of the Commission situated in Gatineau Park not exceeding in any tax year the amounts estimated by the Commission to be sufficient to compensate such authorities for the loss of tax revenue during that tax year in respect of municipal and school taxes by reason of the acquisition of the property by the Commission. 1958, c. 37, s. 15. {Gatineau Park}

FINANCIAL

16. (1) There shall be a special account in the Consolidated Revenue Fund, to be known as the National Capital Fund, to which shall be credited the amounts appropriated by Parliament for the purposes of the Fund. {National Capital Fund}

Payments out of C.R.F.
(2) Subject to subsection (3), the Minister of Finance may, on the recommendation of the Minister, out of the Consolidated Revenue Fund cause to be paid to the Commission such amounts as are from time to time required by the Commission to finance the cost of capital projects approved by the Governor in Council.

Limits on payments
(3) The amounts paid to the Commission under subsection (2) shall be charged to the Fund, but a payment out of the Consolidated Revenue Fund under subsection (2) shall not exceed the balance standing to the credit of the Fund.

Loans
(4) The Minister of Finance may out of the Consolidated Revenue Fund advance to the Commission such amounts by way of loan as are authorized by Parliament, upon such terms and conditions as to interest, terms of repayment and otherwise as are approved by the Governor in Council.

"Capital project"
(5) In this section "capital project" means

(*a*) the construction or acquisition of parks, squares, highways, parkways, bridges, railways, buildings and any other works for the purposes of this Act, or the acquisition of property therefor; or

(*b*) a contribution to a local municipality or other authority in respect of the cost of a project of the municipality or authority. 1958, c. 37, s. 16.

General fund
17. Subject to section 16, the Commission may expend for any of the purposes of this Act any money appropriated by Parliament for the use of the Commission or received by it through the conduct of its operations or by bequest, donation or otherwise. 1958, c. 37, s. 17.

BY-LAWS AND REGULATIONS

By-laws
18. The Commission may make by-laws for the conduct and management of its activities and for carrying out the purposes and provisions of this Act. 1958, c. 37, s. 18.

Regulations
19. (1) The Governor in Council may make regulations for the protection of any property of the Commission and for preserving order or preventing accidents thereon, and may prescribe the punishment that may be imposed on summary conviction for breach of any such regulation, but the punishment so prescribed shall not exceed a fine of five hundred dollars or imprisonment for a term of six months, or both.

(2) Where a vehicle is operated or parked in contravention of any regulation, the owner of the vehicle is liable to the penalties prescribed by the regulations for such contravention, unless at the time of such contravention the vehicle was not operated or parked, as the case may be, by the owner or by any other person with the owner's consent, express or implied. <small>Liability of owner</small>

(3) Where a person is convicted for a contravention of any of the regulations, the convicting court may, at the time sentence is imposed, order that person to pay to the Commission an amount by way of satisfaction or compensation for loss of or damage to property suffered by the Commission as a result of the contravention for which that person was convicted; and the order may, upon the filing thereof in the superior court of the province in which the trial was held, be enforced as a judgment of that court. <small>Damage to property</small>

(4) In a prosecution for a violation of a regulation, a certificate stating that any property described therein is under the control of the Commission and purporting to be certified by the Commission or the Chairman, General Manager, Chief Engineer, or Secretary of the Commission shall be received in evidence without proof of the signature or the official character of the person appearing to have signed the certificate and without further proof thereof, and is *prima facie* proof that the property is under the control of the Commission. 1958, c. 37, s. 19. <small>Evidence</small>

GENERAL

20. The Commission may, if it sees fit, accept any property by way of gift, bequest or devise and may, subject to section 14 but notwithstanding any other provision of this Act, expend, administer or dispose of any such property for the purposes of this Act, subject to the terms, if any, upon which such property was given, bequeathed or devised to the Commission. 1958, c. 37, s. 20. <small>Gifts, bequests, etc.</small>

21. The Commission shall be deemed to be a charitable organization in Canada <small>Commission deemed charitable organization</small>

(*a*) as described in paragraph 69(1)(*f*) of the *Income Tax Act*, for the purposes of that Act, and

(*b*) as described in paragraph 7(1)(*d*) of the *Estate Tax Act*, for the purposes of that Act. 1958, c. 37, s. 21.

22. The accounts and financial transactions of the Commission shall be audited by the Auditor General of Canada. 1958, c. 37, s. 22. <small>Audit</small>

Works for general advantage of Canada

23. All works of the Commission, whether constructed or executed before or after the 6th day of February 1959, are hereby declared to be for the general advantage of Canada. 1958, c. 37, s. 23.

Surplus Crown Assets Act not applicable

24. The *Surplus Crown Assets Act* does not apply to the Commission or to property of the Commission. 1958, c. 37, s. 24.

Agreement approved

25. The agreement entered into between the Federal District Commission and the Corporation of the City of Ottawa on the 7th day of August 1956 respecting the conveyance to the Corporation of the City of Ottawa of a part of Green Island in the Rideau River, is hereby ratified and confirmed. 1958, c. 37, s. 25.

SCHEDULE

DESCRIPTION OF NATIONAL CAPITAL REGION

Those certain parcels or tracts of lands and premises, situate, lying and being partly in the Province of Ontario and partly in the Province of Quebec, and comprising the whole of the Townships of Gloucester, Nepean, Goulbourn, Huntley, March, and Torbolton, and parts of the Townships of Fitzroy, North Gower, and Osgoode, in the County of Carleton, Province of Ontario; parts of the Townships of Pakenham, Ramsay and Beckwith, in the County of Lanark, Province of Ontario; parts of the Townships of Russell and Cumberland in the County of Russell, Province of Ontario; the whole of the Township of Templeton and parts of the Townships of Buckingham and Portland in the County of Papineau, Province of Quebec; the whole of the Townships of Hull and Eardley and parts of the Townships of Wakefield and Masham in the County of Gatineau (formerly the County of Hull), Province of Quebec; the whole of the Township of Onslow and part of the Township of Aldfield in the County of Pontiac, in the Province of Quebec; and including the whole of the city of Hull, in the County of Hull, Province of Quebec, and the whole of the city of Ottawa, in the County of Carleton, Province of Ontario; all of which are more particularly described as follows: Commencing at a point on the south shore of the Grand or Ottawa River where it is intersected by the boundary between the Township of McNab in the County of Renfrew and the Township of Fitzroy in the County of Carleton; thence south-westerly along the said boundary to the line between the north-east and south-west halves of the Lots in Concession II, Township of Fitzroy; thence south-easterly along the last-mentioned line to the line between the south-west half of Lot 21 and the south-west half of Lot 22, Concession II, Township of Fitzroy; thence south-westerly along the last-mentioned line and along the line between Lots 21 and 22, Concession I, Township of Fitzroy, to the boundary between the said Township of Fitzroy in the County of Carleton and the Township of Pakenham in the County of Lanark; thence along the last-mentioned boundary to the line between Lots 21 and 22, Concession XII, Township of Pakenham; thence south-westerly along the last-mentioned line to the line between the north-east and south-west halves of the Lots in Concession XII, Township of Pakenham; thence south-easterly along the last-mentioned line to the line between the south half of Lot 16 and the south half of Lot 17, Concession XII, Township of Pakenham; thence south-westerly along the last-mentioned line and along the line between Lots 16 and 17, Concession XI, to the line between the north-east and south-west halves of the Lots in Concession XI, Township of Pakenham; thence south-easterly along the last-mentioned line to the line between the south-west half of Lot 13 and the south-west half of Lot 14, Concession XI, Township of Pakenham; thence south-westerly along the last-mentioned line and along the lines between Lots 13 and 14, Concessions X and IX, to the line between the north-east and south-west halves of the Lots in Concession IX, Township of Pakenham; thence south-easterly along the last-mentioned line to the line between the south-west half of Lot 7 and the south-west half of Lot 8, Concession IX, Township of Pakenham; thence south-westerly along the last-mentioned line and along the line between Lots 7 and 8, Concession VIII to the line between the north-east and south-west halves of the Lots in Concession VIII, Township of Pakenham; thence south-easterly along the last-mentioned line to the boundary between the Townships of Pakenham and Ramsay; thence south-westerly along the last-mentioned boundary to the road between Concessions VII and VIII, Township of Ramsay; thence south-easterly along the said road to the side road between Lots 20 and 21, Concession VIII, Township of Ramsay; thence north-easterly along the said side road to the line between the north-east and south-west halves of the Lots in Concession VIII, Township of Ramsay; thence south-easterly along the last-mentioned line to the boundary between the Townships of Ramsay and Beckwith; thence south-westerly along the last-mentioned boundary to the line between Lots 16 and 17, Concession XII, Township of Beckwith; thence south-easterly along the last-mentioned line and along the line between Lots 16 and 17, Concession XI, Township of Beckwith, to the north-westerly limit of the right-of-way of the Canadian Pacific Railway; thence north-easterly along the last-mentioned limit to the boundary between the Township of Beckwith in the County of Lanark and the Township of Goulbourn in the County of Carleton; thence south-easterly along the last-mentioned boundary to the boundary between the Townships of Goulbourn and Marlborough; thence north-easterly along the last-mentioned boundary to the boundary between the Townships of Marlborough and North Gower; thence south-easterly along the last-mentioned boundary to the road between Lots 35 and 36, Concession IV, Township of North Gower; thence easterly along the road between Lots 35 and 36 in Concessions IV, III, and II and continuing easterly along the production of the said road to the easterly boundary of the Township of North Gower, being the centre line of the Rideau River; thence northerly following the centre line of the Rideau River to the west boundary of the Township of Osgoode; thence southerly along the last-mentioned boundary to the road between Lots 35 and 36 in the Broken Front Concession, Township of Osgoode; thence easterly along the road between Lots 35 and 36 in the Broken Front and First Concessions and between Lots 34 and 35 in the Second Concession, and between Lots 35 and 36 in Concessions III, IV, V, VI, VII, VIII, IX, X, and XI, Township of Osgoode, and continuing along the road between Lots 5 and 6 in Concessions I, II, III, IV, V, VI, VII, and VIII in the Township of Russell to the road between Concessions VIII and IX of the said Township of Russell; thence northerly along the last-mentioned road to the boundary between the Townships of Russell and Cumberland; thence easterly along the last-mentioned boundary to the road between Concessions III and IV, Township of Cumberland; thence northerly along the last-mentioned road to the line between Lots 1 and 2, Concession III, Township of Cumberland; thence easterly along the last-mentioned line to the west boundary of Lot 10 in the Second Concession from the Ottawa River, sometimes called "The Old Survey", in the Township of Cumberland; thence northerly along the said west boundary of Lot 10 in the Second Concession from the Ottawa River and along the west boundary of Lot 10 in the First Concession from the Ottawa River to the southerly shore of the Grand or Ottawa River; thence northerly across the said Grand or Ottawa River to the point on the northerly shore where it is intersected by the line between Lots 7 and 8, Range I, Township of Buckingham, in the County of Papineau, Province of Quebec; thence northerly along the lines between Lots 7 and 8, Ranges I, II, III, IV, V, VI, VII, VIII, IX, X, XI, and XII, Township of Buckingham, to the boundary between the Townships of Buckingham and Derry, County of Papineau; thence westerly along the last-mentioned boundary to the boundary between the Townships of Derry and Portland East; thence northerly along the last-mentioned boundary to the range line between Ranges III and IV of the said Township of Portland East; thence westerly along the last-mentioned range line to the boundary between the Townships of Portland East and Portland West; thence northerly along the last-mentioned boundary to the range line between Ranges IV and V of the said Township of Portland West; thence westerly along the last-mentioned range line to the easterly boundary of Lot 7, Range V, Township of Portland West; thence northerly along the last-mentioned boundary to the range line between Ranges V and VI, Township of Portland West; thence westerly along the last-mentioned range line to the easterly boundary of Lot 7, Range VI, Township of Portland West; thence northerly along the last-mentioned boundary to the range line between Ranges VI and VII, Township of Portland West; thence westerly along the last-mentioned range line to the easterly boundary of Lot 7, Range VII, Township of Portland West; thence northerly along the last-mentioned boundary to the range line between Ranges VII and VIII, Township of Portland West; thence westerly along the last-mentioned range line to the easterly boundary of Lot 7, Range VIII, Township of Portland West; thence northerly along the last-mentioned boundary to the range line between Ranges VIII and IX, Township of Portland West; thence westerly along the last-mentioned range line to the boundary between the Townships of Portland West and Denholm; thence southerly along the last-mentioned boundary to the boundary between the Townships of Denholm and Wakefield; thence westerly along the last-mentioned boundary to the line between Lots 25 and 26, Range XI, of the said Township of Wakefield; thence southerly along the lines between Lots 25 and 26, Ranges XI, X, IX, VIII, VII, VI, and V, Township of Wakefield, to the range line between Ranges IV and V, Township of Wakefield; thence westerly along the last-mentioned range line to the line between Lots 4 and 5, Range V, Township of Wakefield; thence northerly along the lines between Lots 4 and 5, Ranges V, VI, and VII, Township of Wakefield, to the range line between Ranges VII and VIII, Township of Wakefield; thence westerly along the last-mentioned range line to the boundary between the Townships of Wakefield and Masham; thence northerly along the last-mentioned boundary to the range line between Ranges VII and VIII, of the said Township of Masham; thence westerly along the last-mentioned range line to the boundary between the Townships of Masham and Aldfield; thence northerly along the last-mentioned boundary to the range line between Ranges II and III, of the said Township of Aldfield; thence westerly along the last-mentioned range line to the easterly boundary of the east range of the said Township of Aldfield; thence along the said easterly boundary of the east range of the Township of Aldfield to the line between Lots 14 and 15 of the said east range of the Township of Aldfield; thence westerly along the lines between Lots 14 and 15, east range and west range, Township of Aldfield to the westerly boundary of the west range of the said Township of Aldfield; thence southerly along the said westerly boundary to the range line between Ranges I and II of the said Township of Aldfield; thence westerly along the last-mentioned range line to the boundary between the Townships of Aldfield and Thorne, County of Pontiac; thence southerly along the last-mentioned boundary and continuing along the boundary between the Townships of Onslow and Bristol, County of Pontiac, to the Grand or Ottawa River; thence southerly across the Grand or Ottawa River to the point of commencement; an area of one thousand eight hundred square miles, more or less. 1958, c. 37, Sch.

Appendix A-2

62-63 VICTORIA,

CHAP. 10

An Act respecting the City of Ottawa.

[*Assented to 11th August*, 1899.]

HER Majesty, by and with the advice and consent of the Senate and House of Commons of Canada, declares and enacts as follows:—

Annual grant authorized. 1. The Minister of Finance and Receiver General is hereby authorized to pay out of the Consolidated Revenue Fund of Canada, in the manner and for the purposes hereinafter set forth, the sum of sixty thousand dollars annually, for a period not exceeding ten years from the first day of July, one thousand eight hundred and ninety-nine.

Payable quarterly to credit of the Commission. 2. Such annual payment of sixty thousand dollars shall be made in four quarterly instalments of fifteen thousand dollars each, payable in advance, during the months of July, October, January and April in each year, and the amount of each such quarterly payment shall be paid by the Minister of Finance and Receiver General into a chartered bank, to be designated by him, to the credit of the Board of Commissioners hereinafter provided for, and hereinafter referred to as "the Commission," and no payment shall be made by such bank from any amount at the credit of the Commission except on the joint cheque of the chairman or acting chairman and the secretary or acting secretary of the Commission.

Number of Commissioners and tenure of office. 3. The Commission shall consist of four Commissioners, of whom three shall be appointed by the Governor in Council and shall hold office during pleasure, and one shall be appointed by the Corporation of the City of Ottawa (hereinafter referred to as "the Corporation") and shall hold office for the period of one year from the time of such appointment, or for such period, not exceeding three years, as shall be determined by by-law duly passed by the Corporation: Provided however, that if the mayor or an alderman of the said city is appointed by the Corporation to be a Commissioner, he shall cease to hold office as Commissioner when he ceases to hold office as mayor or alderman, and the Corporation shall thereupon appoint a Commissioner for the unexpired term. *Proviso: if mayor or alderman is a Commissioner.*

4. The Commission shall be a body corporate under the name of "The Ottawa Improvement Commission," and shall have power to make such by-laws, employ such persons, and pay and defray such expenses as are necessary to enable them to carry into effect the purposes for which they are constituted, or any of the powers conferred on them by this Act; but no by-laws so made shall come into force or effect until approved by the Governor in Council, nor shall any alteration, modification or repeal of any such by-law have any force or effect until approved by the Governor in Council. *Incorporation of Commissioners. Approval of by-laws.*

5. The Governor in Council shall designate one of the Commissioners appointed by the Governor in Council to be chairman of the Commission, and he shall hold office as chairman during pleasure; and the Governor in Council shall appoint a member of the public service of Canada to be secretary of the Commission, and the person so appointed shall discharge his duties as secretary of the Commission as a part of his official duties as a member of the public service of Canada. *Chairman and secretary.*

6. The chairman and other members of the Commission, and the secretary thereof, shall serve without remuneration, but they shall be entitled to receive and be paid their actual disbursements for expenses necessarily incurred by them in the discharge of their duties under this Act. *Commissioners and officers unpaid.*

7. The Commission may— *Powers.*

(*a.*) purchase; acquire and hold real property in the city of Ottawa, or in the vicinity thereof, for the purpose of public parks or squares, streets, avenues, drives or thoroughfares; *Acquisition of property.*

(*b.*) do, perform and execute all necessary or proper acts or things for the purpose of preparing, building, improving, repairing and maintaining all or any of such works for public use; *Public works.*

(*c.*) co-operate with the Corporation, or with the Board of Park Management of the City of Ottawa, in the improvement and beautifying of the said city, or the vicinity thereof, by the acquisition, maintenance and improvement of public parks, squares, streets, avenues, drives or thoroughfares, and the erection of public buildings in the said city or in the vicinity thereof; *Improvement of city.*

Expenditure of moneys.

Proviso: as to improvements near Government property.

And for all or any of the aforesaid purposes the Commission may expend the whole or any portion of the sums that are placed at their credit under this Act: provided that in case of local improvements being made by the Corporation in front of or along the line of property owned by the Dominion Government, the Commission may out of such moneys contribute thereto such share of the cost, or may perform such portion of such local improvements, as is agreed upon between the Commission and the Corporation.

Works for general advantage of Canada.

8. All works or undertakings of the Commission under clauses (*a*) and (*b*) of section 7 of this Act are hereby declared to be for the general advantage of Canada.

Acquisition of property.

9. No real property shall be purchased or acquired by the Commission, except with the previous consent of the Governor in Council; and should the Commission be unable to agree with the owner of the property, which they are so authorized to purchase, as to the price to be paid therefor, then the Commission shall have the right to acquire the same without the consent of the owner, and the provisions of *The Railway Act* relative to the taking of lands by railway companies shall, *mutatis mutandis*, be applicable to the acquisition of such real property by the Commission.

1888, c. 29.

Estimates to be approved.

10. The Commission shall from time to time and before making expenditures under this Act, submit to the Minister of Finance and Receiver General detailed estimates of the expenditures proposed to be made by them, which estimates shall be accompanied by such full information as is sufficient to enable the Governor in Council to determine as to the necessity or advisability of such proposed expenditures, or of any portion thereof; and no expenditure shall be made by the Commission under this Act until it has been approved by the Governor in Council.

Annual statement.

11. The Commission shall render to the Minister of Finance and Receiver General and to the Corporation, on or before the first day of September in each year, detailed statements of all their receipts and expenditures up to the last day of June in such year; and copies of such statements shall be laid before Parliament by the Minister of Finance and Receiver General within the first fourteen days of the next following session thereof.

Accounts and inspection.

12. The Commission shall, whenever required by the Minister of Finance and Receiver General, render detailed accounts of their receipts and expenditures for such period or to such day as he designates; and all books of account, records, bank books and papers of the Commission shall at all times be open to the inspection of the Minister of Finance and Receiver General, or of such person as the said Minister names to inspect them.

13. All expenditures by the Commission shall be subject to the audit of the Auditor General in the same manner as in the case of other public moneys. Audit.

14. No member of the Commission nor the secretary thereof shall have any contract with the Commission or shall be pecuniarily interested, directly or indirectly, in any contract or work in regard to which any portion of the moneys at the credit of the Commission is being or is to be expended. Commissioner and secretary not to have interest in works.

15. The annual grant payable under this Act shall be in full payment, satisfaction and discharge of all claims and demands by or on the part of the Corporation on the Government of the Dominion of Canada (hereinafter referred to as "the Government,") in respect of water supplied (including charges for street sprinkling) by the Corporation for use in and on all buildings, lands and premises in the said city of Ottawa (including Major's Hill Park), now owned, rented, leased or occupied, or hereafter to be owned, rented, leased or occupied by the Government, and also for use in and on Rideau Hall and Rideau Hall grounds and the Central Experimental Farm and the buildings thereon, and for use in and on all other buildings, lands and premises in the vicinity of the said city of Ottawa now or hereafter to be owned, rented, leased or occupied by the Government, and for fire protection by the Corporation to any of such buildings or premises, and all payments heretofore made by the Government to the Corporation for water supply, street sprinkling and fire protection shall be discontinued; and the said grant shall also be in full satisfaction and discharge of all other claims and demands on the Government by or on the part of the Corporation. Grant to be in satisfaction of certain claims.

16. Nothing herein shall in any way alter or change the agreement now existing between the Government and the Corporation with regard to the control and possession by the Government of the said Major's Hill Park, the abolition of tolls on and the free use by the public of the Union Bridge over the Ottawa River connecting the cities of Ottawa and Hull, and the maintenance and repair and keeping in repair by the Government of the following bridges and sidewalks in the said city of Ottawa, namely:—the bridges over the Rideau Canal, known as the Dufferin, Sappers', and Maria Street bridges, the bridges over the Chaudière slides, and the sidewalks on the east side of Elgin Street and on the south side of Maria Street Certain agreement not affected except as herein.

in front of and along the side of Cartier Square; or shall in any way alter or change any of the provisions of such agreement except as in this Act provided.

Agreement altered as to Wellington street.

17. So much of the said agreement referred to in the last preceding section as relates to the repair and maintenance and the keeping in repair by the Government of that portion of Wellington Street in the said city between Dufferin Bridge and Bank Street, and the repair and maintenance of good and sufficient sidewalks on both sides of the said portion of Wellington Street, is hereby cancelled, and the following substituted therefor, namely:—That the Government shall repair and maintain good and sufficient sidewalks on the northern side of that portion of Wellington Street in the said city between Dufferin Bridge and Bank Street, and on so much of the southern side of the said portion of said street as is in front of property owned by the Government, and shall keep in repair the roadway of the said portion of Wellington Street between Dufferin Bridge and Bank Street, as it now exists, and should it be deemed desirable that an asphalt or other improved pavement be hereafter placed on the said roadway, such work shall be done by the Corporation in the same manner as similar works are done in other portions of the city, nothing herein contained to be construed as releasing property holders on the said portion of Wellington Street from any obligation imposed upon them by law as regards payment of any taxes or rates in respect of their property on the said street.

Approval of Act by Corporation by-law.

18. The Governor in Council shall not appoint any commissioner under this Act, and no payment shall be made hereunder, until all the provisions of this Act have been accepted and approved by by-law duly passed by the Corporation.

What by-law shall provide.

2. Such by-law shall provide that the Corporation shall at all times while such annual grant is paid as aforesaid furnish an adequate and sufficient supply of water for use in and on all buildings, lands and premises in the said city of Ottawa now owned, rented, leased, or occupied, or to be hereafter owned, rented, leased or occupied by the Government, and also for use in and on Rideau Hall and Rideau Hall grounds, and the Central Experimental Farm and buildings thereon, and for use in and on all other buildings, lands and premises in the vicinity of the said city now or hereafter to be owned, rented, leased or occupied by the Government, and shall also provide an efficient fire protection for any and all of such buildings and premises, and shall also provide for the sprinkling of the streets in front of such buildings, lands and premises, including the bridges in the said city maintained by the Government.

OTTAWA: Printed by Samuel Edward Dawson, Law Printer to the Queen's most Excellent Majesty.

Appendix A-3

THE SUPREME COURT OF CANADA

Harold Munro

v.

National Capital Commission

Coram:—

    The Honourable Robert Taschereau, P.C., C.J.C.
    The Honourable Mr. Justice Cartwright
    The Honourable Mr. Justice Fauteux
    The Honourable Mr. Justice Abbott, P.C.
    The Honourable Mr. Justice Martland
    The Honourable Mr. Justice Judson
    The Honourable Mr. Justice Ritchie
    The Honourable Mr. Justice Hall
    The Honourable Mr. Justice Spence

Appeal heard May 2, 3 and 4, 1966.
Judgment pronounced June 28, 1966.

Reasons of the Court by

    Mr. Justice Cartwright

concurred in by

    The Chief Justice
    Mr. Justice Fauteux
    Mr. Justice Abbott
    Mr. Justice Martland
    Mr. Justice Judson
    Mr. Justice Ritchie
    Mr. Justice Hall
    Mr. Justice Spence

Counsel at hearing:—

    For the appellant—   Mr. B. J. MacKinnon, Q.C., and Mr. Roydon Hughes, Q.C.

    For the respondent—   Mr. D. S. Maxwell, Q.C., and Mr. G. W. Ainslie

    For the intervenant—   Mr. Gerald LeDain, Q.C.
    The Attorney General for Quebec

THE SUPREME COURT OF CANADA

Harold Munro

—v—

National Capital Commission

Coram: The Chief Justice and Cartwright, Fauteux, Abbott, Martland, Judson, Ritchie, Hall and Spence JJ.

Cartwright J.:

This is an appeal from a judgment of Gibson J. in the Exchequer Court pronounced on April 28, 1965, answering in the negative the following question which, by order of the President of the Court, had been directed to be tried before the trial of the other questions raised in the action:

> Whether, on the special case stated by the parties, the expropriation of the lands of the defendant by the National Capital Commission therein referred to is a nullity because the legislative authority of the Parliament of Canada under the *British North America Act*, 1867 to 1960, does not extend to authorizing the expropriation.

On June 25, 1959, the respondent, with the approval of the Governor in Council, expropriated a farm of 195 acres in the Township of Gloucester in the Province of Ontario owned by the appellant. In so doing the respondent was acting under subs. (1) of s. 13 of the *National Capital Act*, Statutes of Canada 1958, 7 Elizabeth II, Cap. 37, hereinafter sometimes referred to as "the Act", which came into force on February 6, 1959.

By information filed in the Exchequer Court on January 31, 1963, the respondent recited the taking of the lands for the purposes of the Act and stated its willingness to pay $200,000.00 by way of compensation.

In his statement of defence filed on October 13, 1964, the appellant asked, firstly, a declaration that the expropriation "was illegal, null and void because it was beyond the jurisdiction of the Parliament of Canada to grant to the Plaintiff (the respondent) powers of expropriation for establishing a Green Belt outside the limits of the said City of Ottawa", secondly, in the alternative, that compensation be awarded to him in the sum of $420,000.00.

By order of the Chief Justice of Canada it was directed that notice of the constitutional question raised in this appeal should be served on the Attorneys

General of the Provinces and on the Clerks of the City of Ottawa, the City of Hull, the Township of Nepean and the Township of Gloucester and a date was fixed for the making of applications for leave to intervene.

By order of Judson J. made on September 9, 1965, leave to intervene was granted to the Attorney General for Ontario and the Attorney General for Quebec. Subsequently the Attorney General for Ontario withdrew his intervention. Counsel for the Attorney General for Quebec filed a factum and presented a full and helpful argument in support of the appeal.

It will be observed that the question which Gibson J. was called upon to decide is limited to whether the expropriation of the appellant's land is a nullity for a single specified reason:

> because the legislative authority of the Parliament of Canada under the *British North America Act*, 1867 to 1960, does not extend to authorizing the expropriation.

The main ground relied on by counsel who support the appeal is that the power of expropriation which the Act gives to the respondent has been exercised, in the case of the appellant's land, for the imposition upon the use of land within the National Capital Region of controls or restrictions of the nature of zoning regulations contemplated by the Planning Acts passed by the Provinces. It is said, more particularly, that the power has been used for the purpose of the establishment of a "Green Belt" in the Region. It is argued that such a use of the power of expropriation is in its nature, character and purpose a use in relation to a matter falling within the classes of subjects assigned exclusively to the Legislatures of the Provinces by the *British North America Act* and that, consequently, if the *National Capital Act* purports to confer such a power upon the Commission it is, *pro tanto*, ultra vires of Parliament.

It is conceded by counsel for the respondent, and so stated in their factum, that the appellant's lands were taken for the purpose of establishing the Green Belt proposed in the Master Plan for the development of the National Capital Region. The constitutional question to be determined is whether it is within the powers of Parliament to authorize the establishment of a Green Belt within the National Capital Region.

The learned trial judge has made a careful review of the legislative history of the *National Capital Act* and of the *Planning Act*, R.S.O. 1960, Cap. 296, and of the development of the Master Plan for the Region. I do not find it necessary to repeat this review because I propose, for the purposes of this appeal, to accept the following conclusions that counsel for the appellant and for the intervenant seek to draw, in part, from that history: (i) that the making of zoning regulations and the imposition of controls of the use of land situate in any province of the sort provided, for example, in the *Planning Act (Ontario)* are matters which, generally speaking, come within the classes of subjects assigned to the Legislatures by s. 92 of the *Briish North America Act:* (ii) that the legislative history of the predecessors of the *National Capital Act* indicates that Parliament, up to the time of the passing of that Act, contemplated that the "zoning" of the lands comprised in the National Capital Region should be effected by co-operation between the Commission established by Parliament and the municipalities which derive their powers from the Provincial Legislatures; and (iii) that it was only after prolonged and unsuccessful efforts to achieve the desired result by such co-operation that Parliament decided to confer upon the National Capital Commission the powers necessary to enable it to carry out the zoning contemplated in the Master Plan.

It is first necessary to consider what is the matter in relation to which the *National Capital Act* was passed and this requires an examination of its terms.

Its full title is "An Act respecting the Development and Improvement of the National Capital Region".

It establishes a "National Capital Region", described in the Schedule to the Act, comprising approximately 1,800 square miles, including and surrounding the City of Ottawa, situate partly in the Province of Ontario and partly in the Province of Quebec. This region is defined as "the seat of the Government of Canada and its surrounding area". It includes the lands of the appellant in the Township of Gloucester.

By s. 3 of the Act, the respondent is created as a corporation to be called the "National Capital Commission" and by s. 27 it and the Federal District Commission are declared for all purposes to be one and the same corporation. By s. 4(1) it is declared that the Commission is for all purposes of the Act an agent of Her Majesty and that its powers under the Act may be exercised only as an agent of Her Majesty.

Section 10 defines the objects and purposes of the Commission and confers the powers to be used for the purposes of the Act. It reads as follows:

> **10.** (1) The objects and purposes of the Commission are to prepare plans for and assist in the development, conservation and improvement of the National Capital Region in order that the nature and character of the seat of the Government of Canada may be in accordance with its national significance.
>
> (2) The Commission may for the purposes of this Act,
>
> (*a*) acquire, hold, administer or develop property;
>
> (*b*) sell, grant, convey, lease or otherwise dispose of or make available to any person any property, subject to such conditions and limitations as it considers necessary or desirable;
>
> (*c*) construct, maintain and operate parks, squares, highways, parkways, bridges, buildings and any other works;
>
> (*d*) maintain and improve any property of the Commission, or any other property under the control and management of a department, at the request of the authority or Minister in charge thereof;
>
> (*e*) co-operate or engage in joint projects with, or make grants to, local municipalities or other authorities for the improvement, development or maintenance of property;

> (f) construct, maintain and operate, or grant concessions for the operation of, places of entertainment, amusement, recreation, refreshment, or other places of public interest or accommodation upon any property of the Commission;
>
> (g) administer, preserve and maintain any historic place or historic museum;
>
> (h) conduct investigations and researches in connection with the planning of the National Capital Region; and
>
> (i) generally, do and authorize such things as are incidental or conducive to the attainment of the objects and purposes of the Commission and the exercise of its powers.

Section 13(1) reads as follows:

> **13.** (1) The Commission may, with the approval of the Governor in Council, take or acquire lands for the purpose of this Act without the consent of the owner, and, except as otherwise provided in this section, all the provisions of the *Expropriation Act*, with such modifications as circumstances require, are applicable to and in respect of the exercise of the powers conferred by this section and the lands so taken or acquired.

Subsection (3) of this section provides that all claims for compensation for lands taken under the section may be heard and determined in the Exchequer Court of Canada.

By section 18, it is provided that the Commission may make by-laws for the conduct and management of its activities and for carrying out the purposes and provisions of the Act.

In my view, it is clear, from a reading of the Act as a whole, that the matter in relation to which it is enacted is the establishment of a region consisting of the seat of the Government of Canada and the defined surrounding area which are formed into a unit to be known as the National Capital Region which is to be developed, conserved and improved "in order that the nature and character of the seat of the Government of Canada may be in accordance with its national significance".

The next question is whether this subject matter comes within any of the classes of subjects which, by s. 92 of the *British North America Act*, are assigned exclusively to the Legislatures of the Provinces.

The only reference to the National Capital of Canada contained in the *British North America Act* is in s. 16, which reads as follows:

> **16.** Until the Queen otherwise directs, the Seat of Government of Canada shall be Ottawa.

The authority reserved by this section to the Queen to change the location of the Seat of Government of Canada would now be exercisable by Her Majesty in the right of Canada and, while the section contemplates executive action, the change could, doubtless, be made by Act of Parliament in which Her Majesty acts with the advice and consent of the Senate and House of Commons of Canada.

The subject matter of the *National Capital Act*, as I have sought to define it above, is not referred to in either s. 91 or s. 92 of the *British North America Act*. In *Attorney-General for Alberta v. Attorney-General for Canada*. (1943) A.C. 356, Viscount Maugham said at p. 371:

> It must not be forgotten that where the subject matter of any legislation is not within any of the enumerated heads either of s. 91 or of s. 92, the sole power rests with the Dominion under the preliminary words of s. 91, relative to "laws for the peace, order, and good government of Canada."

In *In re Regulation and Control of Radio Communication in Canada*, (1932) A.C. 304, Viscount Dunedin had made a similar observation at p. 312:

> Being, therefore, not mentioned explicitly in either s. 91 or s. 92, such legislation falls within the general words at the opening of s. 91 which assign to the Government of the Dominion the power to make laws "for the peace order and good government of Canada in relation to all matters not coming within the classes of subjects by this Act assigned exclusively to the legislatures of the Provinces."

In *Johnannesson v. Rural Municipality of West St. Paul*, (1952) 1 S.C.R. 292, in which it was held that the subject of aeronautics is within the exclusive jurisdiction of Parliament, this Court (at pages 308, 311, 318 and 328) adopted as the true test, to be applied in determining whether a subject matter falls within the legislative authority of Parliament under the general words at the opening of s. 91, that formulated by Viscount Simon in the *Canada Temperance Federation* case, (1946) A.C. 193 at p. 205, in the following words:

> In their Lordships' opinion, the true test must be found in the real subject matter of the legislation: if it is such that it goes beyond local or provincial concern or interests and must from its inherent nature be the concern of the Dominion as a whole (as, for example, in the *Aeronautics* case and the *Radio* case), then it will fall within the competence of the Dominion Parliament as a matter affecting the peace, order and good government of Canada, though it may in another aspect touch on matters specially reserved to the provincial legislatures.

I find it difficult to suggest a subject matter of legislation which more clearly goes beyond local or provincial interests and is the concern of Canada as a whole than the development, conservation and improvement of the National Capital Region in accordance with a coherent plan in order that the nature and character of the seat of the Government of Canada may be in accordance with its national significance. Adopting the words of the learned trial judge, it is my view that the Act "deals with a single matter of national concern".

There is no doubt that the exercise of the powers conferred upon the Commission by the *National Capital Act* will affect the civil rights of residents in those parts of the two provinces which make up the National Capital Region. In the case at bar the rights of the appellant are affected. But once it has been determined that the matter in relation to which the Act is passed is one which falls within the power of Parliament it is no objection to its validity that its operation will affect civil rights in the provinces. As Viscount Simon, adopting what had been pointed out by Rand J., said in *Attorney-General for Saskatchewan v. Attorney-General for Canada*, (1949) A.C. 110, at p. 123:

> Consequential effects are not the same thing as legislative subject matter. It is "the true nature and character of the legislation"—not its ultimate economic results—that matters.

The passage from the judgment of Duff J., as he then was, in *Gold Seal Limited v. Dominion Express Company and Attorney-General for Alberta*, (1921) 62 S.C.R. 424, at p. 460, quoted by the learned trial judge, correctly states the law. It is as follows:

> The fallacy lies in failing to distinguish between legislation affecting civil rights and legislation "in relation to" civil rights. Most legislation of a repressive character does incidentally or consequentially affect civil rights. But if in its true character it is not legislation "in relation to" the subject matter of "property and civil rights" within the provinces, within the meaning of section 92 of the British North America Act, then that is no objection although it be passed in exercise of the residuary authority conferred by the introductory clause.

I have already indicated my view that the matter in relation to which the *National Capital Act* was passed does not come within any of the classes of subjects enumerated in s. 92.

It has been said repeatedly that, in dealing with questions that arise under the *British North America Act* as to the allocation of law-making powers between Parliament and the Legislatures of the Provinces, the court will be well advised to confine itself to the precise question raised in the proceeding which is before it. It is sufficient in this case to say that in my opinion it is within the powers of Parliament to authorize the Commission, for the attainment of its objects and purposes as defined in the Act, to make the expropriation of the lands of the appellant referred to in the question submitted to the Exchequer Court. It follows from this that I agree with the conclusion of the learned trial judge that the question submitted to him should be answered in the negative.

For these reasons I would dismiss the appeal with costs.

Appendix A-4

The Report of the Commission on the Integrity of the Territory of Québec

Rapport de la Commission d'étude sur l'intégrité du territoire du Québec

(CEITQ—The Dorion Report)

The Commission on the territorial integrity of Quebec, headed by geographer Henri Dorion, was given in November 1966 a very broad mandate to study the question of the territorial integrity of Quebec and the development of the Outaouais region. The CEITQ therefore had a double objective in the Outaouais region: to study how the area could be kept as an integral part of Quebec in the face of the large concentration of Anglophones across the Ottawa River, and to recommend the establishment of operating structures that could permit the development of the Quebec region of the National Capital in a harmonious and efficient fashion.

The Dorion Report on the problems of the Canadian Capital Region is a two volume Report of the Commissioners which runs approximately 600 pages. The Commission also published a 118 page synthesis volume, a 550 page volume containing the briefs submitted to the Commission, a 450 page volume containing legal studies by Me André Tremblay, a 200 page volume listing pertinent documentation and a final 227 page volume containing the appendices to the Commissioners' Report.

We list below the postulates and the 37 recommendations of the Commission to the Government of Quebec.

Postulates

(1) Quebec's territorial integrity must be maintained in an absolute way. This implies the rejection of all formulas which are strictly federal and the return of territories which are, at present, the property of the NCC.

(2) Provincial jurisdiction should be maintained in all areas guaranteed under the constitution: justice, education, health, tourism, municipal affairs...

(3) The administration of territory within Quebec under a new regional set up must nonetheless remain entirely within the hands of the Quebec government.

(4) Quebec must control the money invested in the development of its territory.

(5) A more equitable sharing of federal investments, direct and indirect, must be obtained.

(6) Development of the Hull region must be envisaged in a way to avoid that the centrifugal forces in Western Quebec become accentuated by the fact of the presence of the Canadian Capital.

(7) Whatever the nature of the solutions adopted, these should not be irreversible for Quebec.

Recommendations

In consideration of these postulates, The Commission on the integrity of the Quebec Territory recommends:

(1) that the Government of Quebec express clearly its opposition to the creation of any organization body liable to bring about the detachment of part of the territory of Quebec, whether or not such a body bears the title of Federal District.

(2) that the Government of Quebec manifest in a much more tangible fashion than it has to the present its interest in the region of Hull by endowing it with the necessary infra-structure, administrative services and plant up to the limit of the province's financial capabilities.

(3) that the Government of Quebec establish two orders of priority in the action it must take in the region of Hull:

(*a*) the need for development of the Quebec portion of the National Capital Region;
(*b*) the preservation of the territorial integrity of Quebec from both the standpoints of its Territory and the exercise of power.

(4) that until the new structures proposed have been established, future projects, decisions and activities of the National Capital Commission affecting the territory of Quebec be submitted beforehand to the Government of Quebec for its approval.

(5) that the Government of Quebec in accordance with the Governments of Ontario and of Canada prepare in accordance with their respective powers, pieces of legislation and recommendations which are parallel and complementary and which set out the nature, the objectives and the structure of the bodies in charge of the development of the region.

(6) that a permanent tripartite Commission charged with preparation and periodic amendment of a development plan for the National Capital Region be formed.

(7) that the Canadian, Quebec and Ontario Governments enjoy equal representation on this Commission.

(8) that the members be designated by the Governments they respectively represent.

(9) that Quebec representation on this Commission consist of one or more senior officers of the Western Quebec Development Commission whose formation is recommended hereafter.

(10) that the members act on this Commission on instructions of the Governments which they represent, and that they be responsible to their Governments.

(11) that the Commission work at the preparation of a plan which covers:
(a) the formulation of general development objectives for the whole region;
(b) the establishment of large functional areas in the metropolitan area;
(c) the choice of location and route of the main highway corridors.

(12) That the Tripartite Commission study projects:
(a) relating to the visual development of the shores of the Ottawa River;
(b) involving the application of urban esthetic code norms such as those mentioned in recommendation 30;
(c) involving the problem of pollution;
(d) involving alignment and co-ordination of the transportation corridors.

(13) that the decisions of the Commission be adopted by majority with each of the delegations of the three governments having one vote, but that any decision affecting the territory of one of the two provinces concerned cannot be taken without the consent of the Government of that province.

(14) that the provincial Governments have complete latitude in carrying out developments in their respective territories within the provisos of recommendations 11 and 12.

(15) that as soon as possible, the Commission for the development of Western Quebec be formed and charged with:
(a) establishment of policies and projects to be proposed by the Government of Quebec to the tripartite Commission;
(b) preparation of other projects concerning the development and planning of the Western Quebec Region;
(c) the detailed planning of projects deriving from plans accepted by the tripartite Commission;
(d) to oversee the execution of projects by the Quebec departments concerned.

(16) that the Western Quebec Development Commission be formed of representatives of the local municipalities, of regional organizations and of interested departments of the Quebec Government, and in addition of a representative named by the Federal Government.

(17) that the Western Quebec Development Commission avail itself of the necessary technical skills with a staff of full-time specialists.

(18) that joint technical committees be formed grouping technicians attached to the different organizations respectively charged with the development of the Quebec and Ontario sections of the region.

(19) that these joint technical committees assure the necessary mutual information as well as a certain work co-ordination between the different development organizations.

(20) that the Western Quebec Development Commission receive financial, technical and documentary support from the Government of Quebec particularly in the establishment of regional plans concerning provincial and local jurisdictions.

(21) that Quebec undertake the necessary steps to obtain the lands now held by the National Capital Commission in the territory of Quebec, and that this transfer of property be unconditional and without financial compensation.

(22) that certain parcels with particular historical interest for the Federal Government be by exception excluded and remain federal property.

(23) that the Quebec Government exercise control of all property transfers involved in development work and that it continue to be or become proprietor of all the lands which it is judged necessary to acquire for the purposes of development of the Quebec portion of the National Capital Region.

(24) that the regulation and administration of public holdings and territories which have been and will be the object of development in the region be assured by the Quebec Government or by bodies responsible to it.

(25) that the power of expropriation at present exercised by the National Capital Commission as well as the power to create active or passive easements be exercised by the Quebec Government according to the requirements of the Plan adopted and accepted by the tripartite Commission or by the Western Quebec Development Commission.

(26) that all delegation of powers, transfers of stewardship and administration or all agreements involving one department or body of government, or a municipal corporation of Quebec on the one hand and a government other than the government of Quebec on the other, be submitted beforehand to the approval of the Department of Inter-governmental Affairs of Quebec.

(27) that energetic steps be taken in order to proceed rapidly with the restructuring of municipalities in the metropolitan Hull area with a view to reducing considerably the number of municipal corporations preferably down to one single unit.

(28) that a municipal authority (a metropolitan municipality) or a super-municipality (in the case of regrouping of two, three or four municipal entities) be formed in order to constitute a responsible spokesman before the Western Quebec Development Commission and the tripartite Commission.

(29) that there be agreements between the one or several newly consolidated municipalities in the Hull region and the equivalent Eastern Ontario body with a view to unification and joint management of certain public services.

(30) that the Government of Quebec undertake as soon as possible, in co-operation with the Government of Ontario and with the help of competent Federal agencies, the formulation of an urban esthetic code which will ultimately be the object of parallel laws in the two provinces represented in the Canadian Capital Region.

(31) that the Department of Industry and Commerce of Quebec prepare in collaboration with other interested bodies, a firm policy for industrial promotion in the region of Hull through incitements such as fiscal arrangements, the creation and enlargement of industrial parks, increased participation in the provision of infrastructure or the granting of subsidies.

(32) that the Government of Quebec adopt the necessary measures and invest as required to make Hull the dominant French language educational centre in the region especially by extending CEGEP and providing technical and professional schools, centres of popular culture and, eventually, a French language university.

(33) that the Department of Tourism, Fish and Game prepare with the help of the Western Quebec Development Commission a tourist program in Hull especially by increasing tourist plant and services in Gatineau Park.

(34) that the Government of Quebec take urgent measures to avoid the unfortunate consequences of existing sales tax disparity, preferably by way of an agreement with the government of Ontario to prevent the eluding of these taxes.

(35) that the Government of Quebec study the possibility of minimizing the consequences of the inevitable disparities flowing from its taxation system, especially by trying to make the fiscal charges heavier in areas where evasion is more difficult.

(36) that the Government of Quebec demand the abrogation of the "National Capital Act."

(37) that the Government of Quebec rapidly reach an agreement with the Governments of Ontario and of Canada in order to realize as soon as possible the formation of bipartite or tripartite bodies, joint technical committees and parallel legislation suggested in this report.

Appendix A-5

Report of Royal Commission on Bilingualism and Biculturalism—Appendix III to Book V.—The Federal Capital

The essence of a Capital Territory may be stated in three points. First, it could entail the establishment of a new jurisdiction over both the Quebec and the Ontario sectors of the area to be designated as the federal capital. For this area, provincial jurisdiction as it exists today would cease. The provinces of Quebec and Ontario, however, might well continue to have some role *within* the new jurisdiction, depending on the form of government to be established. The important thing is that the present provincial level of government would be replaced by a new body more closely fitted to the requirements of the federal capital.

Second, this new jurisdiction would develop a new governmental structure. This structure could carry out many of the functions presently performed by the provinces. For example, it could administer educational systems, oversee municipal affairs in the area, provide welfare services, exercise taxing powers, and so on. But a territorial government would not necessarily have the same list of powers as the provinces, since the special conditions of the federal capital might well require somewhat different arrangements. For example, while a province may amend its own constitution, the power to amend the territorial constitution might be vested in the federal government rather than in the territorial government.

Third, such a territorial government need not stand in the same relation to the federal government as the provinces do. In Canada's federal system, provinces are autonomous within the jurisdiction allotted to them by the Constitution. The territorial government, while exercising a broad jurisdiction over many of the normal provincial areas of concern, could nevertheless do so subject to limits, guarantees, and general norms established from time to time by the federal government, or through federal-provincial consultation and agreements. To proceed otherwise would be to ignore an important issue basic to this approach: the continuing development of a stronger federal participation in the government of the federal capital.

While the question of a "federal district" has been a frequent topic of discussion in the newspapers and the broadcasting media, and has become even more intensive during the past few years, a good deal of the public discussion has been clouded by emotionalism and false issues. Nevertheless, the real issues should be considered calmly and on their own merits. Therefore, in order to further public understanding and discussion of these issues, some of the more important of them are treated separately in this Appendix in full recognition that the views presented here constitute only a first approach to some extremely complex problems.

From the perspective of bilingualism and biculturalism, the development of a Capital Territory in the long run would be a desirable goal if it can best accomplish the objectives of full equality as our Commission has defined them for the capital area. Some results it might reasonably be expected to accomplish are the following. It could provide a most effective framework for overcoming the present economic imbalance between the Quebec and Ontario sectors. It could radically alter relations in the area—in particular, relations between members of the majority and the minority. It could afford a better chance for the development of a vigorous, selfreliant Francophone community in the capital area, overcoming the present demographic pattern that divides the Francophone population almost exactly in equal parts on either side of the provincial boundary.

Other reasons beyond this perspective have also been advanced for the creation of a federal district or Capital Territory. Perhaps the most important is that such a structure could enable a more effective implementation of urban and regional planning, and especially of the National Capital Plan of 1950. A new jurisdiction over both the Quebec and Ontario sectors could also facilitate closer co-ordination of municipal and regional services, such as a public transportation system and a co-ordinated network of roads.

However, many detailed questions are involved in working out the possible institutional structure of a Capital Territory, such as territorial boundaries, legislative and financial arrangements, linguistic and cultural guarantees, the relations between civil law and common law, the restructuring of educational systems, and others. Most of these questions would have to be settled through complex and far-ranging negotiations between the federal government and the wo "founding provinces" of the Territory—Quebec and Ontario.

As well, there exist at present certain formidable obstacles to the creation of a Capital Territory, upon whose understanding and appropriate resolution the achievement of full equality between Francophones and Anglophones in the capital in great measure depends. The provincial framework, as we noted in Chapter II, is immensely strong in its influence on the outlook and attitudes of residents of the federal capital. Residents in the area therefore tend to view the prospect of a federal Capital Territory in rather different perspectives according to their province of residence. There are corresponding differences between Quebec and Ontario attitudes among those residents outside the capital area itself.

In the province of Quebec, perhaps the first and most obvious characteristic of prevailing opinion is a massive mistrust of any arrangement that would involve the establishment of any new Anglophone majority. Related to this is a deepseated fear of assimilation. Those who share these feelings believe that Canadian history to date affords no example whatever of a successful partnership between Francophones and Anglophones on terms of real and lasting equality. Consequently, in the Quebec sector of the capital there are serious apprehensions that the loss of majority status in the area would endanger the linguistic heritage. Moreover, residents of the Quebec sector would seem to have little to gain from a linguistic standpoint in becoming part of a Capital Territory; their language arrangements are basically satisfactory now.

Beneath this basic suspicion of Anglophone majorities undoubtedly lies a strong scepticism as to the probable efficacy of the federal government's linguistic policy in the capital. Francophones in the Quebec sector doubt that linguistic rights can be guaranteed so that they are fully secure, and they want some evidence of success in the present capital area in order to balance the risks of the larger venture against its advantages.

For the Hull area, a Capital Territory also raises the prospect of being integrated more fully into the economic life of the region. Even this arouses some rather justifiable suspicion. The Quebec sector of the capital has suffered from such a delay in economic development that institutional reforms alone are unlikely to change basic attitudes. Indeed, there is no guarantee that a Capital Territory would automatically bring the Quebec sector parity of economic development with the Ontario sector; some deliberate policy to make up for past neglect would seem necessary.

Finally, the creation of a new jurisdiction of any kind for the federal capital raises the question of the territorial integrity of the province of Quebec. The growth of nationalist sentiment since the 1930's and the Privy Council decision in the Labrador case in 1927[1] have made this a highly sensitive issue. Indeed, the present functions of the National Capital Commission in the Quebec sector, and particularly the Commission's powers of expropriation, have been the target for much criticism locally. The objective of maintaining Quebec's autonomy as fully as possible over its entire territory has become a central tenet for a wide range of public opinion in the province. To find a formula that reconciles Quebec's territorial integrity with the need for an integrated federal capital is perhaps the central obstacle to be overcome. These and other questions are dealt with in full detail from the Quebec perspective in the *Rapport de la Commission d'étude sur l'intégrité du territoire du Québec*, and solutions based on provincial initiatives are advanced therein.[2]

The obstacles on the Ontario side are probably different in both focus and intensity, but they are real nonetheless. The people of Ontario would undoubtedly regret the detachment of the third largest urban area in the province, and the effect on provincial government revenue would be significant. The area in question, while not among the earliest parts of the province to be settled, has

---

[1] *Dominion Law Reports*, 1927, Vol. 2; Re Labrador Boundary (Toronto, 1927), 401–29.

[2] *See* Quebec, *Rapport de la Commission d'étude sur l'intégrité du territoire du Québec*, Vol. 1.2 (Quebec, 1968), 65–79.

strong historical traditions dating back to the early 19th century. Yet there does not appear to be the same sense of distance between the province and the federal government as is felt in Quebec. Recent developments in the province also suggest that there is a willingness in Ontario to accept changes if it can be demonstrated that they advance the cause of Canadian unity.

On the other hand, in the capital area itself there might be a stronger resistance among the Anglophones to the creation of a new jurisdiction. This feeling is compounded of a number of motives. Anglophones will clearly be reluctant to change a system of institutions that has provided efficient government and a high standard of services in the urbanized area. There may be some fear of unknown or imagined alternatives, and particularly fears of a loss of privileges at various levels. Many Anglophones may be hesitant to support bilingual facilities and services when the unilingual English-language ones they know have never caused them personal inconvenience. Finally, the residues of old religious differences still linger in the attitudes of the Ottawa Valley, and to some extent even in the capital area itself. On the whole, the major obstacles on the Ontario side are the local ones; to surmont them, a carefully fashioned structure of government for a Capital Territory would have to be developed.

Apart from its importance for the capital area itself, a Capital Territory would have certain effects outside the limits of its own jurisdiction; these consequences require careful study. The Quebec sector of the capital is the major urban centre for the four counties of western Quebec: Hull, Gatineau, Papineau, and Pontiac. These counties constitute a distinct economic region, somewhat isolated from the rest of the province, and separated by the provincial boundary from the Ottawa Valley counties of eastern Ontario. Since Hull is the only major urban centre in the region, it is clear that its inclusion in a Capital Territory might involve serious adjustments in the regional economy. At the least, these would have to be studied in some depth before a new jurisdiction could be established.

The problems for the adjacent Ontario counties are scarcely the same. Eastern Ontario has urban centres other than Ottawa and good transportation connections. However, creation of a Capital Territory would have consequences for the Francophones scattered throughout the province, for whom Ottawa is a major focus of organizations and associations, a cultural centre, and almost a spiritual capital. The Ontario Francophones outside the capital might ultimately draw inspiration and strength from a régime of equality in a Capital Territory, but the short-run consequences will require study and adjustment nonetheless. In particular, the consequences of removing approximately one-fifth of its Francophone population from direct provincial jurisdiction will require close attention.

The economic problems of western Quebec and the cultural problems of the Ontario Francophones outside the capital are not, perhaps, paramount issues; higher priority could be given to the principle of equal partnership in a federal capital worthy of Canada. Nevertheless, issues such as these show the necessity for careful study, for a new jurisdiction for the capital area ought not to be founded on injustice to smaller or weaker groups that will have to remain outside.

In addition to the rather general obstacles already outlined, there is a range of practical questions involved in creating a workable Capital Territory. As long as these questions remain unsettled, they will constitute an additional source of hesitation for Francophones and Anglophones alike. For example, what arrangements would be made concerning the two systems of private law presently operating in the area, that is, civil law in Quebec and common law in Ontario. What would be done to restructure the complex set of educational systems? What protections would be provided for political rights, and for local interests? The list could easily be extended.

These questions are not just hindrances to be surmounted; a Capital Territory would have to be shown to be capable of improving on existing arrangements in these fields. The present hesitation and mistrust of a Capital Territory are understandable and justified until its structures are worked out and its advantages agreed upon. This consideration applies especially to Francophones living in the Quebec sector. In a federal Capital Territory they would surrender their present position of a linguistic majority; their compensating advantages of full integration in the capital area and adequate linguistic guarantees must be spelled out firmly enough to make the change worthwhile. If the steps recommended in Chapter V for the immediate future prove effective, these obstacles will diminish in significance as mutual trust and co-operative procedures develop. As this occurs, the ideal of a Capital Territory may well emerge as a viable alternative for the capital region.

However, it is obvious that to develop satisfactory arrangements for a Capital Territory would be no easy task. Many diverse interests have to be considered, and much political negotiation would undoubtedly be required on the part of the governments concerned. At this stage there are no final answers or precise formulae to propose; what is set down below may serve rather as an agenda for serious public dialogue.

A. *Geographic Boundaries and the Territorial Integrity of Ontario and Quebec*

Although establishing precise boundaries for a Capital Territory requires specialized knowledge, it is possible to note certain conditions to be fulfilled in arriving at such boundaries.

First, the decision should be made on the basis of the best possible forecast of the long-run development of the capital area. Since changes in territorial jurisdiction are difficult to obtain, a decision for the capital area should be made in view of its expected development over at least the next century, or as far ahead as projections for development can be made meaningful. Several existing federal capitals have outgrown the original districts created for them. In Canada, where a major reason for the establishment of a Capital Territory would be the provision of a guaranteed régime of linguistic and cultural equality for Francophones and Anglophones alike, it would be important that such a régime should extend into the outlying suburban areas, where most new residents of the capital will tend to settle.

For the Ontario sector, there would appear to be a substantial consensus as to the appropriate limits of the capital area. The Ontario portion of the federally defined National Capital Region comprises 1,050 square miles; the provincially established regional municipality of Ottawa-Carleton comprises 1,060 square miles. Though the boundaries are not identical, the two regions overlap substantially and both extend a long way beyond the present built-up areas.[1] Only considerations of development over the very long run would seem to require a significant change.

In the Quebec sector the situation is less clear. The Quebec portion of the National Capital Region, as defined by federal statute, comprises 750 square miles. The 23 municipalities that have been involved in recent discussions about regional government in the Quebec sector, and which are situated wholly within the National Capital Region, together comprise only 540 square miles. The delimitation of suitable boundaries for a Capital Territory in this sector would involve discussions between the Quebec and federal governments based upon a careful consideration of the long-run development of the Quebec sector in relation to the federal capital area as a whole. It seems quite probable that with the removal of physical and jurisdictional barriers this sector would account for an increased proportion of the developed area of the capital.

The question of territory, however, is far more than a matter of suitable boundaries. Creation of a Capital Territory including both the Quebec and the Ontario sectors would require the creation of a new jurisdiction independent of both existing provincial jurisdictions. Correspondingly, the *ordinary* jurisdiction of each province over its own sector would be replaced by the new jurisdiction over the combined Capital Territory.

It is at this point that the case for a Capital Territory encounters one of the strongest arguments advanced against it by many people in Quebec: that a change of this nature would involve an irrevocable cession of Quebec territory and population to an unknown and untried new political unit which would have an Anglophone majority; and that the past history of English-speaking Canada affords no grounds for optimism on this point. It is necessary to recognize the force of this argument and the intensity of feeling that it generates. If a Capital Territory is to become a reality, this issue must be resolved in a way satisfactory to all concerned.

As a first approach towards the discussion of this issue, three comments can be made. First, no outright cession of territory seems to be required. The provincial governments could proceed either by a lease of territory and jurisdiction to the new authority, or perhaps by a delegation of powers alone.

---

[1] In December 1968, the government of Ontario proposed the limits of the regional municipality of Ottawa-Carleton as the "logical boundaries" of the Ontario portion of a formally designated Capital Territory.

Second, whatever arrangement is made need not be made in perpetuity, though it would require sufficient stability to support major developmental programmes by both federal and private interests. In the event that the major objectives of cultural equality were not attained, or that the Canadian Confederation were dissolved or substantially altered, or that the federal capital were transferred elsewhere, both provinces could be guaranteed a clear right of recovery of the territory relinquished in their respective sectors.

Third, it may be noted that by the establishment of a Capital Territory the federal government would not become the absolute owner or proprietor of the land lying within the Territory. In the past, the federal government, acting through the National Capital Commission, has acquired considerable amounts of land simply to control its use. If the federal interest were suitably represented in the governmental arrangements for the Territory, the role of the federal government as a landowner might actually diminish, for its holdings could then be related more directly to its own needs and projects.

B. *Governmental Institutions for a Capital Territory*

The question of a possible form of government for a Capital Territory has given rise to some major misconceptions. All too frequently in Canada, any proposal for a special capital territory tends to be identified at once in the public mind with the system developed in Washington, D.C., which has the oldest and best-known of all federal districts. There are, however, many variations in governmental arrangements for federal capitals, and each federal state must develop a set of institutions to resolve its special problems.

Although a Capital Territory could provide a new setting for the resolution of a whole range of local and federal issues, the pattern of institutions that might be evolved for such a territory need not be vastly different from those existing today. For example, it is likely that residents of the area would retain three distinct levels of government: federal, municipal, and a new territorial government for the Capital Territory itself. The federal and municipal levels would not be greatly affected by the creation of a Capital Territory. In particular, the federal and municipal franchise could continue unchanged. As elsewhere in Canada, members would be elected to the federal House of Commons for capital area constituencies, and similarly the area would be appropriately represented in the Senate.

The territorial level of government raises more interesting questions, because clearly some new body would have to be developed. At the start, two extreme positions can be identified and rejected. On the one hand, it seems unlikely that the territorial government would be under any form of direct federal control, whether that of a parliamentary committee, a ministry, or federally appointed officials or commissioners. Such a system would be too much at variance with the long traditions of self-government of the capital area. On the other hand, the territorial government should probably have rather less autonomy than a province, for otherwise the interests of Canada as a whole in the federal capital would be expressed inadequately. A successful solution must lie somewhere between these extremes.

The proposed government for the Territory can be looked at in a number of different ways. Some have seen it as an enlarged municipal government, a regional municipality, operating under the federal government rather than under a province. Some have seen it more as a substitute for a provincial government. It might also include some elements of both these levels, together with other elements distinctive to its special role as an agency administering a federal capital. It is clear that the problem of allocating responsibilities to the various levels of government is complex, though an eventual solution on these lines might well prove significantly less complicated than the present four-tier arrangement for the area, which includes the federal government, two provincial governments, two regional governments, and a large number of municipal governments—plus the further possibility of an eventual Tripartite Quebec-Ontario-Federal Agency to co-ordinate the policy of all the others.

Discussion of a territorial government must resolve two main questions: its structure and its powers. In both, the central issue would seem to be the question of reaching an appropriate balance between the interests of the resident population and those of Canada as a whole.

Concerning structures, the appropriate legislative authority for the Territory would seem to be a council directly elected by the residents of the area on the basis of single-member constituencies. Such a body would serve to protect regional interests above the municipal level and it would provide the residents with a legislative authority directly responsible to the electorate of the region. It would be in accordance with Canadian electoral practices in other jurisdictions, and it would provide a forum for the integration of the present Quebec and Ontario sectors into a single federal capital.

Electoral constituencies would doubtless be arranged according to population and with some regard to existing municipal boundaries. However, in the short run, the Quebec sector might have an undesirably low representation, and each sector might be guaranteed a minimum proportion of the seats—perhaps one-third—on the same principle that Canadian provinces are guaranteed a minimum representation in the federal House of Commons regardless of population.[1] It must be remembered that Francophone representation will be considerably higher, because half the present Francophone population lives in the Ontario sector.

If a directly elected council assures a voice for the interests of the regional population, there remains the problem of representing the federal interest, the interest of Canada as a whole. It is doubtful that this should be done through federal appointment of officials to the same territorial council: the experience of legislatures that have combined elected and appointed members suggests that such arrangements are seldom satisfactory. It would probably be better

---

[1] By Section 51A of the British North America Act, 1867, as amended by the British North America Act, 1915.

provide a safeguard for the federal interest—that is, for the interests of Canada as a whole in the capital area—either by a power of review of territorial measures vested in a federal parliamentary committee, or by a power of federal disallowance of such measures, or by some similar means. The grounds for exercise of this overriding power could be specified quite explicitly in the constitution of the Capital Territory. The fact of popular election of the territorial legislature should be a sufficient deterrent to misuse of this power and a guarantee of vigorous expression of local interests.

As to the distribution of powers between the various levels of government, only a general indication can be given until the question has been discussed seriously among the levels of government concerned. At the municipal level, a continuing list of local government responsibilities can be visualized. Quite apart from any question of establishing a federal territory, these powers appear to be shrinking as large metropolitan areas move towards regional government. The next level, the territorial government, might be given, first, those powers that, broadly speaking, nowadays fall to the regional or metropolitan governments, and, second, many of the powers currently exercised by the provinces. However, it might be decided that, with respect to the new Capital Territory, some current provincial responsibilities might be left to the federal Parliament on the ground that they relate more closely to the interests of Canada as a whole than to the local population. Possible examples might be the power to amend the constitution of the Capital Territory, or to borrow money, or to construct major public works.

It would be important that the territorial government and the federal government should not stand too far away from one another. There must be some element of flexibility in order to meet the constantly shifting range of regional and federal interests that would have to be reconciled. Most of the ordinary powers of the territorial government could be capable of amendment or redefinition by federal statute, relying upon the political strength of the elected members of the territorial council to forestall undue federal encroachment. Through such a division, a balancing mechanism might be developed to resolve new conflicts between regional and federal interests as they arise.

Certain matters, however, would doubtless be considered too important and too fundamental to be left to the discretion of the federal Parliament. For these matters—and among them linguistic and cultural rights must be included—firm guarantees must be found.

C. *Guarantees for Fundamental Rights*

In the context of this *Report*, the most important single reason for forming a Capital Territory would be that it would create a setting in which might be realized to the fullest degree possible an equal partnership between Francophone and Anglophone Canadians in conducting the affairs of a federal state. To this end it is essential that the linguistic and cultural rights of Francophones and Anglophones in the capital should be placed on a footing of complete equality. If this equality cannot be firmly assured, there would be far less justification in asking the provinces of Quebec and Ontario to co-operate. Indeed, both provinces might insist on firm linguistic and cultural guarantees as part of the agreement by which the Capital Territory would be established.

For this reason it would be essential that there be firm, constitutionally entrenched guarantees for linguistic and cultural rights in any future Capital Territory. These rights should be both specific and enforceable: in a specified range of facilities—including all levels of governmental administration and public agencies, courts and tribunals, all programmes of elementary and secondary education, and publicly supported cultural facilities—services of comparable standards should be freely available in both French and English. This list is merely illustrative; other areas might be added during the negotiations between the governments concerned. It is even worth considering whether similar guarantees ought not to be extended to certain parts of the private sector, such as, for example, services offered by large retail establishments, or services offered to visitors and travellers. Of course, other kinds of rights, such as barriers to discrimination in housing or employment, could be protected in the same way.

Since in the capital area as a whole even the present position of French is precarious, formal legislation setting out a specific policy of language protection and development is needed if the capital area is to afford a base for equal partnership between Francophone and Anglophone citizens. Linguistic rights should be spelled out explicitly and positively in law, and the broad framework of this linguistic régime for a Capital Territory should not be alterable by decisions of a majority of electors in the region but should be firmly entrenched in the constitution of the Capital Territory as a basic and universal right.

In addition, in order to safeguard these basic linguistic rights, a whole series of levels by means of which linguistic equality can be made meaningful would be required. In the first instance, the pattern of political representation would give considerable scope for action at the political level. There would be fairly strong representation of Francophone electors in the territorial council; in all likelihood about 40 per cent of its members would represent predominantly Francophone constituencies. Above the territorial level the federal Parliament could also have the power to review measures affecting the linguistic régime of the capital. A parliamentary committee for this purpose could appropriately give equal representation of Francophones and Anglophones in its membership.

Secondly, there could be a body of formal language legislation, wholly or partially entrenched in the constitution of the Capital Territory, on the basis of which appeals could be made to the courts if the linguistic rights of a citizen were violated or ignored. Such legislation could also contain provisions enabling the federal Commissioner of Official Languages to act as an ombudsman in linguistic matters and so resolve many complaints without resort to formal legal action.

If these combined political and legal safeguards were felt to be inadequate, there remains another possible line of defence. Ontario and Quebec would be the "founding provinces" of the Capital Territory in the sense that their willingness to relinquish territorial jurisdiction is necessary in order to create a new jurisdiction over the capital. Arrangements could be made in the negotiation of the original agreement that changes in the basic linguistic régime of the new Territory would be subject to review not only at the federal level but also by Ontario and Quebec. In this way each linguistic group in the capital could expect some degree of protection on linguistic issues by a senior level of government in which its own language and culture predominated.

In considering safeguards for linguistic and cultural rights, it is important that the guarantees should apply equally to both languages. On the basis of present population patterns it seems highly likely that Francophones would at first be in a numerical minority in a Capital Territory, no matter what boundaries were established. Nevertheless, given the régime of full equality essential for the capital area, it is not impossible that in the long run the linguistic balance in the capital might change. If this happened, it would be important for Anglophones to have at their disposal the same guarantees that are proposed in the shorter run for Francophones.

Above all, the provision of firm linguistic guarantees in the Capital Territory should diminish the psychological effects of "minorization"—the feelings of defensiveness and insecurity that tend to develop within a group in a situation where their own cultural values are under pressure from those of a more numerous or more powerful group. If Francophones in the capital can be made to feel that they are in the fullest sense equal partners with their Anglophone neighbours in the life of the capital and in conducting the affairs of the federal state, this would have a powerful effect not only in the Capital Territory itself but throughout French-speaking Canada.

D. Regional Development

Chapter V touched on the imbalance between the Quebec and Ontario sectors of the capital, and between Francophones and Anglophones within each sector, and indicated some of the remedies that might be initiated at once to reduce these imbalances. In a Capital Territory under a single integrated jurisdiction there would be possibilities for a more complete attainment of equal opportunities between Francophones and Anglophones. This aim should be pursued not for the benefit of the Capital Territory alone but also to demonstrate the possibilities of equal partnership to the whole of Canada.

A policy to give effect to this concept of partnership should be embodied in a formal statement of principle. In this connection one of the constitutional provisions of Finland is relevant. It reads: "The State shall provide for the intellectual and economic needs of the Finnish-speaking and the Swedish-speaking populations upon a similar basis."[1] The effect of this broad declaration of principle is not seen in any formal machinery for its implementation. There is no specific legislation and no particular institution designed to implement it.

---

[1] For the full text of article 14, in which this clause occurs, see *Report of the Royal Commission on Bilingualism and Biculturalism*, I, footnote to §218.

This constitutional clause is simply a general principle that may be appealed to if one cultural group considers itself disadvantaged when political decisions are being made.[1]

The constitutional arrangements for a Canadian Capital Territory should include some similar declaration. As in Finland, such a declaration of principle would have no specific mechanism for its enforcement. However, it would serve as a constant reminder of the earlier agreement to develop a capital based upon the principle of equal partnership.

The consequences of such a declaration would be reflected in various aspects of public policy that might evolve with respect to the planning and development of the Capital Territory. Chapter V indicated some of the aspects of that development that might be relevant during the short run: roads, bridges, and transit systems; the location of future federal buildings; the distribution of federal grant and tax payments to the municipalities of the capital area. As was made clear in that chapter, considerable changes are possible in the short run. However, for the longer-run development of policy in the capital area, the adoption of a formal statement of principle as a basis and inspiration for future development could have a powerful effect.

There remains for consideration the allocation of the costs involved in pursuing the economic and social development of the new Capital Territory. While the measures to promote equal partnership would doubtless have some direct impact on the general prosperity of the capital area, a primary reason for undertaking them is that their benefits would be Canada-wide. For this reason the federal government, and not the regional government, should be prepared to meet the bulk of the costs.

E. Appropriate Financial Arrangements

One recurring problem of governing *any* capital city is how to maintain an equitable balance between the legitimate interests of the local population and the equally legitimate concern of the country as a whole that the capital should appropriately reflect national aspirations and values. The same problem recurs in another form in the financial field. Here, too, there must be an appropriate distribution of financial burdens and control between the local residents and the population of the entire country. Though the problem is universal, its resolution is more difficult in federal states.

One of the arguments sometimes raised against any kind of "federal district" is the danger of fiscal dependency upon a powerful and possibly arbitrary federal government. In the United States, the budgetary dependence of the District of Columbia upon the unpredictable decisions of congressional committees has given considerable substance to this objection. Although the argument as applied to Canada may arise from a simple fear of change to some-

---

[1] In this connection it should be remembered that the Swedish-speaking population of Finland accounts for only 7 per cent of the total.

thing new and unknown, or to suspicions of higher taxes, it is important to recognize that underlying these attitudes is a real problem in intergovernmental financial relations.

If both local and federal interests are to find their due expression in the capital, each must have appropriate areas of financial autonomy. This purpose could best be served in a future Capital Territory by the establishment of clearly defined fiscal responsibilities and corresponding revenue sources for each level of government in the Territory. In this respect the position of the new territorial government might be rather similar to that of a province.

To illustrate the point more specifically, both the municipal government and the territorial government might have their respective sources of tax and other revenues, such as property taxes, gasoline taxes, sales taxes, and so on. These would be levied, at levels determined by the elected representatives of the governments concerned, for the carrying out of municipal and territorial programmes. Unlike the present system for the two provincial sectors of the capital area, the taxes levied by the territorial government would be uniform throughout the Capital Territory. The territorial government would receive certain federal transfer payments, on a similar basis to those of provincial governments, as its share of certain shared-cost programmes in the health care, welfare, or educational fields. In all these respects, the analogy with a province would be close.

In the federal field, the situation is somewhat different, for the federal government would have two distinct roles. First, it would provide to residents of the capital the same range of services and collect the same taxes as it does from residents of the provinces and territories. Further, because of its considerable physical presence in the capital area, it would require municipal services for which it would pay on the same scale as a private individual or corporation. The federal government should not enjoy a more privileged position with respect to payment for services to its buildings and its employees than that of a business firm or a private ratepayer. Making this point, however, does not preclude a revision of the municipal grant structures in the capital area along the lines discussed in Chapter V, so as to bring federal grants into closer alignment with the actual incidence of costs for educational and municipal services.

The other role of the federal government, however, would be more distinctive. A federal capital should reflect both in its physical setting and in its linguistic and cultural image the values of contemporary Canada. This is a concern of Canada as a whole. Therefore the specific costs of developing a Capital Territory worthy in both a physical and a cultural sense to be the capital of Canada should be assumed wholly by the federal government. With respect to physical development, this principle is already substantially recognized in the work of the National Capital Commission. With respect to measures promoting equal partnership in the capital in a linguistic or cultural sense, the responsibility has not yet been fully assumed by *any* level of government. In a Capital Territory, the full financial costs of such measures, including the cost of overcoming the present unbalanced pattern of development of the area, could be undertaken by the federal government.

At this stage it is not easy to say what kind of agency should carry out this special federal role in the development of an appropriate capital for Canada. It is not even clear whether one agency should be responsible for both physical and cultural development, or whether responsibilities should be divided among two or even more agencies according to the type of measure concerned. However, two things do stand out clearly: first, there is a clear policy objective to be pursued from the standpoint of Canada as a whole, and a corresponding federal financial responsibility for meeting the costs; second, in a Capital Territory of the sort in view here, even this special federal role of capital development will require co-operation between federal authorities and the elected representatives of the territorial government, because federal and local objectives must be co-ordinated and reconciled.

In the last analysis, no matter what arrangements are adopted for a Capital Territory, one cannot expect to eliminate all sources of friction in local-federal financial relations. Nevertheless, these frictions might be minimized if the roles and objectives of the different levels of government were clearly defined and each level possessed independent revenue sources appropriate to its responsibilities.

F. Education

Any satisfactory educational arrangements for a Capital Territory would have to fulfil three criteria. First, they would provide parallel, substantially independent educational systems for Francophones and Anglophones, neither one of them being in any sense subordinate to the other. Second, both these systems would provide for transfers of pupils into or out of the Capital Territory with minimum difficulty, in order not to impede the mobility of those who work—or who may wish to work—in the capital area. Finally they would be adapted to the special needs of an environment where two official languages are in widespread use, by giving special attention, among other things, to teaching the second official language.

In terms of structures, two separate educational systems would be envisaged, one for Francophones and the other for Anglophones, in the fields of elementary and secondary education. Each system would operate substantially independently of the other in terms of administraiton, curriculum planning, and teacher training, and each would serve a constituency of students on both sides of the Ottawa River. In one sense, these parallel independent structures would mark a departure from the discussion in Book II. There it was emphasized that minority-language schools should *not* be divorced in administrative or financial terms from the schools of the majority in the province concerned.[1] In a Capital Territory, where neither linguistic group would be in a minority status, relations with other educational jurisdictions outside the capital may prove more important than the interaction of the two systems within the Capital Territory.

Specifically, it seems likely that the French-language educational system in the capital would develop close ties on many different questions with the

[1] *Report of the Royal Commission on Bilingualism and Biculturalism*, II, 33 425–6.

educational system of Quebec, because the latter is the largest and the most dynamic French-language system in North America. Links of this kind would facilitate the most frequently encountered transfers of Francophone students—those between Quebec centres and the federal capital. They would also facilitate admission to Quebec's French-language universities, thus widening the options open to Francophone children in the capital. The Anglophone educational system would no doubt work in close conjunction with the Ontario educational system, but since transfers of Anglophone students to and from other provinces are also numerous, educational planning might take into account the curricula of the other predominantly Anglophone provinces as well. In brief, the two educational systems in the capital must necessarily mesh with the corresponding majority-language systems in the other provinces if the basic requirement of population mobility is to be met.

In terms of size, both educational systems would be large enough to be viable. The Francophone system would probably account for about 40 to 45 per cent of the children in the schools, depending on territorial boundaries and certain other factors. Both systems could easily manage their own teacher-training institutions, although it is to be expected that accreditation agreements with the provinces would supplement local programmes. They would even be large enough to do their own research on the special educational problems and needs of the capital area, while on more general issues they would undoubtedly rely on educational research undertaken elsewhere.

In a capital symbolizing the equality of the two official-language groups, there ought to be a fundamental change in the principles of financing education. Hitherto, the various communities—religious communities in this case—have each been responsible for financing their own school systems, with the result that economic disparities have been directly reflected in disparities in educational facilities, differential tax rates for school purposes, and differences in the salary levels of teachers. All these disparities should disappear. Two basic principles should apply in the financing of education in a Capital Territory: the tax burden on the ratepayer should be identical for both school systems, and the average revenue per pupil for each educational level should be the same in both school systems. On the means of equalization there is clearly room for negotiation, but the principles themselves are central to the whole concept of equal partnership in the capital.

In any restructuring of school systems in a Capital Territory, the issue of confessionality is bound to arise. This delicate issue has already been discussed at some length in Book II.[1] There it was made clear that, without prejudging the question of whether schools should be confessional or non-confessional, the needs of the linguistic communities should receive prior consideration. In the context of a Capital Territory this means that the confessional issue ought to be considered within the context of French- and English-language educational structures respectively.

---
[1] *Ibid.* 33 408–21.

Until recently, practically all French-language education in the capital area has fallen within a confessional framework. Therefore, some element of confessionality would probably continue under any new structure, although one would hope that some arrangements might be made to accommodate the very small number of non-Roman Catholic, Francophone families who are too few in numbers to constitute a separate educational stream. Among the Anglophones, there would be a considerable minority of Roman Catholics—comprising perhaps a third of the Anglophone population—who have had confessional schools in the past and who might wish to continue them in a new structure. At the same time, these schools have laboured under various difficulties in the past, and there might be opposition to extending full public support through the secondary level, since this is not done now in the Ontario sector where most Anglophones live. The issue is obviously difficult. However, it ought to be resolved—in an atmosphere of tolerance and understanding of the minority position—within the framework of an English-language school system.

As mentioned earlier, each of the new educational systems would be able to adapt its curriculum in its own way to the special linguistic situation of the Capital Territory. Nowhere else in Canada would the two languages meet on such a basis of full formal equality. In these circumstances, it is to be expected that both systems would give rather special attention to the problems and methods of teaching the second official language. Even now in the capital area, local educational authorities in both the Ontario and the Quebec sectors depart from provincial norms in a number of ways, including earlier introduction of second-language instruction (in some municipalities at kindergarten level), experimental teaching of secondary-level subjects through the medium of the other official language, and short-term exchanges of Francophone and Anglophone pupils. The school systems of an officially bilingual Capital Territory could do much more in this direction, and the experience so gained would be of benefit not only in the capital but everywhere in Canada.

This is not to suggest that the French- and English-language school systems of the capital will approach second-language instruction with the same emphasis, or in the same way. For the time being, at any rate, the linguistic milieu of the capital area is predominantly English, and this influence is felt even in the Quebec sector. Francophone educators, confident that the milieu itself is a powerful aid to second-language learning, may prefer to give a higher priority to the correct teaching of the mother tongue, at least during the early grades. Most Anglophones derive less assistance from the present capital environment, and there is strong evidence that many English-speaking parents wish their children to become fluent in French through sufficient exposure to it at an early age.[1]

The very strength of this motivation to become bilingual may raise a further problem. Of the 13,800 children in Ottawa French-language separate

---

[1] A recent canvass of 6,300 English-speaking families by the Ottawa Separate School Board showed that 84 per cent wanted their children to become fluent in French by the end of Grade viii, and that 77 per cent favoured a more intensive programme of instruction in French of one hour a day or more. *Ottawa Citizen*, February 11, 1969.

schools in 1968-9, almost 3,000 came from families where English was the main language used at home, and this has given rise to concern among Francophone parents that an influx of these proportions may retard the progress of children who are more fluent in French and may endanger the culture of the minority group. This problem has already been discussed in Book II. There it was recommended that parents of both the majority and the minority group should have the right to choose for their children between a majority-language school and minority-language school, but also that the linguistic and cultural character of minority-language schools should be protected, where necessary, by limiting the numbers of majority-language pupils.[1]

In a Capital Territory, however, neither language would be in a minority status: how, then would this issue be resolved? As far as can be foreseen, there is likely to be continuing and even increasing pressure from Anglophone parents to enrol their children in French-language elementary schools; it seems quite likely that these schools—in some parts of the capital at least—will require measures to protect their linguistic character. On the other hand, there are obvious advantages in having an increased proportion of the capital area population capable of handling both official languages with ease. All of this suggests that in a Capital Territory special arrangements should be made wherever necessary to enable any parents who so choose to have their children educated in the official language of their choice, even if this language is not the normal language of the home.

G. *Legal Systems and the Administration of Justice*

One further question of some difficulty for a Capital Territory arises from the differences between the existing legal systems of the two sectors. These differences arise not merely from the fact that Ontario and Quebec each have their own body of statute law, but also, and more fundamentally, because the private or civil law systems of the two provinces have different origins. That of Ontario is founded on the English common law, that of Quebec on French civil law. Of course, certain other fields of law, including the criminal law, are under federal competence and so apply to both sectors in the same way.

Despite these shared areas, the fundamental question remains: how could the civil-law and the common-law systems be reconciled in a Capital Territory? It would be unreasonable to expect either sector of the new Territory to give up its existing legal system. Each is too deeply rooted in the history and tradition of its respective sector to be surrendered lightly. Each may be said to represent a basic expression of the culture of its area. Nor is it realistic to expect the two traditions to fuse or join together, at least for the foreseeable future. The differences both in content and in thought patterns seem too great. Accordingly it would be preferable for each sector of a Capital Territory to retain its existing legal system. Indeed, this might well be one of the provisions that could be

---

[1] *Report of the Royal Commission on Bilingualism and Biculturalism*, II, §§405,407.

safeguarded by an entrenched constitutional guarantee. In this one respect, a continuing difference would exist between the two geographic sectors of a Capital Territory.

Thus, at the outset, the Ontario portions of a Capital Territory would be subject to relevant Ontario law and the Quebec portion to relevant Quebec law in effect at that date. Both systems would be modified by ordinances or enactments of the territorial government as the systems evolved.[1] In certain areas, the territorial government would be making two kinds of law, one for each sector, as circumstances required. There is no particular juridical difficulty in this, and indeed, as one historical precedent, the Parliament of the Province of Canada did so on a considerably larger scale for the same two legal systems between 1840 and 1867. Of course criminal law, and indeed all federal laws of general application, would be applied in the normal way in both sectors, just as in a province.

Under these arrangements, one difficulty would arise, but it would be of a transitional nature. The Ontario statutes and law reports are available only in English, so that at the outset the Ontario sector's laws would be available only in that language. However, the introduction of written pleadings and other procedures in the French language, the appearance of judgements in that language, and the bilingual version of all "new" law in the form of ordinances, would eventually transform the Ontario sector's law into an effective bilingual instrument. Quebec law is bilingual already.

The structure of the courts would reflect the parallel legal systems. The lower levels of courts having jurisdiction over civil cases—that is, the levels that would correspond to the existing courts of original jurisdiction in each sector—would operate according to the legal system applicable to their sector. Above these courts there would be a common appeal court exercising jurisdiction over the entire Territory. Where appropriate it would sit in separate civil-law and common-law panels, or in any case be structured so that the appeals were decided by judges thoroughly grounded in the legal tradition concerned.[2]

H. Conclusion

The preceeding pages have touched briefly and tentatively on some of the institutional arrangements that might exist in a future Capital Territory. These reflections concern primarily the problems that have been central to the Commission's terms of reference and to its research on the capital. To make the picture complete they must be set beside all the other issues facing the capital region: economic growth, transportation, pollution control, and so on.

From the Commission's vantage point, the most persuasive argument for a Capital Territory is that it would open the way to the eventual attainment

---

[1] The Australian Commonwealth Territory at Canberra began in a similar way, using the state law of New South Wales until this was gradually replaced by enactments made specifically for the Territory.

[2] One brief to the R.C.B. & B., submitted by J. H. MacDonald, an Ottawa barrister, suggested that the existing Exchequer Court of Canada might be assigned a jurisdiction of this kind.

of complete linguistic equality. In a legal and institutional sense, there could be full equality of linguistic rights. With a positive policy of regional development, there could be a reduction of the sectional economic disparities that have characterized the capital area in the past. In time, these measures could produce a psychological climate of equality.

Appendix A-6

The Special Joint Committee of the Senate and the House of Commons on the Constitution of Canada

FINAL REPORT

Chapter 16—The National Capital Area

RECOMMENDATIONS

47. There should be a movement by stages towards the possible creation of an autonomous Canadian Capital.

48. The Canadian Capital should be generally the areas of Ontario and of Quebec now defined in the schedule to the National Capital Act (1959).

A country's capital is an essential instrument of national pride. In a federal, bilingual and multicultural country, it must also be an essential instrument of national unity. It must reflect equitably all aspects of that country's character, and each citizen should have a true sense of ownership in the capital of his country regardless of the distance which separates him from the seat of government.

In Canada this has not been and is not now the case. Ottawa was chosen as capital at a time when the Western Provinces did not exist and Canada had only two of its Atlantic Provinces. It was not granted territorial autonomy but was situated on the territory of one central Province in close proximity to the other.

As Canada grew, so did its Capital, but it did so reflecting the character and the flavour of the Province of which it was a part and on which it was dependent, to the exclusion of the many other characteristics which were already present in, or which were steadily being added to, the fabric of Canada. The absence of a truly bilingual character is particularly marked.

The Federal Government probably first manifested its interest in the capital as a national institution in 1899 with the creation of the Ottawa Improvement Commission but it was not until the late 1920s that a Federal District Commission was set up. Its jurisdiction was limited to the esthetics of Federally owned lands and buildings. It naturally had a low priority on funds during the '30s and '40s. It was restructured in the late '50s into the National Capital

Commission when the Federal Parliament, recognized that the Capital area had expanded in fact beyond the limits of the city and of the Province and therefor adopted the National Capital Act. This Act defined the territory over which the N.C.C. would exert influence.

> The National Capital Region is an area of 1,800 square miles of Ontario and Québec. The Region is home to some 600,000 inhabitants whose cultural backgrounds are proportionate to those of Canadian citizens in general. Centered about the cities of Hull and Ottawa, it includes all or part of 57 local municipal jurisdictions. Its problems are typical of those of most urban communities throughout the country. Moreover, the Region is typically Canadian in its content of farmland, bushland, rocky tree-covered hills and innumerable lakes and streams. (*N.C.C. Annual Report, 1970-71*, p. 2)

The current mandate of the N.C.C. empowers it to acquire and dispose of lands, to undertake joint projects with municipalities. to make grants for various purposes and to conduct research for the planning of the National Capital Region. In our view the Capital Area should continue to be the areas of Ontario and Quebec now defined in the schedule to the National Capital Act (1959).

The Committee is of the opinion that the time has come for the Federal Government to have more voice in the management of the Capital of the country. The Committee also believes that the Capital is not just an Ontario city or an Ontario-Quebec city, but a Federal Capital which aspires to be representative of the people of all 10 provinces, and which can indeed be to all the people an instrument of pride and of unity.

It has been suggested that the national capital should be autonomous. The Committee feels that the present maze of jurisdictional difficulties surrounding this issue have created strong barriers to the establishment of an autonomous capital region. Rather, it would be more expedient to view such an autonomous region as a possible, but not a necessary, final stage of development.

We therefore recommend that a Board comprised of equal numbers of Ministers from the Federal, Ontario and Quebec governments, together with representatives of the Regional Communities concerned, should be established to co-ordinate the activities of governments in the Canadian Capital. This Board should be empowered to promote further municipal rationalization and to impart to the Capital those characteristics which truly reflect the reality of Canada.

Present provincial boundaries and provincial jurisdictions would continue to apply, and residents of the National Capital would continue to elect members of Parliament and members of the Legislature of the Province in which they reside, according to the normal provisions of the respective jurisdictions.

The Committee also suggests, as a second stage, that a single new political structure would be necessary to replace the myriad of local governments found within the National Capital region in order to administer those affairs normally under municipal jurisdictions. Hence, we recommend the eventual establishment of a tripartite Board appointed jointly by the Ontario, Quebec, and Federal governments.

We believe that, having gone through these two stages, the population of the National Capital Area may well consider it advantageous to advance towards fully autonomous status.

We have purposely avoided the term "federal district" because of the bad connotation it generally has. We are convinced, however, that it is within the ingenuity of Canadians to develop a new formula that would achieve the aim of a truly national Capital.

Appendix A-7

OFFICE OF THE PRIME MINISTER — **CABINET DU PREMIER MINISTRE**

PRESS RELEASE / COMMUNIQUÉ

Date: May 17, 1973

For Release: Immediate

Pour Publication:

Mr. Douglas H. Fullerton, Chairman of the National Capital Commission, is resigning his position to carry out a special study for the Government on the future development of the National Capital Region.

The announcement was made jointly today by the Prime Minister and the Minister of State for Urban Affairs, the Hon. Ron Basford.

The terms of reference of Mr. Fullerton's study are "to undertake a study of the most effective arrangements for the future administration of matters directly affecting the National Capital and its development, including the role of the National Capital Commission and its relation to other bodies concerned with the governing of the Capital Region and the coordination of those federal activities which bear upon the development of the Region as a national capital."

Mr. Fullerton, whose term of office would normally have ended August 31st, has submitted his resignation effective May 31st in order to avoid any suggestion of his objectivity being prejudiced by any continuing ties with the Commission.

It is expected that Mr. Fullerton's report will be available within a year.

The Government is giving active consideration to recommending the establishment of a Special Committee in the next session of Parliament, to make a thorough review of present arrangements for administration and development of the National Capital, and Mr. Fullerton's report would provide essential background material for such a Committee study. The last such Parliamentary study was carried out in 1956 by a Joint Committee of the Senate and House of Commons and led to the National Capital Act in 1958 and to the formation of the present National Capital Commission.

The Prime Minister and Mr. Basford said that they welcomed Mr. Fullerton's willingness to undertake this study, and expressed confidence that he will bring to it the same vigour and enthusiasm that have characterized his four-year term of office as Chairman of the Commission.

Advertisement in Ottawa papers on June 16th, 1973, and the following week in Toronto and Montreal papers, and in the largest paper in each provincial capital.

Special Study on the National Capital   Étude spéciale sur la capitale nationale

REQUEST FOR SUBMISSIONS

On May 17th 1973 the Prime Minister and the Minister of State for Urban Affairs announced my appointment to carry out a special study for the federal government on the future development of the National Capital Region. The terms of reference are "to undertake a study of the most effective arrangements for the future administration of matters directly affecting the National Capital and its development, including the role of the National Capital Commission and its relation to other bodies concerned with the governing of the Capital Region and the coordination of those federal activities which bear upon the development of the Region as a national capital."

In furtherance of the objectives of this study, I would welcome the submission of briefs, memoranda or letters from individuals, organizations, or local governments. The submissions should be in typescript form, in English or in French, should relate directly to any or all topics included in the terms of reference, and six copies should be sent to this office before October 1, 1973. Information may be submitted on a confidential basis if so desired.

It is not my present intention to hold public hearings, since these would more appropriately flow from the review of the National Capital by a Special Committee of Parliament, the establishment of which the government is considering recommending at the next Session. However, persons or organizations submitting material to me will be given an opportunity to discuss their proposals.

DOUGLAS H. FULLERTON
June 15, 1973

Box 495, Station A
Ottawa, Canada
K1N 8X9

C.P. 495, Succursale A
Ottawa, Canada
K1N 8X9

613 996-8426

Advertisement in the local papers on October 5th, 1973

RESIDENTS OF THE NATIONAL CAPITAL: YOU HAVE A SPECIAL STAKE IN THIS STUDY. WHAT ARE YOUR VIEWS?

Last June, in an advertisement, I invited your ideas and suggestions about the most effective arrangements for the future administration and development of the National Capital. During the four months we have been in business, my colleagues and I have been discussing many questions about the problems of administering the Capital with a variety of people: Cabinet Ministers, Members of Parliament, Members of Provincial Legislatures, Mayors, Reeves, Controllers, Aldermen, and Councillors, as well as scholars, representatives of community associations and other interested persons. Some of them have suggested to us that the deadline set in June did not provide enough time for the presentation of submissions.

FOR THIS REASON I HAVE EXTENDED THE DEADLINE FOR SUBMISSIONS, BRIEFS AND LETTERS, FROM INDIVIDUALS OR GROUPS, FROM OCTOBER 1st TO DECEMBER 1st, 1973.

A number of questions keep coming up in our discussions, and they may be of interest to you in helping you put your views on paper:

How do you define the Capital? Both sides of the Ottawa River? What form of government would you like to see it have? Do you feel overgoverned now? Does the ordinary citizen have enough to say in decisions taken about his future? Which levels of government do you feel are most responsive to your needs? How should power be divided among them? What kind of government for the Capital would provide both for the interest of residents and those of Canadians from coast to coast? Should an attempt be made to control the size of the Capital, possibly by moving some federal departments or agencies elsewhere in Canada? What do you think of the National Capital Commission? What role should it play in the future? Do you like living in the Capital? Why? Do you feel at home here? Do you feel that the present expansion of governement office buildings on the Quebec side of the region is a good thing or a bad thing? What do you feel about bilingualism and biculturalism in the National Capital? Do you feel threatened by the other main language group? How can the interest of minority groups be protected?

These are a few of the questions to which we are seeking answers. If you have something to say about them, please send them in to me in writing, in English or in French. As residents of the National Capital you have a particular stake in its future and we want your views.

DOUGLAS H. FULLERTON.

Box 495, Station A Ottawa, Canada K1N 8X9 613-996-8426	C.P. 495, Succursale A Ottawa, Canada K1N 8X9

Appendix B

Research Papers and Studies

B-1 Public Opinion Regarding the Restructuring of Government in the National Capital Region
—Professors D. J. Falcone and R. J. Van Loon, Carleton University 288

B-2 The Language Question and the Capital
—James M. Weld 325

B-2A Three Options for the Future Development of Education in the Capital Area
—Professor K. D. McRae, Carleton University 360

B-3 The Government Structure of the National Capital Area
—Murray V. Jones 368

B-4 Local Government and the National Capital Region
—Raymond G. Poulin 376

Appendix B-1

PUBLIC OPINION REGARDING THE RESTRUCTURING OF GOVERNMENT IN THE NATIONAL CAPITAL REGION[*]

by

D. J. Falcone and R. J. Van Loon

Carleton University

This report presents the main findings from a survey project the principal aim of which has been to determine whether a consensus exists among residents of the National Capital Region for a restructuring of government in the Region and, if so, what kind of restructuring is desired. Specifically, we have attempted to measure public opinion regarding the replacement of the present governmental system in the Region with an hypothetical federal territory (or federal district) and to find out what representational form of government likely would be most acceptable, assuming that some sort of government for the territory were to be created. Subsidiary purposes of the study have been to gauge the salience to the public of local political issues; the comparative salience of, and affect towards, levels of government among residents of the Region; and to explore the demographic correlates of these attitudes. The report concentrates on those findings of direct relevance to the principal objective. The format is as follows.

(1) First, we tabulate the percentage distribution of responses to a referendum—type question about the general idea of a federal territory in the NCR. The results provide overwhelming support for the conclusion that there is a consensus in favour of the idea on the part of the residents of the Region. However, since consensus has numerous meanings, we attempt to distinguish three types to enable us to interpret the results more accurately.

(2) Following this brief treatment of definitional problems, we outline in some detail our methods of data collection. This discussion should indicate why we consider our data more reliable and valid than those analyzed in previous research with similar purposes, despite the fact that our sample is smaller than those of all except one of these studies.

---

[*] The research for this study was supported by a grant from the Special Study on the National Capital. We are indebted to Margaret Kipp for her assistance in the data preparation and analysis and to Professor Don Rowat for a critical reading of an earlier draft of the report. The conclusions reached are the authors' as is the responsibility for any errors in the collection, preparation and analysis of the data.

This section can be skipped or skimmed by readers who wish to move immediately to thet "meat" of the analysis but it should be consulted if there is any question abou the methodological orthodoxy of the study.

(3) Then, as a backdrop for the quantitative analyses of answers to the closed-end items in the questionnaire (i.e. those for which response options have been specified), we summarize briefly our impressions regarding the broadly stated responses (or lack of responses) elicited by a few open-end questions. These impressions are not inconsistent with the results of our inspection of the quantified distributions. The former suggest a qualification to our conclusion that a consensus exists in favour of a federal territory only insofar as this consensus is more aptly described as one permitting, rather than demanding, such a change in the government of the Region.

(4) The quantitative analysis of the percentage distribution of responses to closed-end questions forms the bulk of this report. These distributions are displayed by significant sub-groups, such as Quebec–Ontario and income levels. The breakdowns generally fail to produce marked variations in attitudes. For example, in most cases a majority, and in all cases a plurality, of persons in each category favours the idea of a federal territory. However, those few variations that the analyses *do* uncover suggest that, for certain groups in the Region, the consensus for a federal territory may approach the type wherein positive government action is demanded. The groups that stand out most in this respect comprise those persons with high socioeconomic status, high levels of participation in voluntary associations, and Quebecers.

(5) Since the above generalizations apply to opinions toward the fairly amorphous idea of a federal territory, we also examine respondents' opinions about whom should be represented in the event a federal territory were to be established. Naturally, residents of the Region could not be expected to draft a preferred governmental structure. Yet, their attitudes do provide rough guidelines for policy-makers and we note some of the constraints of public opinion in this regard.

The report ends with a summary of the findings of our survey in light of their significance for the concerns of the National Capital Region Study.

Main Findings

Table 1 contains the percentage distributions of responses when interviewees were asked, "which of the following [statements] best reflects your views" on the question of whether the Region should become a federal territory. Labelling items 1 and 2 "favourable", 3 and 6 "neutral", and 4 and 5, "unfavourable", the respective percentages in each category are, approximately; 54, 18, and 28. The fact that the modal category (1) is the most favourable statement and that the ratio of favourable to unfavourable replies is almost 2 to 1, clearly indicate respondents' endorsement of a federal territory. Furthermore, although the number of persons who selected statement 5 does not permit us to describe the distribution as an ideal J-curve, rarely do opinions on anything other than banalities so nearly approximate the classic conception of consensus.

TABLE 1

PERCENTAGE DISTRIBUTION OF RESPONSES TO REFERENDUM
QUESTION ON A FEDERAL TERRITORY FOR THE
NATIONAL CAPITAL REGION

1. The National Capital Region definitely should become a federal territory	31.5%
2. It seems like a good idea but I have some doubts about it	22.5
3. It is difficult to say one way or the other	9.9
4. There seems very little reason to change the present set-up	7.9
5. The National Capital Region definitely should not become a federal territory	20.2
6. I have no opinion	7.9

(n = 275)

A Working Notion of Consensus

For our purposes, the term consensus simply refers to widespread agreement upon a question of public policy or to an opinion distribution that conforms (albeit perhaps crudely) to a J-curve. Thus "defined", a consensus then can be labelled as one of at least three types with respect to its significance for government action. The first of these, "permissive" consensus, describes a climate of opinion that would allow government to act without incurring popular discontent, but that does not necessarily demand positive government action. A second type is "supportive"; i.e., a consensus that underpins existing government policy (or, as may be the case with specific reference to a federal territory plan, what is perceived to be government policy). When widespread opinion suggests the advisability of a particular government response, it represents a third type, the "decisive" consensus.[1] The findings of our survey seem to suggest that there certainly is a permissive consensus towards the creation of some form of federal territory, perhaps a decisive one in some instances. This conclusion finds a solid basis in the analyses of the quantified data presented in this report and is supported by our discussions with interviewers and the two persons who coded respondents' answers to open-end questions (see below, pp. 12 ff). Nonetheless, further study would be needed to categorize authoritatively the nature of the consensus. It may be, for example, that many of those interviewed in our sample perceived that the establishment of some sort of federal territory was a foregone conclusion, and thus their generally favourable opinions could be taken to represent a supportive consensus. Whatever the case, it seems highly unlikely that a decisive consensus exists for a federal territory, but then it is only in very dramatic instances that public opinion can be relied upon to give definite shape to public policy, particularly where government structure is at issue.

---

[1] For a fuller development of this typology and some specific examples of each type see V. O. Key, *Public Opinion and American Democracy* (N.Y.: Knopf, 1965), pp. 28-39.

Methodological Considerations

It can be stated categorically that there never has been a piece of social science research that could not be attacked on some grounds as being "unscientific". Thus the crucial issue in evaluating a study's methodology is not whether the canons of science have been adhered to, but rather whether departures from the ideal damage the conclusions. In this regard, we would contend that, unlike the methodological shortcomings of most previous attempts to determine public opinion about a federal territory in the NCR, those in the present study have not worked to preordain our conclusions.

Previous Opinion Surveys

To our knowledge there have been only five previous surveys measuring opinions regarding the specific question of whether the NCR should become a federal territory.[2] One was national in scope, three were limited to the Ontario sector and one to the Quebec sector. None could be called representative. Unlike our survey which is based on a random sample and home interviews, four of these are based on mail questionnaires with return rates ranging from a poor 17.2% (Municipality of Lucerne, 1969) to a very poor 3.9% (Canadian Studies Foundation, Outaouais Project, 1973). Of course, even if return rates had been considerably higher, one could not rely on the data since in all mail surveys respondents are basically self-selected. The samples are therefore nonrandom, and their probability of error cannot be assessed. However valid and interesting their questions or impressive the sheer numbers of persons who returned questionnaires (eg., 7,000 of 58,000 in the case of R. A. Bell's 1967 study), these studies greatly overrepresent the "attentive" public. Our study probably also tends to overrepresent this group—as evidenced by the fact that respondents' incomes and education levels are slightly higher than would be expected—but hardly to the same extent. We too have experimented with a mail questionnaire sent to a random sample of persons who are in distant parts of the NCR too difficult to reach by our interviews and whose household telephone numbers are in the "Other Listings" section of the *Ottawa-Hull Directory*. The return rate thus far has been about 20% but we have not included the returns in the analyses because of the sources of error thereby introduced. They are, of course, available to anyone who wants to examine the replies.

The one previous study that is based on a selected sample and home interviews, the Scanlon-March survey conducted in 1967, was limited to metropolitan Ottawa and its reliability is somewhat questionable because only 80 completed interviews were obtained. For this limited population, this number does not yield satisfactory error margins and confidence levels (i.e., tolerance interval at a 95% confidence level would be ±11%; at a 90% level, ±9%). An explanation of these terms is presented below, but our point here is that past studies offered little guidance for the design of the present study, and their results can be of little help to the persons who need to know the real climate of opinion on this issue in the entire Region.

---

[2] Some of these are described in Appendix II, "A Report on Public Attitudes," of the *Report of the Royal Commission on Bilingualism and Biculturalism*, pp. 105-108.

The Sample

Sampling Technique and Universe

The findings reported in this study are based on a systematic random sample[3] of 269 persons 18 years old or older whose household telephone numbers are listed in "Section 1" of the December 1972, *Ottawa-Hull Directory*. This universe includes over 95% of the Region's population. A list of the municipalities it encompasses can be found on pp. 20-21 of the 1973 *Directory*. A random number from 1 to 300 was used to designate the first household included in the sample, from which point a step interval of 300 was used to select the remainder. In all, about 750 households were selected. Approximately 150 of these subsequently were excluded because advance letters to households addressed according to the *Directory* listings were returned, indicating in most cases that the persons in the household had moved. Thus, our sample overrepresents the stable population; 66% of those interviewed have lived in the Region for more than 10 years, 40% for more than 20 years.

The approximately 600 households remaining in the sample after those whose advance letters were returned had been removed were subdivided by area according to the same blocking procedure as that used by "Cartex" maps.[4] This gave each interviewer a relatively small area to cover. Household names then were distributed randomly by subdivision to student interviewers. This procedure ensured that at any time after we reached 100 interviews, the data on hand were representative of a wide geographic area. With 269 interviews completed and validated, our sample permits generalization to most of the Region, specifically to residents in areas within the following inclusive bounds:

	Quebec	Ontario
North-South	Templeton West	Richmond
East	Templeton	Orleans
West	Aylmer	Carp

It should be pointed out that Quebec residents are somewhat underrepresented in our sample. They constitute approximately 18% of those interviewed whereas the corresponding population proportion is approximately 24%. Therefore, as is conventional in such situations, we have employed a computer weighting technique that raises the contribution of Quebecers' responses to the overall distributions to conform to population proportions.[5] Thus, the reported number of cases ("n") will sometimes be as high as 288 rather than 269. The *n* will be lower in some instances because cases with missing values for a variable have been deleted.

---

[3] For more information on this method see, Charles Backstrom and Gerald D. Hursh, *Survey Research* (Evanston, Ill.: Northwestern Univ. Press, 1963).
[4] Distributed by National News Co. Ltd., Ottawa.
[5] The technique is a component of the computer routine used, the *Statistical Package for the Social Sciences* (N.Y.: McGraw-Hill, 1970) developed by Norman Nie, Dale Bent and C. Hadlai Hull.

Confidence Levels and Tolerance Intervals

With respect to the accuracy of our reported percentages as measures of parameters in the above universe, given the sampling technique employed and the number of persons interviewed, the figures have a *maximum* expected margin of error of:[6]

$\pm\, 1.96\sqrt{.25/269} = .0598$ (i.e. 6.0%) at a 95% and
$\pm\, 1.65\sqrt{.25/269} = .0503$ at a 90% confidence level.

The *most likely* margin of error for any given proportion (P) would be:

$\pm\, 1.96\sqrt{P(1-P)/269}$ at a 95% and
$\pm\, 1.65\sqrt{P(1-P)/269}$ at a 90% confidence level.

For example, in cases where the figure we report is 20%, the most likely margin would be 0.047, i.e. 4.7%, so that the true figure might be anywhere between 17.7% and 22.4%. The confidence level conventionally refers to the number of times out of an infinite number of samples statistics would measure parameters within the tolerance interval. More roughly, we can say that, in the present study, there is less than a 5% chance that reported percentages will be off the true figures by more than 5.98%, and less than a 10% chance they will be off by more than 5.03%. This is the widest likely margin of error. As percentages move away from 50%, we can expect them to become increasingly accurate representations of population figures. Another factor making the reported margins of error fairly liberal estimates is that, in effect, we have stratified the sample by geographic subdivision, and this tends to shrink the tolerance interval and/or raise the confidence level.

The Interview

Although, as is the case with all interview schedules, ours clearly is not a precision instrument, a pre-test indicated that most respondents were able to understand the questions and that they did not seem constrained to qualify their answers to the closed-end items. Those questions in the preliminary version that provoked extensive qualification, that seemed to contain more than one stimulus, or that were ambiguous for whatever reasons, were deleted from the final schedule. (A copy of the schedule is appended to this report.) Almost all English or French respondents were interviewed in their first language. Several persons were interviewed in Italian. Obviously, however, it simply was impossible to avoid interviewing persons of other groups in other than their native languages.

Depending on a number of variables, the interviews took about 30 minutes to one hour to complete. The interviewers were students from Carleton and Ottawa Universities. All were given training sessions, and many had had previous experience in administering at-home interviews. They were instructed not to paraphrase any of the questions and to be neutral in their reactions to inter-

---
[6] These formulae can be found in appropriate sections of most statistics texts. See for example, Hubert Blalock, *Social Statistics* 2nd. ed. (N.Y.: McGraw-Hill, 1972), pp. 201-18.

viewees' comments, so that the stimuli in the schedule have been standardized as much as possible. Naturally, a sample of those interviewed by each student was checked to verify that he had completed the interviews.

Interviewers were allowed to try to obtain an interview with a designated person in one or the other households adjoining the one chosen at random, if they were unable to interview the designated person in the sample household. It has been shown that, if carefully controlled, this method of substitution does not violate the assumptions of independent, random sampling. We used it since repeated callbacks would have been prohibitively expensive. The substitution was controlled in that students had to follow the grid attached to each interview schedule in selecting the person in each household to be interviewed (see the first page of the questionnaire).[7] The grid ensures that interviewees will be chosen at random with respect to age and sex. Thus, the substitution should not have resulted in traditional causes of unrepresentativeness, such as the fact that housewives tend to be at home more often than persons with other careers, because the interviewers also had to follow the grid in the substitute households.

Open-end Questions

The responses reported in this study pertain to closed-end items only. Time and resources did not permit us to tackle the problems connected with analyzing open-end questions, such as the determination of intercoder reliability and the necessity to empirically derive coding categories. (Some students have been working on intensive analyses of specific items, and these probably will be available later, on request.) However, the coders' impressions from reading the responses to the open-end items provide a basis for some tentative and broadly stated generalizations.

(1) In interviewees' rankings of the most salient problems facing the Ottawa-Hull area today (Question 2), there is almost no mention of political or governmental considerations. Undoubtedly, the latter would have received more priority had the question been at a later time in the interview schedule; i.e., after respondents had been alerted to the political concerns involved in the federal territory proposal. Still, the great majority of those interviewed did receive an advance letter telling them they would be interviewed in a study being conducted by two political scientists, and that their opinions about "local issues" would be elicited. Therefore, there should have been some *a priori* tendency for political considerations to have assumed more salience than they would ordinarily. Despite this, the actual responses indicate that residents of the NCR ascribe most importance to problems such as traffic, pollution, and (to a considerably lesser extent) bilingualism. This is not unexpected in light of Canadians' general lack of concern over political and governmental matters.[8]

---

[7] Six different versions of the grids were used to select interviewees from the sample households.

[8] There is a good deal of literature supporting this point. For an analysis of some empirical evidence, see R. J. Van Loon, "Political Participation in Canada," *Canadian Journal of Political Science* 3 (Sept. 1970): 376-400.

(2) The coders also inform us that answers to the questions probing the "meaningfulness" of the terms "National Capital Commission", "Federal District", and "Ottawa-Carleton Regional Government (Outaouais Region Community)" evinced little detailed understanding of these concepts. For example, the NCC was identified with respect to its public works, not as a federal crown corporation or agency. "Federal District" and "Ottawa-Carleton Regional Government", when they generated any coherent response—and this was in less than one half of the cases—were usually described only tautologically, e.g., "the Ottawa-Carleton Regional Government governs the region". Of course, *prima facie*, this does not indicate that respondents were ignorant of the regional government or that they had no conception of what a Federal District might entail. It simply suggests, as with responses to Question 2, that area residents probably devote little attention to structural features of government. This generalization seems even safer in view of the cue in the advance letter, the slightly above average socioeconomic status of our respondents, and the fact that the stable population of the region is somewhat overrepresented in the sample. With specific regard to reactions to the term Federal District, it should be noted that there is no indication that the term itself has pejorative connotations, not even in the context of a discussion about issues dealing with the structure of local government.

(3) Also indicative of the generally low salience of issues relating to government structure are responses to Question 9. The survey was conducted in November and December of 1973, after the announcement of the Special Study of the National Capital and the proposal for a parliamentary committee on the subject. Although well over one half of those interviewed claimed to have read or heard about proposals for restructuring the government of the Ottawa-Hull region, well under one half of the persons in this group were able to recall anything about the proposals.

Quantitative Analysis of Survey Results

Introduction

In any full scale survey such as this one confronts mountains of data. Thus the major problem in analyzing the material is that of selecting the results which are most likely to be of interest in arriving at policy decisions. We have examined a large amount of data and are presenting here what we believe to be the most interesting and important. However, because many other questions can be answered with the survey results, we have generated numerous other cross-tabulations which are not reported in detail here. These tabulations are available on request and interested persons may find a considerable body of useful information in them.

We have decided to focus this report on seven questions which seem to us to be directly relevant to the purposes of the Special Study. Perhaps the most important question is whether and/or to what extent there exists a permissive consensus in the National Capital Region with regard to the idea of the Region becoming a federal territory. We already have seen in the replies to the referendum-type question that such a consensus exists; that one can say with confidence that at the time the survey was conducted the citizens of the National Capital Region at least were willing to accept the idea of a federal territory. The answers to the question are analyzed in more detail below.

We also go into considerable detail in examining two other questions: have people heard of the ideas for reform of government in the Region; and which government do people in this area "feel closest to"? In somewhat less detail we analyze answers to questions of whether people would favour a retention of local and regional government if a federal territory were to be set up, and whether, in the latter event, they would feel it important to continue to elect M.P.s. Finally, in rather broad strokes we attempt to paint a picture of the climate of public opinion in the region with respect to a wide range of questions that should inform the recommendations of the Special Study.

In the interests of conciseness, we have had to be somewhat selective in the use we have made of independent variables (i.e., those attributes that may help to explain just who holds what opinions). We felt that the most pertinent of these were: place of residence (Quebec or Ontario); mother tongue; socio-economic status (for which income is used as a surrogate); length of residence in the capital region; and the amount of organizational activity in which respondents participate. Not all of these independent variables are used in the written analysis of each question but tabulations for all of them are available.

The Results

Opinions on the National Capital Region Becoming a Federal Territory

As noted previously, all respondents were presented with a referendum type question. The exact wording was as follows:

> For some time now people have been discussing whether or not the National Capital Region should become a federal territory. Which of the following best reflects your views on this question.
>
> The National Capital Region definitely should become a federal territory.
>
> It seems like a good idea but I have some doubts about it.
>
> It is difficult to say one way or the other.
>
> There seems very little reason to change the present set-up.
>
> The National Capital Region definitely should not become a federal territory.
>
> I have no opinion.

The percentages given in Table 1 above indicated that roughly twice as many people in the National Capital Region favour a federal territory as oppose it. The important next question about this result is: does there appear to be any significant variation among sub-groups of the population of the region regarding support for or opposition to the idea? Table 2 summarizes the impact of our major independent variables on this question.

It is clear that respondents from Quebec are more favourable to the idea of a federal territory than are those from Ontario. Some 66% of the former evince general approval of the idea versus 51% of the latter. Moreover, 50% of Quebec residents feel the Region definitely should become a federal territory, whereas the corresponding figure for Ontario residents is 28%. Yet, paradoxically, our French respondents appear to favour the idea slightly less than our English respondents. At first, glance this seems to indicate an overwhelming acceptance of the idea by English-speaking Quebecers, considerable support among French speaking Quebecers, and a comparatively lukewarm endorsement by Franco-Ontarians. However, a further breakdown of opinions, by province and first language (see Table 2a), reveals that, even among Franco-Ontarians, the favourable to unfavourable ratio is well over two to one. The fact that a majority does not endorse the concept obviously is owing to the large number of persons in this subgroup with neutral opinions (44%), rather than to their antipathy to the idea.

The attractiveness of the idea of a federal territory is clearly related to income. Among our lowest income categories the support is weakest although even in this case a majority is favourable. For the upper 20% of our sample, some 75% of respondents favour the idea and only about 17% oppose it. This should be heartening to proponents of the idea since, of course, this is the sub-group whose preferences would be most likely to make themselves felt in decisions on the issue. On the other hand, there is a tendency toward polarization in the distributions of opinions of the $8,000—$9,999, $10,000–$14,999, $15,000–$19,999 groups that tapers off in the case of the $20,000–$29,000 category. As one might expect, this situation probably is owing to the greater extent of opinion crystallization among these groups as evidenced by the smaller percentage of persons who register "no opinion". In any event, in no case do the responses take the shape of a bimodal distribution.

Although there is not a very clear linear relationship between length of residence in the region and the attractiveness of the federal territory proposal, long-time residents tend to give the idea greater support. The final section of Table 2 indicates that the more active a person is in community affairs the more likely he is to favour a federal territory. However, here again, the relationship is neither linear nor particularly strong.

To summarize our findings on the tendency to favour or oppose the National Capital Region becoming a federal territory, we find that about twice as many residents favour the idea as oppose it, that support comes from all of the segments of the community that we have delineated, and that Quebecers tend to favour the idea more than Ontarians. There is also a strong positive relationship between social class and endorsement of the idea (using income to define class).

TABLE 2

VIEWS ON A FEDERAL TERRITORY
(All Figures in Percentages)

Views on a Federal Territory	Place of Residence		Mother Tongue			Income ($/Year) (Social Class)									Length of Residence in region						Level of Organizational Activity (How often attends meetings)				
	Ontario	Quebec	French	English	Other	0-3000	3000-5999	6000-7999	8000-9999	10000-14999	15000-19999	20000-29999	30000 & over	Less than 1 year	1-3 years	3-5 years	5-10 years	10-20 years	over 20 years	Weekly	Monthly	Yearly	Seldom	Never
Definitely or seems OK	51	66	53	57	50	51	53	52	50	49	56	75	76	29	48	48	71	47	53	57	59	65	31	50
Hard to say	11	7	14	9	4	11	6	12	8	11	6	4	0	0	13	10	10	17	5	9	13	0	5	12
Little reason to change or definitely no	30	23	25	28	35	18	20	20	30	33	36	21	8	43	27	23	16	30	33	33	17	29	47	35
No opinion	9	5	9	7	12	20	20	17	13	7	2	0	16	29	13	8	2	6	9	2	11	7	18	2
Total N in column	223	63	76	182	29	12	15	20	27	57	45	48	12	7	24	27	41	74	115	49	48	15	19	157

298

TABLE 2A

VIEWS ON A FEDERAL TERRITORY BY PROVINCE AND MOTHER TONGUE
(Figures in Percentages)

Views on a Federal Territory	Ontario French	Ontario English	Quebec French	Quebec English
Definitely or Seems O.K.	40	52	59	90
Hard to Say	24	10	9	0
Little Reason to Change or Definitely no	16	31	29	0
No opinion	20	7	3	10
Total N in Column	25	161	49	14

Knowledge of the Issue

As already mentioned, a majority of our respondents claimed to have heard about some proposals for restructuring the government of the Ottawa-Hull Region. Approximately 59% answered yes and 41% no to this question. Since it may provide us with a rather good index of who pays attention to local politics in the Region and who does not, the question may be worth analyzing in more detail. Table 3 does this.

Residents of Ontario are somewhat more likely to have heard about proposals for a restructuring of government in the Region than are residents of Quebec. Approximately 61% of the former claimed to have heard or read something on that subject compared to about 50% of the latter. The difference between French and English in this respect is also interesting, with the French respondents being about 14% less likely to have heard about such proposals than the English. Other language groups are about as likely to be aware of such proposals as are the English.

There is a clear relationship between income (or socioeconomic class) and whether a respondent has heard about proposals for restructuring government. Among people whose income is less than $8,000 per year, only 28% claim to have been aware of this issue, while nearly 80% of those whose income is over $15,000 have been aware of the question. This finding is not surprising since many other surveys have shown that, the higher a person's socioeconomic status, the more likely he is to pay attention to political questions of all kinds.

With reference to the other two independent variables analyzed, the relationship between length of residence in the Region and awareness of proposals for a restructuring of government is barely discernible, but the final section of Table

TABLE 3

WHO HAS HEARD ABOUT PROPOSALS FOR RESTRUCTURING GOVERNMENT?

(Figures in Percentages)

Heard about proposals for restructuring	Place of Residence		Mother Tongue			Income ($/Year) (Social Class)								Length of Residence in region						Level of Organizational Activity (How often attends meetings)				
	Ontario	Quebec	French	English	Other	0-3000	3000-5999	6000-7999	8000-9999	10000-14999	15000-19999	20000-29999	30000 & over	Less than 1 year	1-3 years	3-5 years	5-10 years	10-20 years	over 20 years	Weekly	Monthly	Yearly	Seldom	Never
Yes	61	50	49	63	62	32	40	18	67	60	79	71	92	29	79	63	70	53	56	65	67	71	57	60
No	39	50	51	37	38	68	60	82	33	40	21	29	8	71	31	37	30	47	44	35	33	29	43	40
Total N in Column	223	63	76	182	29	12	15	20	27	57	45	48	12	7	24	27	41	74	115	49	48	15	19	157

3 does indicate that the more a person attends organizational functions, the more likely he is to have claimed awareness.[9]

The results of our detailed analysis of this question simply point up the similarity between our respondents and those in countless other surveys with respect to the correlations between socioeconomic status and social activity and awareness of local political issues. For the concerns of this report, that point is important for two reasons. First it tends to affirm the validity of the rest of our findings since our respondents behave "normally". Had we found that lower-status respondents claimed more knowledge of proposals for a change in government structure than did upper-status ones, we would have reason to be suspicious of our other findings. Second, it suggests that the same groups who are least supportive of the idea of a federal territory are those who know least about it, and this should be encouraging to proponents of a federal territory.

Finally it should be pointed out that as issues in local politics go, the federal territory idea has a rather high rate of recognition. Of course, this does not mean that the idea is teeming in the minds of local residents, but—notwithstanding what was said earlier in this report (pp. 12 ff.)—it does indicate substantial interest in the proposal.

Feelings Towards Different Levels of Government

As a measure of the perception of our respondents concerning the relevance to them of the different levels of government in the Region, we asked them: "as a private citizen, which do you generally feel closest to, the federal government, the Ontario (Quebec) government, the Ottawa Carleton (Outaouais)[10] regional government or the (name of municipality) municipal government"? Of those who replied, 62% said "federal", 10% "provincial", 5% "regional" and 25% "local". Partially as a check on this question and because it elicits slightly different information, we also asked people about the salience of different levels of government, or which government they felt most affected their day to day lives. In response to that, 50% said "federal", 20% "provincial", 16% "regional" and 15% "local". Aside from the considerably higher salience of the provincial and regional levels, the responses are quite similar to those regarding the "closeness" of different levels.

Since the question of feelings towards different levels of government provides a valuable barometer concerning how supportive residents may be when it comes to one level or another increasing its influence (as might be perceived to happen were a federal territory chosen as a future mode of government for the area), we analyzed it in more detail in Table 4. The results show that income, length of residence in the region, and level of organizational activity are only weakly correlated with feelings of the closeness of levels of government. The main point of interest in those three parts of the table is that in every category at least a plurality of people feel closest to the federal government.

---

[9] The 71% figure for those who attend meetings "yearly" is based on too small a number of respondents (15) to warrant extensive analysis or interpretation.
[10] The terms in parantheses were used in interviews with Quebec residents.

TABLE 4
FEELINGS TOWARDS DIFFERENT LEVELS OF GOVERNMENT
(Figures in Percentages)

Which Government do you feel Closest to?	Place of Residence Ontario	Place of Residence Quebec	Mother Tongue French	Mother Tongue English	Mother Tongue Other	Income ($/Year) (Social Class) 0-3000	3000-5999	6000-7999	8000-9999	10000-14999	15000-19999	20000-29999	30000 & over	Length of Residence in region Less than 1 year	1-3 years	3-5 years	5-10 years	10-20 years	over 20 years	Level of Organizational Activity (How often attends meetings) Weekly	Monthly	Yearly	Seldom	Never
Federal	65	52	60	64	54	52	86	62	87	49	45	76	68	86	64	48	67	63	60	61	54	65	45	65
Provincial	7	23	17	9	4	0	0	16	4	16	20	0	0	0	11	16	6	7	13	8	10	16	13	9
Regional	6	2	2	6	4	12	0	0	4	9	5	4	0	14	0	8	9	8	1	8	2	7	11	8
Local	23	23	21	22	38	36	14	23	5	26	30	20	32	0	25	27	18	22	26	24	34	13	31	19
Total N in Column	223	63	76	182	29	12	15	20	27	57	45	48	12	7	24	27	41	74	115	49	48	15	19	157

As one might expect, Quebec residents are considerably more likely than Ontarians to feel closest to the provincial government. Over three times as many of our Quebec respondents identify the provincial level as that to which they feel closest, but, even for this group, a majority (52%) of respondents feel closest to the federal level. The difference between French and English speaking residents of the whole Region is not as marked: thus we may infer that Franco-Ontarians do not in general feel much attachment to the Ontario government. These results are consistent with what we know about people's identification with different levels of government from various national public opinion studies carried out over the last few years.

On the whole, these results suggest that, in view of the high level of salience of the federal government in the National Capital Region, there would not be much local public disappointment should the federal government move to increase its control over local and regional affairs. In this sense, the results of this section may be viewed as corroborating the findings of the direct question on respondents' feelings about the Region becoming a federal territory.

Should Some Form of Local and Regional Government Continue?

For anyone who might be considering what form a future government for this region should take, two questions which should be of interest are:

"Well, if the National Capital Region were to become a federal territory,

1. Should there continue to be local municipal governments something like we have now".

2. Should there also be regional governments something like we have now".

Tables 5 and 6 summarize the results of this question, with responses broken down by mother tongue and place of residence.

TABLE 5

SHOULD LOCAL GOVERNMENT CONTINUE?
(Figures in percentages)

Continue Local Municipal Governments?	Place of Residence – Ontario	Place of Residence – Quebec	Mother Tongue – French	Mother Tongue – English	Mother Tongue – Other	Row Total Per Cent
Yes	65	57	64	64	52	61
No	29	34	28	31	33	39
No Opinion	7	9	9	5	15	10
Total N in Column	223	63	76	182	29	

TABLE 6

SHOULD REGIONAL GOVERNMENT CONTINUE?

(Figures in percentages)

Should Regional Government Continue?	Place of Residence		Mother Tongue			Row Total Per Cent
	Ontario	Quebec	French	English	Other	
Yes	40	54	55	41	22	40
No	48	28	29	46	63	41
No Opinion	13	19	16	13	15	19
Total N in Column	223	63	76	182	29	

Tables 5 and 6 can be analyzed together to provide a comparative perspective on regional and local government. Put briefly, local government has a high level of support in the National Capital Region relative to that for regional government. By a very narrow margin our respondents actually reject the idea of continuing regional government. Although the difference of 1% between those favouring and those opposing the continuance of regional government is not statistically significant, the difference of 21% between those favouring a continuation of local government and those favouring a continuation of regional government could be considered highly significant.

The differences by place of residence and by language group are also interesting. There is almost no difference in support for retaining local government between French and English respondents, but Ontario residents tend to be somewhat more in favour of the continuation of local government (though still not highly supportive). With respect to regional governments, Ontario and English residents of the Region vote a modest "no", while French and Quebec residents vote a louder "yes". These findings are difficult to interpret but one could speculate that they are attributable to the comparatively low profile of the OC government, despite the fact that it has been in existence longer than has the Outaouais Regional Community.

When we examined the effect of other independent variables such as income, length of residence in the Region, etc., we found that none of them is correlated with support for local and regional governments. Therefore, the ethnic and location variables are the only ones that seem to be significant.

What does this mean? It suggests that, to achieve maximum public acceptance, any scheme for federal territorial government in the Region should include provision for local municipal government, but that the continuation of the regional government is not as crucial.

Should a National Capital Territory Continue to Elect M.P.s?

The answer to this question, put quite simply from the public's point, is "yes". Referring to Table 7, we see that some 90% of our respondents replied in the affirmative and only 7% said "no", with an unusually small number (3%) of persons undecided. This is about as resounding a "yes" vote as one ever gets in a referendum question of this type.

TABLE 7

SHOULD THE TERRITORY CONTINUE TO ELECT M.P.s?
(figures in percentages)

Should the Region Continue to Elect M.P.s?	Place of Residence		Mother Tongue			Total per cent in Row
	Ontario	Quebec	French	English	Other	
Yes	93	82	89	90	88	90
No	5	14	7	8	4	7
No Opinion	2	5	4	2	8	3
Total N in Column	223	63	76	182	29	

There is no marked difference among language categories with respect to whether or not respondents prefer to continue to elect M.P.s, but there appears to be some difference between residents of Ontario and Quebec. While 93% of those living in Ontario would want to continue to elect M.P.s, "only" 82% of Quebec residents express the same desire. Despite the fact that this difference is significant in a statistical sense, it seems virtually devoid of political significance—at least for the National Capital Region Study—in view of the fact that the proportion of residents who want to continue to elect M.P.s is very large even among Quebecers.[11]

None of our other independent variables is correlated in an interesting or significant way with the desire to continue to elect M.P.s.

The lesson in the responses to this question is patent—no plan for the National Capital Region to become a federal territory that did not provide for the continued election of M.P.s would be acceptable to the residents of the area.

The General Opinion Questions

A large portion of the time spent interviewing our respondents was spent eliciting their opinions in response to a number of statements about local and

---

[11] Besides, attempting to explain the Quebec-Ontario difference on this score could open a virtual floodgate of speculations involving, for example, the relative popularity of current M.P.s.

regional government and about various ideas for a federal territory. A complete list of the statements can be found in Table 8 which presents the basic results. A printout from a computer run of cross-tabulations that accompanies this report contains a much more detailed analysis. We will attempt here only to touch upon the highlights of the findings.

TABLE 8

OPINION QUESTIONS
(figures in percentages)*

*Bracketed figure for each question is the mean score

		Agree Strongly	Agree	Agree Somewhat	No Opinion	Disagree Somewhat	Disagree	Disagree Strongly
16. (a)	The NCC has too much power in National Capital Region Affairs. (4.8)	5	12	15	12	7	40	8
(b)	Ottawa (Hull) should remain under provincial jurisdiction. (3.9)	7	33	6	9	11	29	6
(c)	The government of the National Capital Region should be under federal jurisdiction exclusively. (4.2)	8	21	72	10	10	28	10
(d)	The government of the National Capital Region should include representatives from the federal and Ontario (Quebec) governments. (3.1)	11	49	5	9	7	14	4
(e)	The government of the National Capital Region should have representation from the Federal Government. (2.5)	14	60	7	6	5	7	1
(f)	Since westerners and maritimers are Canadians, they ought to have a say in the government of the National Capital Region. (3.7)	12	33	11	4	10	21	9
(g)	The creation of a federal territory would make Ottawa like Washington D.C. (3.2)	11	38	13	12	9	11	5
(h)	If a Federal Territory were set up people like me would have less of a say in how civic affairs are run. (3.6)	7	35	11	11	13	20	2
(i)	Canada's stature as a nation demands that she have a truly national capital such as Washington, London or Paris. (3.3)	15	35	11	9	11	16	4
(j)	The power of municipal governments like (name of municipal government) should be strengthened. (3.7)	11	28	9	13	15	19	3
(k)	The power of municipal governments like (name of municipal government) is being taken away by the National Capital Commission. (4.1)	4	22	15	14	27	3	15

TABLE 8—*Concluded*

OPINION QUESTIONS
(figures in percentages)*

*Bracketed figure for each question is the mean score

			Agree Strongly	Agree	Agree Somewhat	No Opinion	Disagree Somewhat	Disagree	Disagree Strongly
(l)	The power of municipal governments like (name of municipal government) is being taken away by the Ottawa-Carleton Regional Government)	(3.9)	5	26	17	17	5	26	4
(m)	Government is getting too big to control	(3.7)	12	28	14	9	7	26	4
(n)	Parliament should have some say in how the Ottawa-Hull area is governed	(3.1)	12	41	18	6	3	18	1
(o)	The present system of government in the Ottawa-Hull area is becoming so complicated that a person like me really can't understand what is going on	(3.0)	22	35	15	2	5	17	3
(p)	The Ontario government neglects the Ottawa region and pays too much attention to Southern Ontario, OR the Quebec government neglects the Outaouais region and pays too much attention to Montreal and Quebec City	(3.1)	23	33	7	10	6	20	1
(q)	The Federal Government is building too many offices in the Hull area	(4.7)	5	18	6	9	10	45	9
(r)	Generally speaking, the provincial government is doing a good job in the National Capital Region	(4.3)	2	26	23	10	11	27	11
(s)	Generally speaking, the federal government is doing a good job in the National Capital Region	(3.1)	6	45	17	11	6	13	12
(t)	Generally speaking, the National Capital Commission is doing a good job	(2.6)	12	55	12	11	1	5	2
(u)	Generally speaking, the Ottawa Regional Government (Outaouais Regional Government) is doing a good job	(3.9)	2	28	14	22	11	18	6
(v)	Generally speaking, the (specific municipal government) is doing a good job	(3.2)	4	43	23	8	9	13	2
(w)	English Canadian culture has too much influence in the Ottawa-Hull area	(5.8)	5	10	8	7	12	47	11
(x)	French Canadian culture has too much influence in the Ottawa-Hull area	(4.6)	7	17	9	5	11	44	8
(y)	I find municipal politics highly interesting	(4.6)	2	17	17	4	11	36	12
(z)	The Province of Ontario has too much to say in how the Ottawa-Hull area is run	(4.5)	3	16	11	18	11	39	2
(aa)	The Province of Quebec has too much to say in how the Ottawa-Hull area is run	(4.7)	3	15	5	15	10	46	5
(bb)	The Federal Government has too much to say in how the Ottawa-Hull area is run	(4.5)	4	14	13	12	11	43	3
(cc)	I think the efforts being made to move government offices to Hull and to move heavy industry out should be continued	(3.5)	10	36	16	5	9	16	9

Two points need to be made at the outset in analyzing these questions. The first is that most respondents have some tendency to positive "response set bias". That is, other things being equal, they will tend to agree rather than disagree with a statement. Thus the mean (average) score for a question on which feelings were essentially neutral would be slightly less than the central point of 4.0. This problem can be partially circumvented by reversing some questions. For example, question (a) invites the respondents to agree that the NCC is too powerful. That they in fact disagreed is indicative of a rather high degree of public affection for the NCC.

The second point is that relatively small differences in mean scores are fairly significant. The very lowest mean we found was 2.5 and the next lowest was 3.0 (agree somewhat) while the highest was 5.0 (disagree somewhat). In general, differences of 0.5 in means indicate that we have found a statistically significant difference.

The first impression on looking through the opinion questions is that they are inconsistent. This should not be surprising; there are literally scores of public opinion surveys which indicate a similar or higher level of inconsistency. In this case, we find that there is very slight agreement with the statement "Ottawa (Hull) should remain under provincial jurisdiction" (question a) while there is quite strong agreement that the provincial governments are neglecting the region (question p). Moreover, the provincial governments get the most negative rating among various governments active in the region (question r). Yet, a second thought about these apparent inconsistencies will suggest that it is possible for people to rate the provincial governments relatively low without wishing to eliminate their influence altogether. That is, the impression we might take away from this subset of questions simply is that, in setting up a federal territory, the role of the provincial governments could be diminished, but that the public probably would not accept the complete elimination of provincial government influence in the area. This speculation is buttressed by responses to question (c), which indicate modest disagreement with the suggestion that the area should be under federal jurisdiction exclusively and by responses to question (d), which show that people opt quite strongly for representation from both federal and provincial governments. It should be pointed out in this respect that the score of 2.5 on question (e), which asserts that the federal government should be represented in the government of the Capital Region, is by far the highest level of agreement found for any question in this section and corroborates our earlier assertion that there is, at the very least, a clear permissive consensus for a territorial government. Question (n) replicates question (e) with nearly the same results.

The relatively high affect for local government and the relatively low affect for the region shows up in questions (j), (l), (u), and (v). In question (j) there is some support for an increase in the strength of municipal government and in (l) there is agreement, again modest, that regional government has been eroding that strength. The regional governments get a barely positive rating in question (u), while the municipal governments are viewed considerably more positively in (v). In this regard, it should be noted that the federal government and, particularly the NCC, get very high ratings for their activities in the region. Question (a) indicates substantial disagreement that the NCC has too much power, question (s) gives the federal government a very high (second highest) rating in the job it is doing in this region. Question (t) gives the NCC an exceptionally high rating. The activities of the NCC may well be responsible for the permissive consensus to which we have alluded repeatedly in this report.

Several other opinion questions get at the question of the citizen's efficacy in civic politics. Question (o) suggests considerable agreement that the system of government in the Ottawa-Hull area is too complicated to understand and question (m) might suggest some feeling that government is getting too big to control. Reactions to statement (h) indicate that people feel this tendency would be exacerbated by the establishment of a federal territory. Yet we know that people nevertheless are willing to go ahead with such a plan. Again, these results are consonant with those of surveys conducted elsewhere in suggesting that people are less disturbed than intellectuals sometimes think about their loss of personal efficacy, provided they feel that government is being well conducted.

Taken in sum, and even allowing for some apparent inconsistencies, the reactions to statements a-cc generally reinforce our earlier conclusions about the positive feelings residents of the Region have concerning the question of a federal territory. There are some differences between residents on one side or the other of the Ottawa river, between French and English, and between the other categories of our independent variables, but in no case do they constitute a basis for qualifying the main conclusions to this study.

Summary

We began this report by presenting a working definition of a permissive consensus in which the latter is conceived as a climate of public opinion, in favour of, but not necessarily demanding, an hypothetical form of government action. From our impressionistic reading of answers to open-end questions, and from our quantitative analyses of the responses to closed-end items, it seems that this term admirably describes public attitudes in the National Capital Region toward the general idea of turning the Region into a federal territory. Widespread agreement in favour of a restructuring of government clearly is evident but the intensity with which opinions about government structure are held seems too low to warrant describing the consensus as "decisive", in the sense that overall public opinion in the Region is demanding such a change.

Comparisons of the opinions of significant subgroups in the sample revealed that a permissive consensus characterizes attitudes in each one of these. In general, the variations in support for a federal district territory by sub-groups are politically, if not statistically, insignificant. However, there is a reasonably strong positive relationship between socioeconomic status and support for a federal territory and between the latter and the extent of participation in group activities. *In fact, among the highest income and activity groups, the consensus we have described as permissive might conceivably be termed "decisive"*. This finding is significant because, as numerous studies have shown, there are the groups forming the "attentive public" or that segment of the population with the greatest political influence.

The examination of opinions regarding whether, within a federal territory, the Region's residents should continue to elect M.P.s, indicated an overwhelming desire to do so. There also appears to be strong support for the retention of local governments but only very lukewarm sentiment for the continuation of the regional governments such as they now exist. Furthermore, the analysis suggested the advisability of representing the two provincial governments in any form of government for the Region, despite the relatively low salience of this level for our respondents.

These conclusions as well as others reached in the text obviously are only as sound as the data upon which they are based. For this reason, at the beginning of this report we discussed any factors that could affect the validity of the data, and concluded that none of them was likely to influence the results to a significant extent. In the analyses, it was pointed out that the credibility of the data is enhanced by the fact that our findings regarding classic relationships, such as that between socioeconomic status and group activity, are as expected. It was noted that our sample is not perfect. However, those groups that tend to be over-represented, i.e., the stable population and, to a lesser degree, high socioeconomic strata, are those whose opinions one might want to consider the most important in relation to the main questions posed by this survey.

PUBLIC OPINION REGARDING THE RESTRUCTURING OF GOVERNMENT IN THE NATIONAL CAPITAL REGION

by

D. J. Falcone and R. J. Van Loon

Carleton University

The material which follows in this report contains the written instructions given to interviewers, including the procedure to be followed and the precise questions to be asked.

INSTRUCTIONS TO INTERVIEWER

1. For each interview you should have one questionnaire and sheets which you will hand to the interviewee at the appropriate time in the interview.

2. Follow the introductory format down to the interviewee selection. If the selected respondent is not home, make an appointment or ascertain the time at which the respondent is usually home.

3. Be polite but confident. You can assume you will get an interview since over 50 percent of people are pleased to be interviewed.

4. Never indicate approval or disapproval of any answer.

IF PERSON AT DOOR IS NOT THE DESIGNATED RESPONDENT

According to the research method used in this survey, I have to ask a few questions of the (woman) (youngest man) (etc.) in your household. Would you please call (him) (her) to the door.

IF PERSON AT DOOR COULD BE CORRECT RESPONDENT

According to the research method used in this survey, I have to ask a few questions of the (man) (oldest woman) (etc.) in your household. Would that be you?

WHEN THE CORRECT RESPONDENT ARRIVES AT THE DOOR REPEAT THE INTRODUCTION.

C12 REASONS FOR NO INTERVIEW: APPOINTMENT. WRITE: _____

CHECK 1 ___ vacant
       2 ___ no qualified adults
       3 ___ refused (describe over)
       4 ___ not at home
       5 ___ appointment

Day/Hour of appointment—or times when usually home

Name _____

Address _____ Apt _____

Phone (home) _____ (bus.) _____

C13 NUMBER OF CALLBACKS

CIRCLE: 0   1   2   3   4

1. About how long have you lived in the Ottawa-Hull area?
   C14
   C15 _____ years

2. Judging by your experience, or by what you read or hear, what do you think are two or three of the most important problems facing the Ottawa-Hull area today?

3. Can you tell me the name of the municipality you live in?

   | WRITE IN ANSWER | C16   1 _____ correct

                              2 _____ incorrect

                              9 _____ DNA

4. As a private citizen, which do you generally feel closest to?
                                                          | READ LIST |
   C17 1 _____ the Federal Government
        2 _____ the Ontario (Quebec) Government
        3 _____ Ottawa-Carleton (Outaouais) Regional Government
        4 _____ Name of Municipality
        9 _____ DNA

5. As a private citizen, which government do you think most affects your day-to-day life?
   | READ LIST |

   C18 1 _____ Ottawa-Carleton (Outaouais) Regional Government
        2 _____ the Ontario (Quebec) Government
        3 _____ Name of Municipality
        4 _____ the Federal Government
        9 _____ DNA

6. In your estimation, who is the single most important spokesman in civic affairs in (name of municipality)?

      C19
      C20 _____ DNA

7. What does the term "National Capital Commission" mean to you?

> IF RESPONDENT DOES NOT RECOGNIZE GO TO 8

>> IF RESPONDENT CLEARLY RECOGNIZES

7a. Probe: What does the National Capital Commission do?

7b. Have you ever had any personal dealings with the National Capital Commission?

      C21   _____ Yes
          _____ No

> IF NO, GO TO 8

>> IF YES

7c. What would these have been?

8. What does the term "Ottawa-Carleton Regional Government" ("Outaouais Regional Government") mean to you?

> IF RESPONDENT DOES NOT RECOGNIZE, GO TO 9

>> IF RECOGNIZES

8a. Probe: What does the regional government do?

9. Have you read or heard about any proposals for restructuring the government of the Ottawa (Hull) region?

      C22   _____ Yes
          _____ No

> IF NO, GO TO 10

>> IF YES

9a.   Do you happen to recall what some of the proposals might have been?

10.   What does the term "Federal District" mean to you?

10(I).   For some time now people have been discussing whether or not the National Capital Region should become a federal territory. Which of the following best reflects your views on this question?

C23
1. ___ The National Capital Region definitely should become a federal territory
2. ___ It seems like a good idea but I have some doubts about it.
3. ___ It is difficult to say one way or the other.
4. ___ There seems very little reason to change the present set-up.
5. ___ The National Capital Region definitely should not become a federal territory.
6. ___ I have no opinion.
9. ___ DNA.

10(II). Well, if the National Capital Region were to become a federal territory,

a. Should there continue to be local municipal governments something like we have now?

	C24	1 ___	Yes
		2 ___	No
		3 ___	No opinion
		9 ___	DNA

b. Should there also be regional governments something like we have now?

	C25	1 ___	Yes
		2 ___	No
		3 ___	No opinion
		9 ___	NA

c. Should the region's residents continue to elect members to the federal Parliament?

	C26	1 ___	Yes
		2 ___	No
		3 ___	No opinion
		9 ___	NA

10(III). Suppose a government of some sort were to be set up for the whole National Capital Region . . . perhaps a federal territory or perhaps some other form of government . . . about what percentage of the power do you think should be held by the federal government? What about the Ontario government? And the Quebec government? What about the municipalities?

	DO NOT POINT OUT TO THE RESPONDENT IF HIS FIGURES TOTAL OVER 100 PER CENT

        C27 _____ Federal government
        C28 _____ Ontario
        C29 _____ Quebec
        C30 _____ Municipalities
        C30 _____ DNA ... 09 (code)

11. About what percentage of the Ottawa-Hull area would you guess to be French-speaking?

        C31
        C32 _____ %

In a minute I'd like to get your opinion on several issues, but just before I do that I'd like to ask you a couple more information questions.

12. First of all, could you tell me who is your Federal MP?

        C33 Name _____

13. And who is your provincial (MPP if Ontario) (MNA if Quebec)?

        C34 Name _____

14. What about the mayor or reeve of this municipality?

        C35 Name _____

15. Finally, could you very briefly tell me what each of the following people do?

    a. Denis Coolican   C36

    b. Pierre Benoit   C37

    c. Douglas Fullerton   C38

    d. Oswald Parent   C39

    e. John Turner   C40

    f. Jean-Marie Seguin   C41

    g. Leon LeBlanc   C42

> HAND OPINION SHEET TO RESPONDENT

Now I'd like to read you some statements people have made about civic affairs in this area. As I read them could you please tell me which response on the sheet best describes your own reaction to the statement.

> THERE IS "NO OPINION" OPTION ON THE RESPONDENTS' SHEET

	Agree Strongly	Agree	Agree Somewhat	No Opinion	Disagree Somewhat	Disagree	Disagree Strongly

16. a) The NCC has too much power in National Capital Region Affairs .... — — — — — — —
    C43

   b) Ottawa (Hull) should remain under provincial jurisdiction .... — — — — — — —
    C44

   c) The government of the National Capital Region should be under federal jurisdiction exclusively . — — — — — — —
    C45

   d) The government of the National Capital Region should include representatives from the federal and Ontario (Quebec) governments .... — — — — — — —
    C46

   e) The government of the National Capital Region should have representation from the Federal Government .... — — — — — — —
    C47

   f) Since westerners and maritimers are Canadians, they ought to have a say in the government of the National Capital Region .... — — — — — — —
    C48

   g) The creation of a federal territory would make Ottawa like Washington D.C. .... — — — — — — —
    C49

   h) If a Federal Territory were set up people like me would have less of a say in how civic affairs are run .... — — — — — — —
    C50

   i) Canada's stature as a nation demands that she have a truly national capital such as Washington, London or Paris .... — — — — — — —
    C51

	Agree Strongly	Agree	Agree Somewhat	No Opinion	Disagree Somewhat	Disagree	Disagree Strongly

j) The power of municipal governments like [name of municipal government] should be strengthened
C52

k) The power of municipal governments like [name of municipal government] is being taken away by the National Capital Commission
C53

l) The power of municipal governments like [name of municipal government] is being taken away by the Ottawa-Carleton Regional Government
C54

m) Government is getting too big to control
C55

n) Parliament should have some say in how the Ottawa-Hull area is governed
C56

o) The present system of government in the Ottawa-Hull area is becoming so complicated that a person like me really can't understand what is going on
C57

NOTE OPTION

p) The Ontario government neglects the Ottawa region and pays too much attention to Southern Ontario, OR the Quebec government neglects the Outaouais region and pays too much attention to Montreal and Quebec City
C58

q) The Federal Government is building too many offices in the Hull area
C59

r) Generally speaking, the provincial government is doing a good job in the National Capital Region
C60

	Agree Strongly	Agree	Agree Somewhat	No Opinion	Disagree Somewhat	Disagree	Disagree Strongly

s) Generally speaking, the federal government is doing a good job in the National Capital Region
C61

t) Generally speaking, the National Capital Commission is doing a good job
C62

u) Generally speaking, the Ottawa Regional Government [Outaouais Regional Government] is doing a good job
C63

v) Generally speaking, the [specific municipal government] is doing a good job
C64

w) English Canadian culture has too much influence in the Ottawa-Hull area
C65

x) French Canadian culture has too much influence in the Ottawa-Hull area
C66

y) I find municipal politics highly interesting
C67

z) The Province of Ontario has too much to say in how the Ottawa-Hull area is run
C68

aa) The Province of Quebec has too much to say in how the Ottawa-Hull area is run
C69

bb) The Federal Government has too much to say in how the Ottawa-Hull area is run
C70

cc) I think the efforts being made to move government offices to Hull and to move heavy industry out should be continued
C71

| RETRIEVE OPINION SHEET |

17. Do you think the extent to which French is recognized as an official language in the Ottawa area is too much, about right, or too little?

        C72   1 _____ Too much
                  2 _____ About right
                  3 _____ Too little
                  4 _____ No opinion
                  9 _____ DNA

18. Now I'd like to end the interview by asking you a few questions about yourself. Do you own this residence or do you rent?

        C73   1 _____ Owns
                  2 _____ Rents
                  9 _____ NA

19. How long have you lived in this particular residence?

        C74   _____ Years

                    _____ Months

20. How often have you moved in the last five years?

        C75   1 _____ No times
                  2 _____ Once
                  3 _____ Twice
                  4 _____ Three times
                  5 _____ Four or more times
                     _____ DNA

21. Where were you born?

        C76   _____ Country
        C77   _____ Province
        C78   _____ Locality

22. Where did you spend your primary school years?

C79 _____

C80 _____

23. In what places did you attend secondary school?

C-2-15 _____
C-2-16 _____

24. a) What is the name of the last school you attended? _____

b) What was the last grade you completed in school?

                C-2-17   1 _____ 0-8 years
                             2 _____ 1-2 years high school
                             3 _____ 3-5 years high school
                             4 _____ 1-2 years college
                             5 _____ 3-4 years college
                             6 _____ more than 4 years college
                             7 _____ Other

                        | SPECIFY IF OTHER |

                             9 _____ DNA

25a. What is your job . . . your occupation?

| PROBE UNTIL YOU GET ACTUAL NATURE OF RESPONDENT'S WORK e.g. CIVIL SERVANT IS NOT SPECIFIC ENOUGH . . . WHAT DO YOU ACTUALLY DO? |

                          C-2-18
                          C-2-19

25b. Who is your employer?

26a. Do you belong to any organizations . . . that is groups like Home and School, clubs, church groups, unions and so on?

| PROBE | any other?   C-2-20   C-2-30

26b. How often would you attend group meetings of any sort?

        C-2-31   1 _____ once a week or more
                        2 _____ once a month or more
                        3 _____ once a year or more
                        4 _____ seldom
                        5 _____ never
                        9 _____ NA

27. What language is your mother tongue?

   1 _____ French
   2 _____ English
   3 _____ Other

   SPECIFY OTHER

   C-2-32   9 _____ NA

28. How would you rate your ability in
   SPECIFY FRENCH OR ENGLISH, OPPOSITE OF INTERVIEWED

   C-2-23   1 _____ None
             2 _____ Quite weak
             3 _____ Fair
             4 _____ Good
             5 _____ Bilingual

29. What is your age?

   DO NOT PROBE. IF RESPONDENT HESITATES RECORD AN ESTIMATED AGE WITH A QUESTION MARK.

   C-2-34 _____ years

30. Here is a card showing different income groups. SHOW CARD. Just give me the letter of the group your family is in.

   Yearly Income of Family (Confidential)

   A Under $3,000   1 _____ A
   B $3,000-5,999   2 _____ B
   C $6,000-7,999   3 _____ C
   D $8,000-9,999   4 _____ D
   E 10,000-14,999   5 _____ E
   F 15,000-19,999   6 _____ F
   G 20,000-29,999   7 _____ G
   H Over 30,000   8 _____ H
                            9 _____ DNA
   C-2-35

31. What was your father's nationality? _____ C-2-36

32. What was your mother's nationality? _____ C-2-37

| OPINION SHEET TO BE GIVEN TO RESPONDENT |

(as referred to on pages 316 and 320).

	Agree Strongly	Agree	Agree Somewhat	Disagree Somewhat	Disagree	Disagree Strongly
a) The NCC has too much power in National Capital Region Affairs C43	—	—	—	—	—	—
b) Ottawa (Hull) should remain under provincial jurisdiction C44	—	—	—	—	—	—
c) The government of the National Capital Region should be under federal jurisdiction exclusively C45	—	—	—	—	—	—
d) The government of the National Capital Region should include representatives from the federal and Ontario (Quebec) governments C46	—	—	—	—	—	—
e) The government of the National Capital Region should have representation from the Federal Government C47	—	—	—	—	—	—
f) Since westerners and maritimers are Canadians, they ought to have a say in the government of the National Capital Region . C48	—	—	—	—	—	—
g) The creation of a federal territory would make Ottawa like Washington D.C. C49	—	—	—	—	—	—
h) If a Federal Territory were set up people like me would have less of a say in how civic affairs are run C50	—	—	—	—	—	—
i) Canada's stature as a nation demands that she have a truly national capital such as Washington, London or Paris C51	—	—	—	—	—	—

	Agree Strongly	Agree	Agree Somewhat	Disagree Somewhat	Disagree	Disagree Strongly
j) The power of municipal governments like [name of municipal government] should be strengthened C52	—	—	—	—	—	—
k) The power of municipal governments like [name of municipal government] is being taken away by the National Capital Commission C53	—	—	—	—	—	—

Etc. (for complete list of questions see pages 317 to 319).

Appendix B-2

The Language Question and the Capital: an Analysis

THE LANGUAGE QUESTION AND THE CAPITAL: AN ANALYSIS

1.	The basic premises	326
2.	Experience to-date with respect to the Capital	326
3.	Bilingualism vs multiculturalism	327
4.	French as an international language	327
5.	The B & B problem in the Capital today	328
6.	The assimilation question: how serious is it?	328
7.	The federal public service	334
8.	The provinces	338
9.	The local governments	339
10.	The teaching of French in Canada: general issues	341
11.	The local educational scene: an overview	347
12.	Ottawa-Carleton (second-language study)	347
13.	Ottawa-Carleton (minority-language)	350
14.	Outaouais (minority-language)	351
15.	Outaouais (majority-language)	352
16.	Post-secondary institutions in relation to the French character of the Outaouais	354

Appendix B-2

The Language Question and the Capital: an Analysis

James M. Weld

In any study of Canada's capital the language question bears examination for two reasons: one negative and practical; the other hopeful and optimistic.

The negative and practical reason for facing up to the language issue is that it won't go away. Stripped of its philosophical and ethical aspects, the policy of equal partnership advocated by the Royal Commission on Bilingualism and Biculturalism is the only practical political path for Canada today and for its capital.

The positive reason for attaching importance to the language question relates to finding ourselves. We have always seemed to be resisting having another identity fitted on to us: first a British one and now an American one. We should recognize that our linguistic duality and the squabbles between English and French Canadians are part of us and have been for two hundred and some years. Bilingualism is not a bore, but a boon, and is as Canadian as compromise. It makes us different in an increasingly standardized North American world and, although we have been slow to recognize it, it has always been a key element of our national personality.

2. Experience to-Date With Respect to the Capital

The history of the Capital reflects the importance of linguistic equilibrium. Kingston (1840-43) did not work as the Capital of the United Provinces because of this lack. Montreal (1843-49) had the ethnic balance but failed because of the burning of the Parliament Buildings and other violence stirred by the Rebellion Losses Bill. The wandering Capital between Toronto and Quebec (1849-65) also reflected cultural balance, but was considered impractical for the same reasons that an oscillating Capital in Switzerland at about the same time was found inconvenient.[1] In recommending Ottawa to the Queen in 1857, Sir Edmund Head underlined not only its advantageous geographical position on the border between Upper and Lower Canada, but also its favourable racial mix of the two major cultures.[2] That the Queen's choice was a wise one is evidenced by the fact that after Ottawa was chosen as capital by the Fathers of Confederation following four moves in less than 25 years (1840-64), there has been no subsequent pressure to move the Capital to any other location in more than a century.

3. *Bilingualism vs Multiculturalism*

Few would disagree with the present federal and parallel provincial policies regarding multiculturalism. Essentially, these consist of encouraging "New Canadians", within the framework of our laws, to keep as much as they wish of the cultural heritage they brought with them to Canada.[3] The policy is based on the enlightened view that the country will be the richer by reflecting many cultural strains and that the newcomer will be a better citizen if he is secure in his identity and proud of the inheritance he brings to his new land.

Bilingualism and multiculturalism grow from the same root and that is human dignity. Every Canadian is encouraged to take pride in what he is. But to what extent can the state offer services to take account of the cultural separateness of each of its citizens? Clearly some compromises have to be made. Concentration is an important factor. Although Italian-speakers form only 8% of the Swiss population, they are concentrated in one canton (Tessin) which assures them of their own government and public services. In many districts of our Western provinces, there are concentrations of German- or Polish- or Ukrainian-speakers and these provinces have responded favourably to requests from school boards for schools in these languages. But it is clear that service by the federal or provincial governments in many languages is not generally possible for the several million immigrants who have come to Canada over the last three quarters of a century and before that, and who are scattered throughout the length and breadth of our land.

The Study received one or two briefs which argued that too much was being done for "the French" and not enough for those whose mother-tongue was neither English or French. But the Study also received briefs from persons of "third" linguistic communities which stated specifically that it was only practical for Canada to have two official languages.

It is difficult to resist the logic of this position. The Capital, in its monumental and visual aspects, as well as in its pageantry and display, could perhaps reflect more effectively than it has in the past, the contributions of Canadians other than the British and French. But it is hard to conceive a formula whereby Canada's cultural pluralism could be reflected in the governmental structures of the Capital.

4. *French as an International Language*

The valiant recent efforts of the Federal, Quebec and Ontario Governments to encourage the French language must be viewed against the background of a net retreat of French as an international language relative to English. This is largely due to politico-economic factors. If the adage "trade follows the flag" is true, "language follows power" would seem to be an appropriate corollary. Latin spread throughout the ancient world on the heels of Roman power and deteriorated into various "vulgar" tongues when the power of Rome collapsed. French was the language of diplomacy in Europe in the eighteenth century and enjoyed enormous prestige at the time in large measure because France was the strongest land power in Europe and the court of Versailles was the greatest centre of the arts. The largest nineteenth century empires were those of Britain and of France, a further factor in spreading French throughout the world. With the "decolonizing" policies of Britain and France in the decades following the end of the Second World War, the prestige of both these languages would, no doubt, have plummeted, were it not for the fact that the United States, which had emerged as a superpower, also happened to be an English-speaking country. Certainly, the forces to dislodge the old "colonial" tongues and to revive the indigenous languages in the former British and French colonies are strong, and the main reason for the retention of English and French is their practical utility as a *lingua franca* among many often conflicting dialects. Where a highly structured "colony" language exists (e.g. Arabic in North Africa), the future of French over the long term may be more uncertain. Most significant of all is the relative decline of French in Europe. Despite its being the working language in the European Economic Community, its position is slowly weakening measured by any of the usual criteria: its teaching as a second language in European schools or its use in science and diplomacy and at international conferences. Even the small army of French language teachers sent abroad by the Cultural Affairs Directorate of the French Foreign Ministry is suffering slow attrition, while at an international conference in Dakar in 1973 on the preservation of French outside of France, only 9 of 25 French or partially French-speaking countries were represented and France and Canada between them sent more than three quarters of all the delegates.[4]

5. *The B & B Problem in the Capital Today*

The bilingual problem or "Kulturkampf" as it relates to the Capital today can be simply stated. The Francophone fears that he will be assimilated, but the Franco-Ontarian, and the "nationaliste" of the Outaouais québécois may have different ideas as to what to do about this threat. The English-speaking Canadian on the other hand fears for his job. The federal public service in Ottawa is no longer the English-speaking preserve it once was and, in the contest for jobs, the linguistic vulnerability of the unilingual English-speaking civil servant becomes readily apparent. Let us examine each of these problems in turn.

6. *The Assimilation Question—How serious is it?*

The assimilation battle has been fought, over the years, with Census of Canada statistics, and succeeding censuses have developed and refined measurements of social characteristics. Thus the censuses before 1901 measured only ethnicity derived from paternal origin. At the time, this was probably not too inaccurate a measurement because French communities throughout Canada were relatively close-knit both for language and religious reasons. After the 1901 census, "mother-tongue" was adopted as a more accurate tool to measure language differences. Mother-tongue is defined as the language one learned as an infant and can still understand. Finally, as a result of prodding from the

Royal Commission on Bilingualism and Biculturalism, the 1971 census adopted the notion of the language spoken at home or the language most commonly used. In the tables which follow, it must be recognized that figures comparing a regional population by French ethnicity in 1871, mother-tongue in 1911 and language-most-often-spoken in 1971 provide only a rough statistical tool. It is a case of comparing apples and oranges and peaches and then generalizing about fruit. Secondly, census areas, most notably the area of the Capital, can change from census to census. Third, migration can also affect the apparent assimilation picture. A drop between 1961 and 1971 of French mother-tongue in a given region does not necessarily mean assimilation. Some French mother-tongue residents may simply have moved away. Fourth, in figures showing Canada as a whole, it should be recalled that the entry of Newfoundland into Confederation in 1949 automatically meant a minor drop in French demographic percentages beginning with the 1951 census. Fifth, in many mixed (Anglophone-Francophone) marriages parents insist on speaking both languages in the home, so that even the latest, most refined statistical tool loses its edge in these cases. Finally, next to unemployment statistics, language characteristics statistics have been the most exploited for political purposes. It is useful to those favouring an independent Quebec to be able to point to "scientific" evidence that Francophones are fast disappearing through assimilation.

A serious and objective presentation on the subject of assimilation is found in Richard Joy's short work "Languages in Conflict".[5] The thesis he develops

MAP I — THE SOO-MONCTON BILINGUAL SET

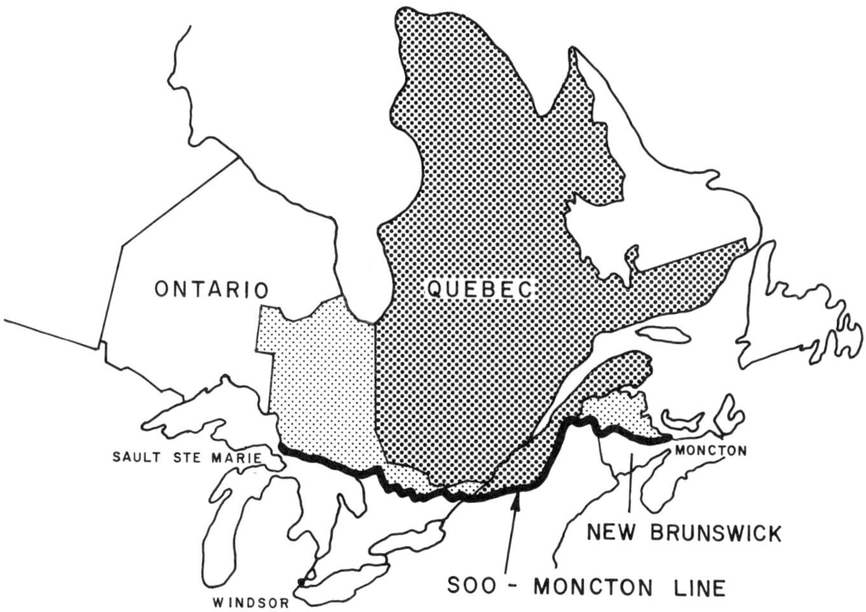

Hatching shows areas of important Francophone population in Ontario and New Brunswick. The isolation of traditional French centres, St. Boniface, Windsor, Yarmouth, Fall River may also be seen.

MAP II — FRANCOPHONE EXPANSION

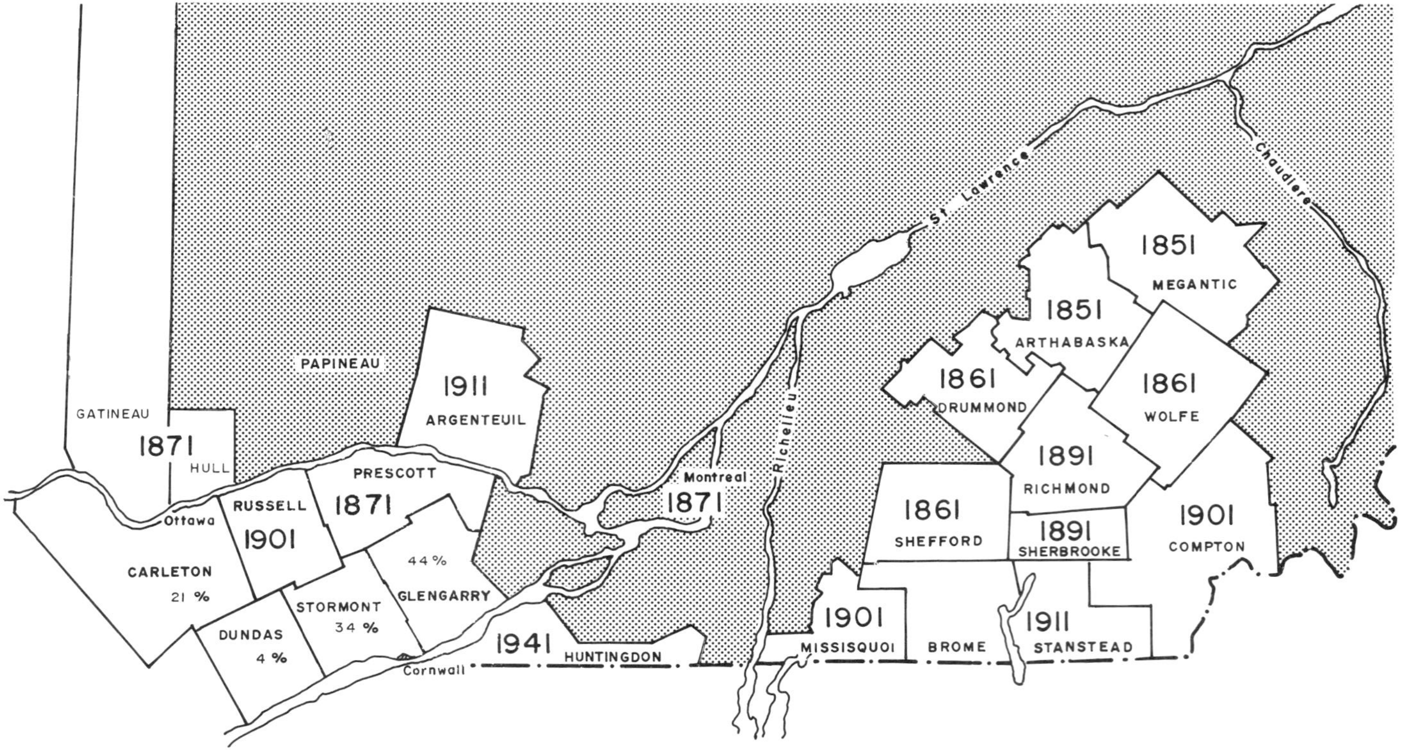

Black areas had French majority before 1851. The census year in which other counties achieved a French majority is shown. The percentage of Francophone (mother-tongue) in certain adjacent Ontario counties where they constitute somewhat less than a majority is also given (1971 census).

from an analysis of census figures is that while there was a relatively wide dispersal of both the English population in Quebec and the French population outside Quebec at the time of Confederation, there is now a strong tendency toward linguistic segregation. Between the Francophone Quebec heartland and English Canada properly speaking, there is a bilingual belt; a line drawn from Sault Ste Marie to Moncton marks the boundary between English Canada and this bilingual belt.

Francophone outward expansion occurred largely in the latter half of the nineteenth century and consisted of opening up new farmland in Quebec and adjoining provinces or providing labour for the mines and mills of the industrializing areas in Quebec or adjacent New Brunswick, Ontario, or New England.

The French tide stopped at the Soo line at about the turn of the century and it was largely waves of European immigrants and settlers from Western Ontario who peopled the West in the succeeding decade. Table A below[6] illustrates the shrinking percentage of Francophones living outside the Soo-Moncton line.

TABLE A

PERCENTAGE OF FRANCOPHONES* LIVING IN VARIOUS PARTS OF CANADA

	1911	1941	1971
Quebec Province	78 %	81 %	84 %
Adjacent Ontario	6.5	6.5	5.7
Adjacent New Brunswick	4.5	4.5	3.5
Outside the Soo-Moncton line	11	8	6.8

* By ethnicity 1911, by mother-tongue 1941 and 1971.

Where have the Francophones living outside Quebec and adjacent areas gone? Despite the caution with which one should handle such statistics, it is impossible to resist the conclusion from Table B below that a substantial degree of assimilation has taken place.

TABLE B

DISTRIBUTION OF CANADA'S FRENCH POPULATION, ACCORDING TO THE THREE ALTERNATIVE CRITERIA OF ETHNICITY, MOTHER-TONGUE AND LANGUAGE MOST OFTEN SPOKEN—1971 CENSUS

	Ethnicity	%	Mother-tongue	%	Most often spoken	%
Quebec Province	4,759,000	77.0	4,867,000	84.0	4,870,000	88
Adjacent Ontario	398,000	6.4	330,000	5.7	281,000	5
Adjacent New Brunswick	208,000	3.4	201,000	3.5	192,000	3.5
Outside Soo-Moncton line	814,000	13.2	396,000	6.8	203,000	3.5
Canada	6,180,000	100%	5,794,000	100%	5,546,000	100%

Of persons of French ethnic origin who live outside the Soo-Moncton line, it will be noted that, in 1971, fewer than one in four reported French as the language most often used in the home.

With respect to the National Capital Region, further figures from Mr. Joy suggest that Francophones, especially on the Ontario side, are vulnerable to assimilation. Persons of French ethnic origin made up 40% of the population in 1971 but there has been a significant discrepancy between this figure and those speaking French at home on the Ontario side of the river. The 1971 census found 238,495 persons of French origin, as compared to only 203,595 who gave French as the language of the home, with the following distribution:

TABLE C

	Fr. ethnic	Fr. language of home	Difference
Living on Ontario side	115,695	82,115	29%
Living on Quebec side	122,805	121,480	1%

Apart from assimilation, it must be recognized that the French component in the Canadian population has risen and fallen since Confederation. It is interesting to compare figures for the country as a whole and for the Ottawa-Hull Census Metropolitan area.

TABLE D

FRENCH-SPEAKING POPULATION vs. TOTAL POPULATION 1871–1971

Canada	1871	1901	1941	1971
Total Population	3,486,000	5,371,000	11,507,000	21,568,000
French(1)	1,083,000	1,649,000	3,355,000	5,794,000
French/Total %	31.1	30.7	29.2	26.9
Ottawa-Hull Census Metropolitan Area (2)				
Total Population	22,000	80,000	215,000	603,000
French(1)	7,000	35,000	87,000	220,000
French/Total	33%	44%	40%	36.6%

Note (1): "French" by origin in 1871 and 1901,
    by mother-tongue in 1941, 1971.
  (2): using boundaries in effect at the time.

The French-speaking proportion of the population of the National Capital Region has generally been larger than that of the country as a whole, but the decline of both in relative numbers following 1941 is apparent. The Ottawa Valley was part of the French expansionist movement of the late nineteenth century, as described in a previous paragraph and illustrated in MAP II. Just as the relative decline of the Francophone population in the country as a whole was due to the force of English-oriented immigration, so the relative decline in French in the Capital Region is due in large measure to the "immigration" here of English-speaking civil servants in large numbers. The relative weakness of Francophone migration to the Capital can be attributed to a variety of reasons which have changed from decade to decade. In the past veterans' preference played against the Francophone, as did the nature of the civil service examinations. Again, until recently, there was the necessity to adjust to the "English" atmosphere of the Capital and the lack of qualification for many of the technical public service jobs. In more recent times, the stigma attached by many Québécois to working for "le fédéral" and other considerations of a political or psychological nature must be borne in mind. The dramatic decline in the birth rate, the lowest in Canada, which affected Francophones both in the Capital area as well as in the country as a whole, has no doubt also accentuated in part the relative weakness of the Francophone component in the Capital as reflected by the most recent census figures. I should emphasize the word "relative", however, since, in absolute numbers, the French population of the region is increasing at a healthy clip, as the last table illustrates.

If it is not too difficult to diagnose the problem, solutions are harder to come by. There has been collaboration between the federal and provincial governments with respect to the encouragement of Francophone immigration to Canada, but there are few signs on the horizon that the birthrate in Quebec is likely to increase dramatically in the near future. Indeed, there is reason to suspect the proportion of French to the total population is likely to go down again marginally in the next decade.

This *in itself* is not likely to affect the Frenchness of Canada. What is upsetting to French-speaking Canadians is that, *within the Province of Quebec*, French is still not the language of business and of prestige, and that immigrants given the free choice have been inclined to send their children to English- rather than French-speaking schools.[7] In this connection, it should be noted that migration has always been a factor in the Quebec population equation and is likely to be the dynamic element in the middle future, according to that province's well known demographer, Robert Maheu.[8] The overall picture as it emerges in the Gendron report, however, is positive from the point of view of the demographic stability of the Quebec French-speaking community which, from 1871 to 1971, moved from 78% to 79%.[9] Messrs. Maheu and Charbonneau prepared a study for the Gendron Commission taking the birth rate as a constant and using net immigration as the variable. The projection for 1991 gives the following picture of the Quebec population[10]:

TABLE E

Assumed net annual migration of:	A (−10,000)	B (+2,500)	C (+15,000)
Population Projection for 1991			
French Mother Tongue %	84.5	82.1	79.1
English %	11.2	12.2	13.8
Other %	4.3	5.7	6.9
Total	100	100	100

Hypothesis B above corresponds most closely to the actual migration figure averaged from 1921 to 1971 which shows a net positive migration to Quebec of just under 5,000 persons per year.[11] An optimistic conclusion is therefore justified that, despite "world pressures" against the French language, it seems likely to hold its own in Quebec at somewhat over 80%. The effect of new language legislation might even increase this figure. A research officer of the Census Branch, Statistics Canada, Mr. John M. Kralt, has recently produced tables showing languages spoken in the home by residents of Canada simultaneously cross-tabulated by ethnicity, mother-tongue and place of birth. These figures generally confirm the thesis of this paper. Thus for those persons born and residing in Canada outside Quebec, of French ethnicity and mother-tongue, 73% still speak French at home. Persons born and residing in Quebec of French ethnicity and mother-tongue, speak French in the home at the level of 99%.

7. *The Federal Public Service*

We are now at a second stage in the application of bilingualism in the public service of Canada. The Royal Commission on Bilingualism and Biculturalism (1963-1970) performed an essential task in making us aware of the extent to which the federal public service in the Capital was an English-speaking enterprise and of the difficulty for the Francophone to work or to be served in his language, or to be fully at home in his cultural milieu.

The first major thrust of the government aimed at establishing certain language targets in all employment categories, judged sufficient to assure bilingual services and to permit members of either major language group to work comfortably in their mother-tongue. Functional bilingualism was the order of the day. In theory, this meant that, in any normal government office, relatively few individual bilinguals were required but, by carefully combining unilingual Anglophones and unilingual Francophones, a bilingual service would be provided. Thousands of Anglophones and hundreds of Francophones, nevertheless, attended government language schools to improve their second language capabilities; bilingualism advisers were appointed to departments and agencies; and administrative notices and circulars began to appear regularly in French as well as English, where this practice had been previously largely honoured in the breach. An active campaign of recruitment of Francophones was undertaken. The facilities of the Translation Bureau were greatly increased.

This immense government effort certainly caused an awareness of the language problem. But few would deny that instead of having merely discontented Francophones on its hands, the new policies succeeded, somehow, in alienating many Anglophones without basically satisfying the Francophone complaint.

Anglophone resentment lay in the belief that the rules had been changed in the middle of the game. Their jobs suddenly appeared jeopardized by the threatened imposition of a language requirement which, to many, seemed unnecessary because their work had always previously been carried out quite satisfactorily, from their standpoint, in English. Further, cyclical language school courses were difficult to reconcile with continuing job responsibilities and the drop-out rate was high. Some unilingual English-speaking stenographers bristled at the 7% premium pay accorded to bilinguals, while the same stenographers' bosses might inwardly burn at Francophones who they believed were "parachuted" into senior positions and whose views on the nature of Canadian federalism might differ from their own.

Guided by a resolution in the House of Commons adopted on June 6, 1973, by a vote of 214 to 16, the government revised its policy. The new target date for a functionally bilingual public service has been fixed for 1978, and in the meantime all public service positions must be identified as falling within one of four categories: bilingual, unilingual English, unilingual French, or either English or French. Contrary to the earlier somewhat easy concept that functional bilingualism could be achieved without many individual bilinguals preliminary information given to the Study regarding the new approach suggest, that a high proportion of the public service positions for the Ottawa-Hull area will call for bilingual capability.[12]

While this news might appear upsetting to the Anglophone community, the new approach, generally, seems to be much more acceptable to this group than the previous one. In the first place, identification of a position only makes it "potentially" bilingual. A bilingual incumbent need not be found for it until it is "designated" bilingual and departments have until 1978 to designate positions. Further, position identifications are discussed with the appropriate public service unions. Again, for each bilingual position there is a bilingual profile and many of these profiles may require only passive bilingual skills (i.e. reading and understanding rather than writing and speaking). Finally, if a unilingual (either Anglophone or Francophone) wins a competition for a bilingual job, he has up to a year (depending on the bilingual profile of his job) to learn the second official language. Likewise a "grand-father clause" protects long-service uniligual employees.

The Public Service Commission has also been actively pursuing its recruitment of Francophones to bring the language balance if possible somewhat closer to the national population ratio. In this endeavour, the Commission has been highly successful with respect to young university graduates.[13]

TABLE F

UNIVERSITY RECRUITMENT INTO THE CANADIAN PUBLIC SERVICE

	1968	%	1969	%	1970	%	1971	%	1972	%	1973	%
Appointments	531		462		384		847		851		961	
Anglophones**	424	80	329	71	294	77	449	53	610	72	676	70
Francophones**	107	20	133	29	90	23	398*	47	241	28	285	30

* Special Francophone recruitment programme.
** In this and other tables, this means the first or preferred language of the individual concerned.

Six year average Francophone university recruitment = 29%
Francophones (language of home) to total Canadian population (1971 census) = 25.7%

Recruitment of Francophones at the university level is on average better than their position with respect to all appointments.[14]

TABLE G

TOTAL APPOINTMENTS TO PUBLIC SERVICE 1971 TO 1973

	1971	%	1972	%	1973	%
English	53,237	79.8	69,566	78.6	76,937	78.1
French	13,438	20.2	18,918	21.4	21,578	21.9
Total	66,675	100	88,484	100	98,515	100

Three year average: Francophones/total appointments = 21.2%
Francophones/total population = 25.7%

There is an even sharper drop with respect to senior positions.[15]

TABLE H

CLASSIFICATION OF POSITIONS OF EXECUTIVE APPOINTMENTS 1971–1973

	1971 Number	%	1972 Number	%	1973 Number	%
Anglophone	127	83	182	71	211	58.3
Francophone	—		4	2	2	0.6
Unspecified or bilingual	26	17	71	27	149	41.1
	153	100	257	100	362	100

Assuming that half of the "unspecified or bilingual" senior positions are occupied by Francophones (which generally corresponds to published information[16]), the above figures averaged over the three year period suggest that 85% of these positions would normally go to Anglophones or Francophones willing to work in English, and only 15% to Francophones or Anglophones willing and able to work in French. As of February 28, 1974, 171 of the 909 officers in the executive category or 18.8% were Francophone, despite the fact that 38% of executive appointments in 1973 to the public service from outside the public service were French speaking.

There has, I understand, been a difficult problem with respect to the attracting of senior Francophone officers to the Capital. This cannot be ascribed to any lack of effort by the Public Service Commission, as the resistance to moving to Ottawa by any well-established French Montreal or Quebec family is usually strong. Nevertheless, the resulting situation is unfortunate and one of the most discouraging things for the bright young Francophone coming to the Capital is to be unable to communicate "upward" effectively in French. If there are five Anglophones and five Francophones at a meeting in Ottawa and all but one Anglophone are bilingual, the meeting will normally take place in English. If he decides to stay in Ottawa, the young Francophone will resent this for the first year or so and then shrug his shoulders and, to this extent at least, accept the pattern of working in English.

One way to help these young officers would be the encouragement of passive bilingualism. This means that each person should understand the other official language but not necessarily speak it. It also implies that at meetings one would address a colleague in one's own language and receive a reply in his. This may appear artificial when first tried, but practice has shown that it works. Departmental directives encouraging this practice would certainly make it easier for young Québecois officers who, as things stand, tend to be somehow cast in the role of linguistic fanatics, merely by insisting on speaking their own language.

A word about French Language Units or FLU's which work entirely in French save for contacts with certain interacting units. FLU's undoubtedly are ideal for that young Québecois coming to work in the Capital. But, by its very nature, any headquarters must serve the whole organization. The offices in the Capital must be able to do business with the whole country. It is therefore hard to conceive a form of organization in which very many branches or divisions of departments or agencies can be designed to work in one language only at the governmental nerve centre of the nation. Passive bilingualism offers more hope, but this option, it must be recognized, implies a continuance of the government language schools, until the regular school system in Canada turns out persons capable of understanding spoken French.

In summary, there exists at the present time the political will to make the federal public service a reflection of the bilingual reality of Canada. A new administrative effort of massive scale is underway in consultation with the parties most directly concerned: the departments, the unions, the individuals.

While the proportion of Francophone public servants in all categories is not in balance with their numbers in the population, this proportion is growing. At the same time Anglophone fears of imminent disaster are not as vocal as they were before the new approach. Everyone seems to recognize that it will be a long haul but no one is now saying that it can't be done.

To conclude on a hopeful note, figures received from the Public Service Commission relating to appointments to the public service in 1973 *in the National Capital Region* show that the proportion of Anglophone/Francophone appointments corresponds almost exactly to the linguistic balance in the country as a whole.

PUBLIC SERVICE APPOINTMENTS JAN-DEC 1973 IN
THE NATIONAL CAPITAL REGION

Claimed Working Language of Employee	New Appointments	Appointments within Public Service	Total	%
French	2,847	5,723	8,570	25.8
English	7,678	17,000	24,678	74.2

Francophones/total appointments = 25.8%
Francophones/total population = 25.7%

8. *The Provinces*

The Ontario position with respect to bilingualism rests first on a brief prepared by the Province and a statement by Premier Robarts for the Constitutional Conferences in 1968 and 1969.[17] Latterly, the policy statement of Premier Davis of May 3, 1971, provides the operating guideline.[18] Of first importance in Ontario policy is that the "legitimate requirements" of Franco-Ontarians be met. Apart from significant action in the field of education, dealt with in the following sections, the aim is to provide over-the-counter service in French in French-speaking areas of the Province; to establish a priority list of official documents for printing in both English and French; to help municipalities in their efforts to bilingualize; to expand the provision of bilingual judicial services, both oral and written; to encourage the use of French in the Ontario Legislature and to improve the Province's translation services. Although rejecting the notion of bilingual districts, the Davis statement committed the Government of Ontario to do its part to assure that the National Capital is a place which all Canadians can be proud.

In implementation of this policy, the Ontario Government entered into an arrangement with the federal government whereby provincial and municipal officials take language training at the federal language bureau in the Capital in exchange for the training of federal officials at the provincial language school in Toronto. In general it would be fair to say that, while Ontario interpretation and translation services have been of excellent quality with respect to conference services and public documents, most ministries seem to be making haste slowly in the matter of giving substance to the bilingualism objectives set out by Premier Davis.

Constitutionally, the language position of Quebec differs from that of Ontario in that it is, to some extent, regulated by the British North America Act. Section 133 of that document provides for the use of English and French in the legislatures and the courts of Quebec and of Canada. In addition to the fact that Quebec legislation must be published in English and that English may be used in Quebec courts, the Anglophone there enjoys the benefits of the Quebec Cities and Towns Act which provides that municipal notices must be published in both languages. Generally speaking, Quebec provincial services in the Outaouais area are bilingual, although we did hear from Anglophones from English-speaking townships that regulations and instructions relating to various acts of the Quebec legislature were usually received in French only.

In any direct comparison, however, it is difficult to resist the conclusion that Ontario's bilingual services have some way to go to compare with those of Quebec.

Viewed in another way, the situation in Ontario and Quebec is similar, in that it is French, the minority language in Ontario and the majority language in Quebec, which feels threatened in both provinces. Indeed, it was to this question which the Gendron Commission addressed itself for a period of three years. As of this writing, the country is awaiting a comprehensive statement of the Quebec Government's language policy promised in the 1974 Throne speech. This policy, when announced, should be examined not only in terms of the protection and guarantees it accords to the minority language (English), but also bearing in mind that many Québécois believe, rightly or wrongly, that French is vulnerable even within their own Province.

9. *The Local Governments*

In his Study on the Federal Capital conducted in 1965–67 for the Royal Commission on Bilingualism and Biculturalism, Professor Kenneth D. McRae records the considerable difficulties his research team experienced with City of Ottawa to obtain information on the representation of Francophones on City staff and on the language of communication both within municipal departments and with the public.[19] The subsequent turnaround in attitude by the City with regard to Canada's official languages has been most impressive and entirely in keeping with Ottawa's special status as the image of the nation both to Canadians and to the representatives of other countries in the Capital. Two by-laws were passed by the City in 1970[20]. The first recognized the equality of the English and French languages within the municipal administration, provided for notices to the public in both languages where deemed necessary or advisable, and assured employees that their careers would not be impaired or affected because of their language capability. The second by-law provided for the substitution of bilingual signs or symbols for the old unilingual traffic signs when these require replacement. Further, a bilingualism adviser and a translator were hired. At the present time most of the by-laws have been translated, several hundred civic employees have had language training and simultaneous interpretation has been introduced as a regular feature at Council meetings, following a symbolic joint gathering with Hull City Council to introduce the new service. In its own way, a Quiet Revolution has taken place at City Hall between 1970 and 1973 although there is still some way to go to achieve full bilingual services.

The City of Hull, though it clearly has a high bilingual capability, nevertheless does have some gaps. Its bylaws, for instance, are only in French. The Outaouais Regional Community (CRO) has recently engaged a fulltime translator, however, whose services will be available to the City of Hull. In one sense, Hull might be considered to be moving away from bilingualism insofar as the Hull Council passed a recent resolution[21] declaring itself in favour of the predominance of French in the matter of signs. This should perhaps be viewed in the context of a desire to preserve the French character of Hull which is considered vulnerable in view of the large numbers of Anglophone public servants now in Hull and new businesses which have sprung up in the wake of the major federal building programme there.

The federal government established a small programme administered by the National Capital Commission to provide financial support for bilingual development within the municipalities of the region. This has been a useful catalyst not only for a number of municipalities and other local bodies but also for private associations and groups seriously interested in increasing their bilingual capability.

Professor Lyne Langlois, of the University of Ottawa, conducted a study[22] on the degree of bilingualism reached by various authorities in the region. This was measured under fifteen headings: official letterheads, public notices, by-laws, information services, traffic signs, fire service, police, library, recreation, language of council meetings (simultaneous or consecutive interpretation), documents at council meetings, bilingual staff (actual), hiring policy, and language courses for personnel. The results of these interviews show, on the Ontario side, that only Vanier and Ottawa are bilingual in any full sense of the word. In descending order thereafter, but with some degree of bilingualism, are Gloucester, Cumberland, Nepean, Richmond and Fitzroy. The other eleven municipalities in Ontario do not score at all.

All five local Ontario police forces claimed to be bilingual but the Ontario Provincial Police, which serves thirteen municipalities, refused Professor Langlois an interview, despite repeated attempts. Her personal observation (police tickets, telephone calls, etc.) suggest to her that the organization is rather rigorously unilingual. (On the other hand the report issued in early 1974 by the

Ontario Task Force on Policing[23] recommends that police services in Ottawa-Carleton be bilingual and that a recruitment policy favouring bilinguals or candidates expressing a willingness to be bilingual is the way to move forward in this area.)

On the Quebec side, Miss Langlois found, to her surprise, that the situation, while better than in Ontario, had big gaps. She qualifies twenty of the thirty-two municipalities as bilingual. "The three municipalities offering most bilingual services are Aylmer, Eardley and Templeton East, followed by Buckingham North, Hull West, Lucerne and Templeton West. Certain other municipalities also offer substantial bilingual services: Hull, Gatineau Point, Perkins and Templeton Village. Some bilingual services are offered by Aldfield, the Town of Buckingham, Gatineau, Touraine, Wakefield Village, Deschênes, Buckingham South-East, Portland West and Quyon."

Seven municipalities offer services substantially in French: Notre-Dame-de-la-Salette, Angers Village, Wakefield East, Masson, Templeton East, Ste-Cécile-de-Masham, and Angers parish.

Five municipalities offer services substantially in English. They are North Masham, South Onslow, North Onslow, Wakefield Township and West Buckingham.

Professor Langlois notes that, save for a few of the smaller French municipalities, all Quebec municipalities in the region have bilingual employees and their policy is to recruit bilingual personnel. On the other hand, she regrets that she was not able to interview the Chairmen of the regional bodies (Regional Municipality of Ottawa-Carleton, Outaouais Regional Community, Outaouais Planning Corporation) and in general she feels that these organizations are not as bilingual as might be expected of institutions serving a wide community.

Miss Langlois' study is largely based on interviews with the Mayors or officials of the municipalities, and time did not permit her to check out "on the ground" the stated bilingual capabilities. I would be inclined to question the degree of bilingualism claimed in several instances. Nevertheless, I think the study does show that some progress in bilingualism is being made.

10. *The Teaching of French in Canada: General Issues*

The Study found that the weight of opinion as expressed both in briefs and in personal interviews favoured the strengthening of second-language teaching at the school level as the basic answer to the language problem in Canada.

Several reasons have been put forward to explain our weakness in this area. First, there has been a disposition by the provinces to teach a second language at the secondary school level, although evidence of linguistic and medical specialists suggests that a language is learned most easily from infancy until about the age of ten.

TABLE I

SECOND LANGUAGE* TEACHING AT ELEMENTARY LEVEL 1972-73

Canadian Province	% Students Studying Second Lang.*	Trend** Up ↑ Down ↓ No Trend X	% Time in School on Second Lang. Study	Trend** ↑ ↓ X
Newfoundland	31.6	↑	6.3	↑
Prince Edward Island	32.5	↑	6.4	X
Nova Scotia	14.4	↑	5.8	↓
New Brunswick	56.0	↓	5.9	↓
Ontario	43.9	↑	6.6	X
Manitoba	34.1	↑	5.9	↑
Saskatchewan	5.1	X	8.3	X
Alberta	28.1	↑	5.4	X
British Columbia	6.3	↑	5.0	X
Nine English-Speaking Provinces	33.3	↑	6.4	X
Quebec	33.4	↓	11.1	↑

* English in Quebec; French in all other provinces.
** As of past three years.

Table I above[24] shows the position of second-language teaching in Canada at the elementary level in 1972-73. It will be noted that, while one-third of Canadian children in the English-speaking provinces studied their second language, this was on average for only 6.4% of the time, or some twenty minutes a day. The Chairman of one of the area school boards told the Study that twenty minutes a day was worse than useless, in that it gave the token impression of devotion to the second language without imparting enough knowledge to be of any practical use to the child emerging from the primary system. It should be noted in this connection that, although the same percentage of Quebec elementary students study English as primary students in the other provinces study French, the Quebec elementary students study English almost twice as long, i.e, about thirty-five minutes a day.

In the so-called French "core" programmes on the Ontario side of the National Capital Region, experiments are being made with differing periods of second-language study at the elementary level. While it is too soon to speak of proven results, I have the impression that the local boards will eventually come around to something like forty to sixty minutes a day all through elementary to produce a potential bilingual, provided adequate funding is available.

There seems to be a general policy among ministries of education in Canada to move away from compulsory curricula at the secondary level and to give students the widest latitude in the choice of subjects as long as they obtain a certain number of "credits". In this "credit" system both English and French have tended, in the English speaking provinces, to go by the boards. As long as the universities demanded English and French as entry subjects, the line could be held to some extent, but as the universities dropped this standard, the numbers studying English and French at the high school level went down. The pendulum now may be swinging the other way. In Ontario for instance English as well as Canadian studies will be compulsory in high school beginning 1974-75 but there is a disposition to draw the line there. If French were made compulsory, a senior Ontario official told the Study, there would be pressure to make physical training and other subjects compulsory and the educational system would be in the old straight-jacket as of yore. It should be noted, however, that the Quebec authorities have found it possible to make English compulsory from Grade 5 upwards and that they are now giving grants to interested school boards for its extension to the earliest primary grades.

The watchword in the English-speaking provinces is "motivation", with respect to second language study. But this policy does not seem to have met much success except in certain areas like the Ontario side of the National Capital Region. Table J below illustrates that, as far as second-language study is concerned, the trend is down without exception, although the record of the Maritime Provinces is good with two students out of three studying French for about an eighth of their school time. This "best" English-speaking record compares with Quebec's record of one hundred percent (100%) for one-seventh of school time to study the English language.

TABLE J

SECOND LANGUAGE* TEACHING AT SECONDARY LEVEL 1972-73

Canadian Province	% Students Studying Second Lang.	Trend** UP ↑ Down ↓ No Trend X	% Time in School on Second Lang. Study	Trend** ↑ ↓ X
Newfoundland	58.2	↓	10.8	↑
Prince Edward Island	66.6	↓	10.8	↑
Nova Scotia	65.0	↓	12.9	↓
New Brunswick	70.9	↓	14.7	↑
Ontario	39.4	↓	13.0	X
Manitoba	45.3	↓	11.9	X
Saskatchewan	55.7	↓	11.3	↑
Alberta	34.5	↓	10.3	X
British Columbia	57.2	↓	11.3	X
Total of English-speaking Provinces	47.0	↓	12.0	X
Quebec	100	X	14.2	X

* English in Quebec; French in all other provinces.
** As of last three years.

The approach in the English-speaking provinces toward French instruction places great emphasis on oral/aural skills with endless repetition yet somehow without producing effective communication as an end product. The current pedagogy does not seem to challenge or inspire the student of today and it is legitimate to ask if both stick and carrot are not essential to human motivation. The most obvious "stick" is to make French compulsory in the English speaking provinces as English is in Quebec from the fifth grade to high school graduation. The "carrot" would be to make French interesting and exciting for students as it now obviously is not, judged by the trends illustrated above. Educationists recognize integrative and instrumental attitudes with respect to language learning: the former being a desire to discover a literature, a culture, another world; the latter being some specific objective such as a job in the federal public service. Educational guidance officers could evoke interest in both areas in their important work of student orientation. Bilingual service to the public in both the government and the private sector is a fact of life in South Africa today. Is this because a student there cannot obtain his high school leaving certificate without having passed his second-language examinations, English or Afrikaans as the case may be?

Minority-language education means studying in English by the English-speaking minority in Quebec and studying in French by the French-speaking minority in all the other provinces. This question also merits attention in the national educational context.

Table K below illustrates the stage which has now been reached with respect to minority-language schools at the elementary level.

TABLE K

MINORITY LANGUAGE** AS LANGUAGE OF INSTRUCTION-ELEMENTARY
1972–73

Province	% of Students Studying in Minority Language in relation to Mother Tongue Minority Language Population in that Age Group	Trend* Up ↑ Down ↓ No Trend X	% Time Spent in Study of Minority Language	Trend* ↑ ↓ X
Newfoundland	0	↓	—	↓
Prince Edward Island	42	↓	100	↑
Nova Scotia	113	X	78	↓
New Brunswick	85.4	↓	99.9	X
Ontario	119.5	↑	94.3	↓
Manitoba	62.3	↓	70.4	↑
Saskatchewan	21.3	↑	80.8	↑
Alberta	69.3	↑	33.2	X
British Columbia	9.8	↑	39.7	X
Nine English-Speaking Provinces	99.2	X	92.3	↓
Quebec	133.4	↓	100	X

* Based on figures 1970-71 to 1972-73.
** English in Quebec; French in other provinces.

It will be seen that the picture in Ontario, Quebec, New Brunswick and Nova Scotia appears encouraging. Indeed figures for Nova Scotia, and Ontario suggest that some Anglophones or children of other non-French mother tongues, are attending French-language schools, and that in Quebec some Francophones or children of other non-English mother tongues, are attending English-language schools. At the secondary level the picture is different as will be noted from Table L.

TABLE L

MINORITY LANGUAGE** AS A LANGUAGE OF INSTRUCTION—SECONDARY
1972-73

Province	% Students Studying in Minority Language in relation to Mother Tongue Minority Language Population in that Age Group	Trend* Up ↑ Down ↓ No Trend X	% Time Devoted Study of Minotiry Language	Trend* ↑ ↓ X
Newfoundland	27.7	X	100	X
Prince Edward Island	25.0	X	100	X
Nova Scotia	57.1	X	76	X
New Brunswick	62.1	↑	100	X
Ontario	38.3	↑	82.5	↑
Manitoba	35.6	↓	46.3	↑
Saskatchewan	4.1	X	69.7	↑
Alberta	125.9	↑	9.4	↓
British Columbia	—	—	—	—
Nine English-Speaking Provinces	47.5	↑	79.6	X
Quebec	88.6	↑	100	X

* Based on figures 1970-71 to 1972-73.
** English in Quebec; French in other provinces.

It will be seen that less than one half of Francophones outside Quebec go on to high school in their mother-tongue and even here the percentage holds up because of relatively strong figures in New Brunswick and Nova Scotia. The figure for Ontario is low but the trend there is up.

The senior education department officials from the Western Provinces, with whom we spoke on this subject, were quick to point out that most French-speaking Canadians in their respective territories did not wish *all* the secondary education for their children to be in French but mostly wanted half the subjects taught in English to assure the students' successful integration into an English-speaking milieu. It will be noted that this conforms to Mr. Joy's picture of French assimilation outside the Soo-Moncton line described in earlier paragraphs.

Since 1970 the Department of the Secretary of State in implementation of recommendations of the Royal Commission of Bilingualism and Biculturalism has provided funds to the provinces to strengthen second-language teaching, minority language education, language-teacher training and a number of related subjects. The programmes have been renewed for another five years until April 1979. They are based on an across-the-board formula of 9% of the costs of a full-time minority language student and 5% of the costs of second-language teaching plus assistance in other areas. As the programme has worked out in its first three years, Quebec has received 55% of the $167 million dollars in grants and Ontario and Quebec between them almost 85% of the total. In view of the fact that a good minority-language (English) school system has been in existence in Quebec since Confederation and Quebec also has had compulsory second-language (English) teaching from the fifth grade, it is possible to ask if the special federal government programme is not merely supporting the status quo. Yet in our talks with senior education officials in Alberta, Manitoba and Saskatchewan, which together receive only $4\frac{1}{2}$% of federal grants, there was little support of the idea that these grants should be negotiated bilaterally on the basis of specific improvements or extensions of service in the area of minority or second language teaching, and there was general agreement that a formula which could be applied to all provinces was the best approach. Ironically, we found that it was in Ontario, a major beneficiary under the existing formula, that senior education officials argued for more flexible arrangements. We unfortunately did not have discussions with educationists from British Columbia, Quebec or the Maritime provinces.

Bearing in mind that education, including language education, is a purely provincial responsibility, federal assistance, in my view, should be directed at improving existing standards which, in the matter of second-language learning, have been depressingly low in the past. The Study received several comments that federal language grants were not even being used by provinces for language purposes. All the senior education officials with whom we spoke, however, assured us that the federal money was being devoted to language education, while the federal government assures us that "adequate accounting information will be provided to the public"[25] on the specific grants as well as on the achievement of objectives. However this may be, doubts can still exist as to the optimum use of federal funds. A school board in Province "X", aware of the existence of federal funds, can arrange for a gap in its budgeting with respect to second or minority language which the province will dutifully fill with federal grant money. This, in fact, is what is happening in a number of cases, I was told by one provincial official. While looking good on paper, this merely continues the status quo, and its net effect is really to permit the school board in question to spend on something *other than language education*, because the federal monies, in the example given, merely replace what the board itself would have done in language education without the federal bonanza. Efforts should be bent in the view of the writer of this paper to assure that federal monies are devoted to an extension of language-teaching beyond the existing norms and curricula.[26]

11. *The Local Education Scene: an overview*

Whatever the future may hold with respect to the form of government for the Capital area, the systems of education and of law are likely to be the last to be changed. I propose in this paper to deal with immediate practical matters affecting Ontario and Quebec where the possibility of progress exists. This is not to say that the Capital is not a metropolitan area for some educational purposes. The University of Ottawa and Algonquin College serve students from the Outaouais québecois as they do their own Ontarians. Likewise, there have been instances of informal cooperation between boards of education in the area, of which the 1973 summer exchange programme for second-language learning is a good example. But such cooperative ventures tend to be on the margin of education and not in the heartland of curriculum and pedagogical approach. Despite the highly structured and regulated nature of the Ministries of Education of Quebec and Ontario, it is possible to believe that formal interprovincial educational cooperation within the National Capital area can be extended. The Study has been told that there is an acute shortage of French immersion teachers in Ottawa-Carleton and yet the certificates of Francophone Quebecers are only recognized if the Quebec teacher has followed an academic and pedagogic programme that is exactly the equivalent of that required in Ontario. Bearing in mind the 1969 agreement between Ontario and Quebec on Education Cooperation, would it be too radical to conceive of a reciprocal recognition of certificates at least in the area of language and on a "quota" basis? The paper of Professor Kenneth McRae (Appendix B-2A), a companion-piece to this report, analyses in depth the opportunities which are open in the National Capital area in the domain of education structures. This paper will comment on the local scene as it exists today.

12. *Ottawa-Carleton (Second-Language Study)*

I begin with three premises that I believe are generally accepted at this time. The first is that English education and French education should be separated. There were widespread hurt feelings among the "liberal-minded" Anglo-Ontarians here a few years ago when the French would not have anything to do with a bilingual high school which was proposed by the Ottawa Board of Education and to which it was hoped both the English and the French communities would send their children. The English "liberals" now at least understand the fear of assimilation by the French, the stark reality of which was brought out in Section 7. Such is the pressure of the English language that, in extra-curricular activities, in any French/English concentration of less than four or five to one, the likelihood is strong that English will be spoken. (As now planned "bilingual" high schools in the Ontario side of the Capital will be for Anglophones wishing to become fully proficient in French).

My second assumption is that the present confessional system will remain for some time yet. A former local school board chairman of broad experience who also happens to be Francophone suggested to the Study that there be three school boards for the Ontario side of the Capital region: one English public; one French public; and one English/French confessional. This system, he explained, would have the advantage of giving a home to the French-speaking Protestants who now have to choose between an English school system or a Catholic one at the primary level, as was also the case, until recently, in Quebec. The confessional school system would also, he explained, be able to accommodate academically denominations other than Roman Catholic, whereas they too, now, have no means of public financial support. This idea is interesting, but I do not intend to pursue it.

My third assumption is to accept, with qualification, the equality principle which forms the basis of Ontario and Quebec educational philosophy at the present time. By the equality principle, I refer to the notion that all children of Ontario (or of Quebec) are entitled to the same basic education. Private schools are not banned but the intention is that the public school education will be sufficiently excellent to allow the student to develop to the fullest extent of his capabilities. In Ontario, equality is introduced by means of "per pupil ceilings", i.e., a fixed dollar amount per public school student and a fixed dollar amount per high school student. A predetermined tax on the assessment base of the school board region will provide a certain proportion of the "per pupil ceiling", while the province pays the rest. The province may pay less than 40% in "rich" areas like Toronto and more than 70% in less prosperous communities. School boards have had up to 1973 complete freedom with respect to curriculum[27]. The wealthier boards of the province are inclined to want to "break" their ceilings for a variety of reasons to improve the quality of education offered, whereas the Ministry of Education, fearing the flood if the gate is opened, has been most insistent that boards live within their ceilings.

Having set down my premises, I turn to the education of English-speaking children in the Ontario portion of the National Capital. The imaginative and flexible approach taken by all four Boards (Ottawa, Ottawa Roman Catholic, Carleton, Carleton Roman Catholic) has been very effective in advancing the standards of French (second-language) learning. The numbers of students and percentages of time devoted to second-language learning are far greater than the Ontario average shown in Tables I and J above. Each Board has had original ideas and experiments, a number of which are still going on. The description which follows gives a composite but fairly faithful picture. All boards have a basic "core" French programme varying from twenty to seventy-five minutes a day, followed by all children except those in immersion. Core French, taken through public school and high school, is intended to produce a potential bilingual: i.e., a person who on graduation, when exposed to a bilingual milieu and perhaps with some "finishing", would be capable of working in both official languages in most types of jobs.

Most boards also have "immersion" programmes, where the children work entirely in French except for English-language studies. The various boards started with a kindergarten class and worked out curricula each year for a subsequent year. The Ottawa Separate School is the farthest advanced in this respect, with classes up to grade 4. A total of 4,338 immersion pupils are enrolled in all four boards up to the grade 3 level out of a total kindergarten to grade three population of 52,606. This amounts to more than 8%, while 5,458 pupils out of 51,347, or 10.6% are expected in 1974–75. The immersion programmes are carefully monitored[28] and all the research so far indicates that any losses the immersed child suffers in his mother-tongue skills are quickly recouped so that at the grade three level he is equal to the grade 3 English (core) student with an extra language to boot.

Boards are also experimenting with an immersion stream beginning at grade 6 or 7 and a bilingual high school.[29]

The Ontario Government agreed to allow the federal government to contribute over $4 million over a two year period to assure the development and expansion of this language teaching experiment. Many persons from the Ontario side of the National Capital have spoken enthusiastically to Study members about it. The aim of the various boards is to obtain relief from "ceiling pressure" sufficiently long to have a complete range of immersion classes (k-8) and a bilingual high school (9-13). There is every reason to argue that continuing support should be given this experiment, which is in many ways unique, until a wider range of programmes is established and research results are available to permit an effective long-term future orientation for second-language study. This is in line with the approach discussed earlier that the federal monies now distributed to Departments of Education to promote language learning be allocated on the basis of specific initiatives such as *extending* the existing teaching of French or introducing new experimental programmes of the type described above.

Once the immersion stream structure is established, the adoption for the primary and secondary levels of a system like that applied to Algonquin College and the University of Ottawa might be considered. It will be recalled that these institutions justify to the Ministry of University and Colleges the *extra* costs involved in running bilingual institutions. Running two English streams, one "core", one "immersion", at the public and high school levels, is likely to add marginally, but only marginally, to costs. The Ontario Boards, with full bilingual services in the Capital area, might apply to the Ministry of Education for relief from these marginal costs, following the Algonquin/University of Ottawa pattern. Perhaps the federal government could share in the additional marginal charges.

The federal government should, in any case, in my view continue to seek cooperative arrangements with the provinces to assure the highest standards of language training in the Capital. There is a precedent for this in Switzerland where, though education is a cantonal responsibility, the federal government has taken measures to assure that the French-speaking federal public servants are able to educate their children in French in Bern.

The federal government should also, as I see it, give encouragement, where necessary and desirable, to certain specialized activities or institutions which favour second-language learning. One example is exchanges, where students are twinned with opposite numbers of the "target culture". Another example is the Cours Claudel, a private French school with high standards of excellence, whose presence in Ottawa has helped to attract many senior Quebecers since its establishment in the 1960's.

Should the existing Ottawa-Carleton school board structures reflect any changes that may be made in the political structures of the National Capital? Mr. Fullerton (Chapter 15) and Professor McRae (Appendix B-2A) analyse the options which may be open in this area. From my rather closer perspective, present board sizes seem just about optimum and the friendly competition of existing boards in the area of second-language programmes has been healthy and productive of exciting educational experiments.

13. *Ottawa-Carleton (Minority Language)*

The liberal educational policy[30] which saw English, French, German, Gaelic and Algonquin schools happily co-existing until 1867 and, except for Algonquin, until 1876, was gradually replaced by a frankly assimilationist policy in 1890. Regulation 17 of 1912, which forbade teaching through the French language after the third grade and which was on the books for a generation, is graven on the heart of every Franco-Ontarian. Indeed it was not until 1968 with the amendment of the Secondary Schools and Boards of Education Act[31] that publicly-supported French high schools were authorized in Ontario. Even after this break-through (for which the name of John Robarts is particularly revered by Franco-Ontarians), the sailing was not smooth. While the new law provided for the creation of French-language advisory committees to be attached to school boards in which French programmes were introduced, there was no guarantee that the Boards would accept the Committees' advice. Disagreements arose usually over the establishment of a detached French school (favoured by the advisory committees to guard against assimilationist tendencies of students) as against the running of a "bilingual" school with parallel English and French streams (favoured by boards for a variety of reasons). Although emotions ran fairly high in Ottawa in two instances, the Franco-Ontarians succeeded in obtaining detached high schools there, but in Sturgeon Falls an impasse was reached. The Minister of Education, the Honourable Robert Welch, set up a Minister's Commission of Enquiry under Professor T. H. B. Symons, President of Trent University on September 15, 1971. Among the latter's recommendations[32] was a system for the adjudication of disputes between French-(or English-) language advisory committees and boards of the district *majority language*. Along with another recommendation for the creation of a Standing Committee on French at the Ministry of Education with a Chairman of Assistant Deputy Minister rank, the basis was laid for a

French school system in Ontario paralleling the English system. A French-speaking assistant deputy minister was named in early 1972 and an adjudication system basically similar to that recommended by the Symons Commission was made law[33] in late 1973.

In a recent seminar on the future of Franco-Ontarians, one of the panelists[34] declared that in the past the three strongest forces to preserve French-Canadian culture in Ontario were the home, the church, and the school. In the context of modern society, home and church influence had been weakened as cultural bastions, she analysed, but a major break-through had occurred with respect to the school. I would agree with this analysis and although considerable upgrading remains to be done, it is my view that the French-language school system in Ontario is solidly based. It will be recalled that 38.3% of mother-tongue Franco-Ontarians in the relevant age group went to French high schools in 1972-73 (Table L above), and the trend was up. The future of Franco-Ontarians will depend in large measure on the will of the youth to keep the arrow pointing upward.

14. *Outaouais* (*Minority Language*)

The Quebec government's application of the "equality principle", described above, has been even more rigorous than that of Ontario, so that at the present time there is very little financial discretion left to Quebec Boards. By means of "balancing" or "equalization" grants from Quebec City, each Board in the province receives the same revenue for "authorized expenditures admissible for grants". Boards can raise money by supplementary school taxes for "authorized expenditures not admissible for grants" but this scope for financial discretion is very narrow. The impression we gathered from our conversations with Outaouais English-speaking school trustees and officials was that there was not enough slack in the system to permit adjustments in the pupil-teacher ratio required for more effective second-language programmes. We were also told by one official that while the local Quebec Protestant system considered itself once well ahead of the Ontario side in French, they were, as a result of the immersion programmes in Ottawa and Carleton, losing this advantage.

The Study was informed that the federal government has been unable to make a contribution for French second-language teaching in the Outaouais québecois on grounds that it subsidizes only the minority language (mother-tongue or second language) and that, in Quebec, French as the *majority* language cannot be aided. One can argue that this was the right decision for the wrong reason. If French is the "threatened" language in Canada, it should be helped regardless of the geographical location of the need. But if Quebec has already received more than half of the federal language subsidies, would it not be just that some of this money be used to build up a structure of immersion schools on the Quebec side of the National Capital? It is understood changes along these lines are being negotiated between the federal and Quebec governments.

Two important avenues are open to assure the survival and progress of French in Canada. First, the French-Canadian himself will have to take pride in his language and not drift away from it. Second, more Anglophones will have to learn to speak French, not haltingly, but easily and joyfully. I believe that immersion is the path to produce this fluently bilingual Anglophone. I further think the French character of the Quebec side of the Capital will be maintained much more surely when this kind of Anglophone is around in greater numbers. I am therefore persuaded that the Quebec Government has every bit as great an interest in imaginative and experimental programmes to incite the Outaouais Anglophones to become fluently bilingual, as Ontario has in its Ottawa-Carleton special programmes. It can be argued of course that with many bilingual Anglophones around, assimilation of the French would be even more rapid. But if more widespread bilingualisation led to more Anglophone/Francophone marriages, the normal law of probabilities and of free choice would suggest the "bilingual children" of such unions would fit readily within either language group and that the overall ethnic balance would be preserved, while French would be in a less threatened, defensive position.

15. *Outaouais (Majority Language)*

A fair number of French Quebecers attend English-language schools in that province. A large majority of immigrants to Quebec choose the English language stream.[35] These have been disturbing questions to the government of Quebec and to many French-speaking Quebecers.

In the face of these developments the government has, for some time, taken a liberal view despite strong and emotional opposition. Bill 63 leaves freedom of choice to all residents of Quebec to choose the English or French language stream for the education of their children. The policy of the Quebec Government in the words of the Minister of Education in the National Assembly on December 20, 1973, is "to promote the teaching of French (mother-tongue); to promote the teaching of English and of French (second languages); and to establish structures to welcome immigrants". The Government's view in a nutshell is that English is indispensable as the majority language on the North American continent and that the best way to encourage the immigrant to Quebec to assimilate toward the French is by receiving him warmly rather than compelling him by law to send his children to French language schools.

In this connection, it should be noted that the Quebec Ministry of Education has provided additional funds to establish "classes d'accueil" or "welcoming classes", specially geared to assist immigrants to learn the French language. The Hull-Outaouais School Board has established such a centre. This Board has also since 1971 conducted a pilot project for the Quebec Ministry of Education involving the study of English from the first year of elementary school. Hull parents have shown themselves strongly favorable to this programme, as have other parent groups throughout Quebec. The Quebec Ministry of Education is using federal funds destined for second language teaching to extend to lower grades the teaching of English to those school boards who so request, following the success of the Hull experiment. The strengthening of English-language teaching will, it is hoped, attract more New Canadians to the French-language stream since in this way children of a cultural background that is neither English nor French will have the opportunity to leave school with a firm grasp of both Canadian official languages, as well as the one they have learned at home.

The strong feelings engendered by immigrant schooling has not affected the Outaouais. This region, unlike Montreal, has not been a traditional centre for receiving overseas immigrants. The attached table shows the small percentage of "other" mother-tongue students at the schools of the region:

TABLE M[36]

STUDENTS IN THE OUTAOUAIS QUÉBECOIS

Mother Tongue	1972/73 French	English	Other	Total
Number	61,082	12,264	524	73,870
%	82.7%	16.6%	0.7%	100%

It will be seen in the next table that more English mother-tongue students are studying through the medium of the French language than vice-versa. Further, while more "other" students are studying in English rather than French, the numbers are so small as to be insignificant from the point of view of ultimate cultural influence.

TABLE N

STUDENTS IN THE OUTAOUAIS QUÉBECOIS

1972/73

French Students Studying in French	French Students Studying in English	French Students at Bilingual Schools	Total French Students
54,648	494	5,940	61,082
89.5%	0.8%	9.7%	100%

English Students Studying in English	English Students Studying in French	English Students at Bilingual Schools	Total English Students
8,949	1,029	2,286	12,246
73%	8.4%	18.6%	100%

"Other" Students Studying in English	"Other" Students Studying in French	"Other" Students at Bilingual Schools	Total "Other" Students
309	180	35	524
58.9%	34.4%	6.7%	100%

As of this writing the Quebec Government has not announced the details of its new cultural policy. In contrast to past policies of Ontario, Manitoba and certain English speaking provinces, Quebec has traditionally pursued a very liberal policy in allowing its citizens to choose freely between French and English schooling. Certainly from the perspective of this paper it is hoped that this liberal outlook will be maintained. At the same time, it must be borne in mind that many French-speaking Quebecers consider their language is threatened, even in Quebec, and there is a strong popular feeling that at least the children of new immigrants to Quebec should be guided toward a study of the majority language. If changes are to be made, might there not be special provisions for the National Capital Region, so that new Canadians on either side of the Ottawa River would continue to have freedom of choice?

16. *Post-Secondary Institutions in Relation to the French Character of the Outaouais*

The problems of French education at the post-secondary level on the Ontario side are interesting. Some Franco-Ontarians and Quebecers in the student and teaching body at Algonquin College and Ottawa University would like to carry the idea of linguistically separated institutions to the post-secondary level. There should be a French, not a bilingual university, in the Capital, and at least a French Campus for Algonquin College; so the argument runs.

Separateness is no doubt a good thing in high school so that Franco-Ontarians who want to maintain their culture can have a thorough grounding in French. At the post-secondary level, it seems to me more difficult to justify this separateness in the Province of Ontario since, after college, the Franco-Ontarian will have to face the "real world" and it is legitimate to ask if he will not be disadvantaged if he has had no formal exposure to English beyond his second-language studies in primary and secondary school. Although I recognize that the matter is one of lively debate on the campuses of Algonquin College and the University of Ottawa, the balance of advantage, in my view, lies with bilingual post-secondary institutions of which Algonquin and the University of Ottawa are viable examples. As I see it, the thrust should be to have more and more courses available in French, even if these courses may be in some cases only carbon copies of an English course (e.g. a French course in Common Law or in engineering). Algonquin and the University of Ottawa are now receiving certain monies representing the extra costs for running a bilingual institution. It is essential that this funding be continued.

Quebecers play a useful part both at the University of Ottawa and Algonquin College in maintaining a French atmosphere and it is hoped that the liberal attitude of the Government of Ontario in encouraging their presence will be maintained.

Born of two English parents (the Eastern Ontario Institute of Technology and the Ontario Vocational Centre) it is remarkable that Algonquin College in the course of only seven years has 39 courses in French and is able to satisfy the demands of most Francophones as is shown in Table 0.[37] This increasing

Enrolment / Inscription

- ■ College total / Total du collège
- ■ Mother tongue, french / Français, langue maternelle
- ☰ Requested instruction in french / Demandes d'enseignement en français
- ☰ Received instruction in french / Reçoivent enseignement en français

	1969	1970	1971	1972
College total	3088	3060	4500	5150
Mother tongue, french	561	592	862	1339
Requested instruction in french	N.A.	161	567	1012
Received instruction in french	97	194	499	767

Table/Tableau **M**

bilingualisation touches administrative as well as teaching staff: 45 of 110 administrative positions are occupied by bilinguals as of March, 1974, according to information given to the Study.

The recommendations on bilingualism in the Report of the Ontario Commission on Post-Secondary Education[38] are also worthy of attention by serious students of the subject. Generally, these deal with the progressive expansion of French-language courses at the post-secondary level and of cooperative arrangements between French-language post-secondary institutions to make a wider range of programmes available at minimum cost.

It has been argued that a French-speaking university in Hull would go a long way toward strengthening the French character of the Outaouais Québécois. A Hull campus of the University of Quebec has been in existence for some time but the number of courses offered, as of this writing, has been extremely limited. At the same time, more than a third of the enrolment of the University of Ottawa consists of Quebecers.[39] While it might be culturally advantageous for the Government of Quebec dramatically to expand the Hull Campus of the University of Quebec, this would certainly be expensive in relation to the present rather cozy arrangement whereby many local Quebec students are educated under an Ontario umbrella. There is also the question of how many major universities a metropolitan area like Ottawa-Hull can expect to support within the next twenty years and what the projected pattern of the now declining university enrolments is likely to be in this time-frame. It is legitimate to ask whether some form of rationalization might not be worked out between Carleton University, Ottawa University, and the University of Quebec (Hull Campus) to offer the widest range of disciplines in both languages in the over-all, but to avoid attempting to duplicate all disciplines in all universities. This would, it seems to me, reinforce the reality of the situation that we live in one metropolitan area. Cooperation between the three universities, the Hull French and English CEGEPs and Algonquin College could be held up as a goal for the Capital without affecting the special role which each plays in the community. Indeed a small beginning has been made on this road by the creation of the Ottawa Valley Education Liaison Council, but to date this only extends to the Universities, Community Colleges and Boards of Education on the Ontario side of the River.

The opening paragraph of this report laid down its basic premises. The review which followed of the current state of English and French in the Capital, in the federal public service, and by extension in the country has led me to the conclusion that we are on the right path. If much remains to be done (particularly in the area of education), progress has also been steady in the last few years. And if the pattern of Francophone concentration may change in the country in the years ahead as it has in the past, the Capital is likely to continue to be a faithful reflection of our linguistic duality.

May I express my appreciation to the many federal, provincial and municipal officials, the school board trustees, academic administrators, professors, teachers, and interested persons who kindly gave me so much of their time and counsel in the preparation of this analysis, as well as to the critics who have read the typescript and who have variously suggested that the paper has an overall "Anglophone", or contrariwise "Francophone", bias!

Whatever new policies may be developed at the federal, provincial or local levels in the area of official languages, it is to be hoped that the National Capital Region will merit special consideration in order to assure that, in the words of the agreed conclusion of the eleven Prime Ministers at the Constitutional Conference of February 1969, the two official languages and the cultural values common to all Canadians be recognized *by all governments concerned* in Ottawa and Hull and in the Capital Region in general.

James M. Weld,
Ottawa,
April, 1974

Footnotes

1. *Royal Commission on Bilingualism and Biculturalism*, Vol. 5, p. 13, and Rowat, D.C. (ed.), *The Government of Federal Capitals*, University of Toronto Press, 1973, p. 286.

2. Eggleston, Wilfrid, *The Queen's Choice*, The Queen's Printer, 1961, p. 102.

3. The Statement in the House of Commons by the Rt. Hon. P. E. Trudeau on October 8, 1971, and document tabled on that day which sets out the federal government's response to Book IV of the Royal Commission on Bilingualism and Biculturalism, give the basic federal position on multiculturalism.

4. Article by Donat Valois, *Le Droit*, December 10, 1973.

5. Joy, Richard J., *Languages in Conflict*, published by the author, 1967, McClelland & Stewart Ltd., and also available at Carleton Library, No. 61. The Study is grateful to Mr. Joy for permission to reproduce Maps I and II.

6. Mr. Joy was kind enough to up-date tables from his book to take account of the 1971 census figures. The Study is indebted to him for Tables A, B, C and D.

7. *Documents: Démographie scolaire*, n° 9-14, Gouvernement du Québec, Ministère de l'éducation.

8. *Rapport de la Commission d'enquête sur la situation de la langue française et sur les droits linguistiques au Québec* (hereinafter called *Gendron Commission Report*), Vol. III, p. 173.

9. The figures have been taken from Table 8 (p. 146) of Vol. III of the *Gendron Report*, updated to take account of 1971 census figures.

10. ibid, p. 177.

11. ibid, Table 30, p. 170. In a paper presented in November 1973, Mr. Maheu stated that net migration in 1961-71 was much stronger out of Quebec than shown in the Gendron report. The average net migration into Quebec 1921-1971 using Mr. Maheu's figures would be 4,100 rather than 5,000.

12. cf. Press Release of the Hon. Charles Drury of February 19, 1974.

13. *1972 Annual Report, Public Service Commission of Canada*, Table III, p. 10. (The Study has added figures for 1973 obtained from the Public Service Commission and calculated the percentage figures for convenient comparative purposes).

14. ibid, Appendix 2(c), p. 61, with additions mentioned in footnote (13).

15. ibid, Appendix 2A(i), p. 57, with additions as above.

16. ibid, Table II, p. 9, shows that of a total of 308 appointments of bilingual senior officers between 1968 and 1972, 151 were Anglophones and 157 were Francophones.

17. Statement by Premier Robarts at first meeting of Constitutional Conference, February 1968, p. 19-53 of Official Report; *Revised propositions of the Government of Ontario* as of December 1968, paras. 5.6.11—5.6.13. (Conference document)

18. *Ontario Legislative Debates*, 4th session, 28th Legislature.

19. McRae, Kenneth D. (ed.), *The Federal Capital*, Vol. I, Appendix D, p. 223-43, Information Canada 1969.

20. By-laws 358-70 and 359-70 of October 19, 1970.

21. Resolution No. CE-74-60 of Hull City Council of February 1974.

22. The National Capital Commission agreed to fund part of the cost of this Study and copies are available from the NCC.

23. Government of Ontario, *Task Force on Policing in Ontario*, Ontario Government Bookstore, Toronto.

24. Figures for this table are taken from Vol. 2, No. 4 of the *Statistics Canada Service Bulletin* of April 1973, (Cat. No. 81-001), written by L. Steingarten and L. Catin. The form of presentation is our own. We are also indebted to this Bulletin for Tables J, K and L. Several educationists and experts who have seen our manuscript in draft have questioned one or more of these figures. We therefore think it desirable to include the following note from the bulletin by the authors:

    > These data have been collected primarily to serve a data requirement of a federal provincial agreement made in 1970, by which the federal government provides financial support for minority language education on a per pupil cost basis. Therefore, the 1970-71 period is the first year for which such data are available.
    >
    > The method of collection of the data varies by province. For the 1971-72 period, data for six provinces (Nfld., P.E.I., N.S., N.B., Man., Sask.) was obtained from a survey of individual schools carried out by Statistics Canada. Data for the remaining provinces (Que., Ont., Alta., B.C.) was provided by the provinces using their own methods of collection. For 1970-71 the majority of provinces provided data to Statistics Canada based on their own studies.

25. News release, Department of the Secretary of State, March 27, 1974.

26. Several Francophones, whose opinion I hold in high respect, disagree with this general argument, and see nothing wrong in the fact that Quebec, which has the strongest minority-language and second-language school structure, should receive by far the largest proportion of federal grant money. They argue that this rightly rewards past concern for minority-language schooling there and that maintenance of the status quo will, in fact, meet federal objectives in Quebec.

27. As noted above Canadian Studies and English will be compulsory as of the 1974-75 academic year in Ontario high schools. It should also be observed that the financial arrangements described in this paragraph are basically for the public rather than the separate school system although the province aims at effective equality between the two systems.

28. The Ottawa Roman Separate School Board was first in the field of immersion in the Capital area. Its programme has been monitored by Dr. H. P. Edwards and Miss M. C. Casserly who have conducted a major study, financed by the Ontario Ministry of Education and with the participation of Ottawa University and the Ottawa Separate Board.

All the other Boards have equally distinguished persons monitoring their second-language experimental programmes. Dr. H. H. Stern, Director of the Modern Language Centre at O.I.S.E. is presently synthesizing the findings of the research being conducted in the National Capital area.

29. The strategy developed by the Ottawa Board of Education for a long range bilingual programme including a bilingual high school is set out in its *Report of the Committee on Teaching French to English-Speaking Students* of May 1971. Although somewhat overtaken by events, this document is interesting in giving insights into the broad curriculum planning which has resulted in the efflorescence of second-language programmes in the Capital.

30. Cf. the paper of Professor C. J. Jaenen of the University of Ottawa prepared for the workshop "Language and Education", Ottawa, May 25 1972, preparatory to the Heritage Ontario Conference in June of that year.

31. Bill 141, 1st Session, 28th Legislature, Ontario, 17 Elizabeth II, 1968, "*An Act to Amend the Secondary Schools and Boards of Education Act*.

32. *Ministerial Commission on French Language Secondary Education*, The Queen's Printer & Publisher, Toronto, 1972, Identification No. 1040-70.

33. Bills 180 and 181, 3rd Session, 29th Legislature, 22 Elizabeth II, 1973, *An Act to Amend the Secondary Schools and Boards of Education Act.* and *An Act to Amend the Schools Administration Act*.

34. Mme Régine Wyczynski at a panel discussion sponsored by the Institut canadien-français d'Ottawa, January 20, 1974.

35. Gouvernement du Québec, Ministère de l'Éducation, *Documents: Démographie scolaire* n° 9-14.

36. ibid, p. 74, tableau 3.1.1.8, The figures for Table N were also taken from this source.

37. *Not as a Burden*, Report of the Ad Hoc Committee on Bilingualism, Algonquin College, April 1973, Appendix 2, Chart 2.

38. Published by the Ontario Ministry of Government Services, Toronto, 1972, (Ontario Government Bookstore).

39. 2931 full-time undergraduates in the academic year 1973-74 out of a total undergraduate enrolment of 8300.

Appendix B-2A

Three Options for Education in the Capital Area

A supplementary note on the language question

Kenneth D. McRae
Carleton University

1. *Preliminary Considerations*

At the outset certain goals and constraints may be identified that would apply to Anglophone and Francophone educational structures in the capital area no matter what forms its governmental arrangements might take. The most important of these may be considered under three headings:

(1) equality between educational systems
(2) linkages with the rest of English Canada and French Canada respectively, and
(3) special needs of education in the capital area.

(1) Equality may be viewed from a number of different perspectives, including (*a*) equality of school financial resources, as measured by expenditure or revenue per pupil; (*b*) equality of financial burden on ratepayers supporting different educational systems within any one municipality; (*c*) equality of financial burdens among ratepayers in *different* municipalities of the capital area, or on different sides of the Ottawa River; and (*d*) equality in physical plant, capital assets, and general facilities available to the respective school systems.

It is worth noting that while the main goal in Ontario in the 1960's was to equalize (*b*), that is, mill rates for ratepayers, school legislation in Quebec in those years moved first to equalize (*a*), that is, revenues and expenditures per pupil. The most difficult policy area is probably (*d*), especially as it relates to the general quality and intellectual atmosphere of different school systems. One can visualize some capital grants and perhaps developmental grants to overcome past inequalities of physical plant and even of teacher qualifications, but there are limits here imposed by considerations of equitable financial arrangements between systems, by difficulties of measurement, and by the need for each educational system to have reasonable autonomy as to its own values and goals of education.

More important, there is a problem in reconciling equality in a wider sense with a degree of autonomy sufficient for each system in the capital to determine its own educational goals and priorities. It will be recalled that Volume II of the Report of the Royal Commission on Bilingualism and Biculturalism—the volume dealing with education—was premised on a majority-minority relationship for education in every province, that is, each province would have schools for the official-language minority in that province that offered approximately the same educational services in the minority language as would be available in the majority language in the other schools of the province. I suggest that this formulation should be modified in its application to the capital area. In the capital the only premise consistent with complete equality is that *Anglophone and Francophone educational systems should be in no sense subordinate one to the other*, for only in this way can they have room to develop according to the goals and priorities of the respective language communities. Of course, this does not rule out cooperation and exchanges between systems.

We may conclude from this that equality in the educational context should mean primarily equal access to financial and fiscal resources for each system; beyond this point the systems must have considerable discretion to allocate resources and establish priorities as they see fit.

(2) In the second place, the educational systems in the capital, no matter what their structures, must have strong and easy linkages with other parts of Canada. Given the nature of employment in the capital area, the systems must serve not only a resident population but a substantial mobile population of families whose child-raising years will be spent in several two- or three-year postings in several cities. For example, the annual reports of the Ottawa Public School Board show that in 1967 and 1968 the proportions of registered pupils withdrawing each year to schools outside of Ottawa were 9.7 and 10.4 per cent respectively. With this level of mobility, there must be easy transfers from one system to another for both Anglophones and Francophones moving into or out of the capital area. Moreover, such transfers should be seen not as a disadvantage but as part of an integrative process whereby Canadians from all parts of the country enlarge their understanding of other regions. This integrative role of the capital is important, and it should be reflected in educational structures no less than in government or industry.

We may envision the capital area schools as serving three population groups: (*a*) a "local" population of longer-term residents, who in recent years have become aware of an increasing need for bilingual capacity in many sectors of the capital area work force, (*b*) a more mobile Anglophone population who will have lower commitment to bilingualism and whose career plans include residence in other provinces or even abroad, and (*c*) a more mobile, more unilingually oriented Francophone population which also considers residence in Ottawa as temporary and has career plans involving a return to Quebec or other Francophone countries. This third stream has been small hitherto, but it must grow and find accommodation in the school system if the capital area is to fulfil its integrative role properly and if Francophones are to occupy positions in the public service proportionate to their numbers in Canada as a whole. The relative sizes of these streams are important to educational planning: based on a figure of 10 per cent annual outflow from the public school system and allowing for some multiple moves, we may make a rough estimate that in a five-year period perhaps 30 to 40 per cent of families move away from the region and are replaced by newcomers.

(3) The third consideration is that the capital's educational system, no matter how organized, must continue to reflect certain special needs of the area in its role as federal capital and meeting place for French-speaking and English-speaking Canadians. There will be a need for the best possible forms of second language teaching, of bilingual educational programming, and of research on how to get improved results from such programmes in the specific local setting of Ottawa. Correspondingly, at least equivalent research will be needed on how best to stabilize, reinforce and enrich the mother tongue of Francophone children in the Ottawa milieu (especially on the Ontario side where the linguistic environment poses special problems for French-language education). Finally, financial equity for pupils, teachers and ratepayers in the capital is important because the federal government, as the area's largest employer and grant-payer to local authorities, is indirectly underwriting and sanctioning these educational systems through its payments of municipal grants in lieu of taxes. In a wider and more symbolic sense these educational systems must work fairly and equitably because the capital area is the showplace of the Canadian federation as a whole, both within Canada and with respect to other countries. Injustices or inadequacies in its educational structures are ultimately a reflection on the Canadian federal system itself.

II. *Basic policy choices*

In the light of the above goals and constraints, we can go on to identify and evaluate the broad policy options that arise with respect to educational systems in the capital area at a time when its governmental structures are under review. For convenience of analysis we may identify three broad options: (1) a continuation, basically, of present educational structures and of present machinery for federal involvement in the capital; (2) a continuation of present provincial educational structures in a setting of special governmental and administrative status for the capital, such as would exist if some form of overarching governmental structures were developed for the Ontario and Quebec portions of the capital area; and (3) the establishment of new educational structures within a capital territory having its own legislative and administrative jurisdiction. The first of these options, the continuance of the status quo, does not require further elaboration at this point.

Under option 2, the educational systems would remain much as they are now with respect to organization, curriculum, teacher training, and similar matters, or at least changes in these areas would be at the discretion of the provinces. However, any new overarching authority for the capital area might take some initiatives in the following areas:

(a) It could enlarge educational choices by paying the fees now charged when pupils transfer from one system to another, including transfers between provinces or between language streams.

(b) It could modify current provisions for federal grants in lieu of taxes so as to provide for full financial equality among the various educational systems. This would require federal legislation to amend the present Municipal Grants Act, or at least the establishment of alternate arrangements for the capital area.

(c) Within certain limits it could provide grants for special purposes, pilot projects, and educational research on topics of special relevance to the capital (as the federal government does now in support of minority-language schooling and second-language teaching).

Probably most of these activities could also be carried out to some degree under option 1, but in the absence of some form of special status capital area projects that ran counter to provincial policy would be more likely to be sources of friction. Besides, under option 1 there would be no agency to formulate proposals and press for their implementation.

A more extensive possibility under option 2 would be for the overarching authority to negotiate and arrange for *both school systems to operate on both sides of the Ottawa River*. This would mean that the choice of school systems available to the individual family would be wider than at present, and it would have the effect of providing, throughout the capital area, linkages for those expecting to move from the capital to other parts of Ontario and Quebec.

The third option would be the creation of a new educational system and new structures for the capital area alone. Presumably a new system would begin from the existing base, but it would develop as a direct reflection of capital area needs. In many respects it would be analogous to a provincial educational system, but subject to the requirements of equality of status between its Anglophone and Francophone segments as discussed above.

III. *Analysis of policy choices*

We can now assess these three policy choices briefly from a number of standpoints, including particularly (1) structures, (2) curriculum development, (3) staffing, and (4) connections with post-secondary education.

(1) *Structures*. It is clear that if the capital area retains its present governmental framework (option 1) changes in educational structures would be likely to remain minimal. Option 2 offers somewhat more flexibility but educational structures would remain substantially the present provincial ones. There could be further decentralization than now exists but the structures themselves would probably be little changed. On the other hand the financial policy of the new coordinating authority could largely eliminate fiscal inequalities between educational systems. Further, the range of effective choices could be widened by arranging for both provincial systems to operate throughout the capital

area to the extent that demand warrants. This might help to diminish the feelings of either Francophones or Anglophones that a given educational system is in a minority position in the capital.

Option 3 involves the creation of a complete new educational administration for the capital area. In terms of population served, it would be analogous to the ministries of the smaller provinces, approximately equivalent to those of Newfoundland or New Brunswick, and several times larger than that of Prince Edward Island. Its form raises several questions. First, since the prime goals of the system include equality and autonomy for Anglophones and Francophones, it should undoubtedly be organized on a dual basis with sufficient administrative separation of the two linguistic segments that neither feels pressed or threatened by the other.

Second, since confessionality is the major line of division in existing systems of education in the capital, its continuance should be expected in some form in any new system. But it would seem that confessionality could be handled, with legal guarantees if necessary, within a basic framework of linguistic dualism. The Francophone sector would seem to have few problems in accommodating the very small percentage of non-Roman Catholic Francophones (as it does now), but the more diversified Anglophone sector might require special guarantees for confessional schools to ensure the rights of religious minorities. A slightly different alternative to publicly administered confessional schools (the usual Canadian pattern) would be to subsidize confessional and also other private schools on the basis of fiscal equality or near-equality with the public, non-confessional systems (as in Belgium or the Netherlands), subject to some degree of control in terms of inspection, curriculum standards, and teacher qualifications. This alternative would recognize current public dissatisfaction with large, monolithic school systems and the desire expressed by some groups to experiment with various new—or traditionalist—approaches to education.

A third problem concerns bilingual education. Presumably all education in the capital area would stress the acquisition of the second official language commencing at an appropriate level—which for sociolinguistic reasons would probably differ according to sectors, earlier for the English sector, later for the French. But many families would want more intensive linguistic training through full-scale bilingual or immersion programs—and these are being developed even now at several grade levels. On present evidence, it seems clear that both the need for such programmes and public interest in them lies almost entirely on the Anglophone side, and currently most programme development and research is being done by English-speaking boards. Therefore, until a significant demand arises for bilingual programmes on the Francophone side, such programs should remain within the Anglophone sector. It should be clearly recognized, however, that up to now the present linguistic environment of the capital has been more effective in forming bilingual Francophones than formal educational programmes have been in creating bilingual Anglophones.

(2) Curriculum development. The factors influencing curriculum development include the demands of the employment market and admission require-

ments for post-secondary education. Students educated in the capital in either language stream must be able to meet these requirements and to compete effectively with graduates of the same language stream educated elsewhere. In addition they would have to meet any additional language requirements of the capital area labour market if they work there.

Under options 1 and 2 both programme options and curricula would be tied to existing provincial systems, though one could visualize some variations arising from decentralization and development undertaken by local boards of educational, especially under option 2. The chief practical result of option 2 (as compared to option 1) is that the Quebec educational system could be available as an option to the entire Francophone population of the capital (as would the Ontario system to all Anglophones). In particular this would facilitate the entry of Ontario Francophones into post-secondary programmes in Quebec universities, and could operate to diminish the psychological gulf between Franco-Ontarians and Québécois in the capital area.

Under option 3 the Anglophone and Francophone sectors of the capital would each develop its own curriculum, adjusted in each case to its special needs but also firmly linked to post-secondary opportunities in the wider context of English and French Canada respectively. In order to promote the fullest development of the Francophone sector and maximize the range of choices at the post-secondary level, it is to be expected that this sector would become fairly closely linked with the educational system of Quebec. Of course these arrangements would not exclude transfers from one system to the other for students who are linguistically competent to make them, but the curricula should undoubtedly be devised for the great majority that would complete all their education within one linguistic sector. The separate educational structures envisaged by option 3 could also provide a better environment for educational research and innovation appropriate to the bilingual setting of the capital than would be available under other options.

(3) *Staffing and teacher qualifications.* In a period of declining birth-rates, the need for new teaching staff will probably be small, and for the short-term future this consideration will be a dominant one. Under options 1 and 2 recruitment of teachers would continue through existing channels of training and certification by Ontario and Quebec. One can visualize departures from provincial norms by local boards only to a limited degree, but one possible task for the new overar-ching authority for the capital under option 2 would be to explore the certification of Quebec-trained teachers in Ontario and Ontario-trained teachers in Quebec, especially in the area of second-language instruction.

Under option 3 the new educational authority would become responsible for certification of teachers, but with a more or less stationary enrolment of pupils it becomes difficult, and probably unnecessary, to visualize an independent training programme for capital area teachers. It would seem to be healthier for the educational system, and more suited to the integrative role of the capital, tor the new authority to accept as a basic norm suitable levels of certification by the provinces, to be *supplemented* by summer or part-time courses to acquire whatever further skills were deemed appropriate. By this means teachers from other parts of French and English Canada could be introduced to the cultural duality of the capital, and teacher mobility could be preserved and perhaps even expanded.

It does not seem realistic to expect all capital area teachers to have special qualifications in the two official languages. To do so would restrict mobility at a time when competent bilingual personnel will be in high demand in many other sectors. For the near future it is to be expected that most second-language instruction in both linguistic sectors can be better performed by specialists.

(4) *A note on post-secondary education:* The post-secondary level need not be fully explored here, but certain points concerning linkages may be helpful. Under option 1 the post-secondary level would remain entirely in provincial hands, as it is now. Under option 2, while the elementary and secondary levels would remain under provincial organization and control, the post-secondary level might either remain as it is under provincial control or alternatively it could become one of the responsibilities of the new capital area authority. If the latter, the two major existing universities could become in some sense federal institutions roughly analogous to the Australian National University. The other publicly supported institutions in the post-secondary sector, Algonquin College and the CEGEP de Hull, could be similarly treated, though it must be remembered that the latter—or a similar institution—would have to continue its present role of bridging the gap in Quebec between secondary level and the Quebec universities. Under option 3 post-secondary education, like the lower levels, would have its own distinctive universities and other post-secondary institutions under the control of the education authority for the capital. Given the size of the population to be served, most of the standard university disciplines, technological options, and even the major professional programmes could be offered in English and in French, but for the less common ones it would be necessary to attend outside institutions.

If the capital area assumed control of its own post-secondary institutions under either option 2 or option 3, it would be important not to restrict transfers into or out of the new system. In order to fulfil its integrating role with respect to Canada as a whole the post-secondary institutions of the capital should be open to qualified candidates from across the country, and correspondingly secondary level students in the capital should be able to qualify for any post-secondary program in their own language anywhere in Canada.

IV. *Review and conclusion*

In the event that present provincial boundaries and jurisdictions remain unchanged (option 1), the educational systems will remain substantially as they are now and there will be limited room to pursue educational changes consonant with the special needs of the capital. In the event of significant governmental changes, there is a case for weighing the respective advantages and drawbacks of options 2 and 3.

Option 2, which envisages the continuance of provincially organized educational systems, requires very little in the way of new educational structures. It builds on what exists now, but it could open up choices not available now to the linguistic minorities on both sides of the Ottawa River. Perhaps more important, this widening of choices offers some prospect of building a stronger and more united Francophone community from a population that is currently divided into two groups of almost equal size by the provincial boundary. Because of the continuing linkage with provincial systems, any gains and achievements under option 2 would have an immediate direct impact on the entire educational systems of the two largest provinces. Finally, this option might also have advantages as an interim solution pending the development of a system oriented primarily towards the needs of the capital area.

Option 3, on the other hand, would produce an educational system built explicitly for the capital area and its cultural imperatives. It would be specially tailored to capital needs, and would transform the capital region from one that consists essentially of two separate, peripheral areas, both remote from their respective capitals, into a new coherent centre. It would counteract the extreme fragmentation of present educational regimes in the capital, and it could reduce the feelings of subordination, lack of autonomy, and financial disparity that arise from the present system. Further, it could open the door to research and experimentation in the capital area on the perennial problems of promoting and maintaining cultural equality in a plural society.

To summarize in terms of the goals outlined at the beginning, option 3 appears preferable in terms both of equality of educational systems and of the special needs of the capital area, but option 2 has some inherent advantages in terms of linkages with other areas, at least in the short run. Option 3 has the potential for comparable linkages and could perhaps serve as a powerful example of educational equality for the rest of Canada, but this could be achieved only over a period of time by patient and deliberate effort.

Kenneth D. McRae
Department of Political Science
Carleton University.   March, 1974.

Appendix B-3

The Governmental Structure of the National Capital Area

A Report by Murray V. Jones

to

Douglas H. Fullerton,

Special Study on the National Capital

January, 1974

Introduction

The nature of the "research and analysis" undertaken for this Report makes it desirable and appropriate to express the results in a personal manner and consequently, I have chosen to use the first person singular throughout. While the views expressed are my own, I cannot say how much they have been influenced by the many discussions I had with your staff and other consultants. Similarily, since most of my "research" was conducted by way of numerous interviews with knowledgeable and articulate persons in the area, I am sure that the comments which follow will reflect many of the persuasive arguments they presented. I have also carefully studied all of the written submissions and, while these were of a mixed quality, I was impressed with the sincerity of the views expressed and some aspect of these views are incorporated in my own.

It will be obvious from what follows that it was not my intention to conduct an exhaustive piece of research and analysis into all aspects of the political and administrative arrangements for the Capital Area, and consequently my Report is short and contains assertions based on the nature of the "research" I did conduct; these are intended to provoke discussion in any forum that may be created to follow from the Special Study.

I would particularly like to thank André Guibord for his assistance. His knowledge and understanding of circumstances and outlook in the Outaouais part of the region were most valuable. In addition, his recognized abilities as a journalist proved extremely helpful in preparing reports of all of the inverviews

Assumptions

I have made a number of underlying assumptions resulting from my own biases but which are shared, I believe, by at least a majority of the people in the area.

1. I assume that some form of democratic, local government is an essential component of any government structure in the Capital Area.
2. Because it contains the seat of government for Canada, I assume there is a national interest in the Nation's Capital, however varied or ill-defined that interest may be.
3. I assume there is a Federal Government interest in the Federal capital of Canada. Although related to the national interest and in part at least an expression of it, the two are nevertheless, not synonymous.
4. I assume that whether the area continues to have many of the characteristics of a "company town" or whether its economy becomes more diversified, there will be an increasing interdependence among the people of the urban region. Consequently, any effective and satisfactory government structure must encompass the urban region on both sides of the Ottawa River.
5. I assume that the provinces (Ontario and Quebec) will be willing through time to decrease their role in the Capital Area mainly by way of delegation of authority to competent local government.
6. I assume that it will be in the national interest as well as in the interests of the people living in the area to recognize and maintain the historic differences in parts of the area in such fields as law, education, and culture generally. I make this assumption despite the influences at work in a growing metropolitan (and therefore interdependent) area tending to modify the "purity" of the culture of any group.

While many other assumptions could be stated, it seems to me that these bear most directly on the question of the form and structure of government in the Capital Area.

Attitudes

I have not conducted an attitude survey as such, but I think it relevant to record my impressions of current attitudes as gleaned from the interviews and submissions. I appreciate that a survey was commissioned and it may well be that the results will differ from my most unscientific approach. Even though there was a wide variation in the opinions expressed, the following constitute what I consider to be the most important and relevant to the issues at hand.

1. It is obvious that general public awareness of issues and the individual's relation to them has been sharpened considerably in the last few years. More people than ever are aware of the implications of general development policies or lack of them as well as of the merits or otherwise of specific projects. This means, among other things, that the issues of the

Study are now more capable of being considered and a positive response elicited than ever before. One of the important implications of this growing awareness is that it not only becomes possible to propose alternatives for future change but also that alternative proposals can be more effectively debated and a consensus reached.

2. There is a wide gulf between those whom I will call the "centralists" and those who have a strong attachment to "local autonomy". I suspect there are a great many people, both English and French, who are confused by the complexity of urban life, myriads of government, and various layers of bureaucracy and who react by expressing a desire for a simpler arrangement, one they hope they could better understand and even influence. In the short term, at least, these people want to reduce the number of governments and centralize more power in the hands of the Federal Government, particularly in its agency, the N.C.C. Others have a strong attachment to local self-determination and react strongly to the conflict they see between the "federal company town" and their role as local citizens of an urban area. There are, of course, opinions which range between these extremes.

3. I found an ambivalent attitude in the Outaouais region as expressed, on the one hand, by those who felt they were part of the national capital, recognized the interdependence between the two sides of the river and were ready to consider some form of institutional arrangement that would express this reality; and by those, on the other hand, who were concerned about the protection of a unique cultural heritage and were suspicious of any moves that might be construed as a "takeover" either directly by way of an institutional arrangement or indirectly by way of the continued expansion of the Federal bureaucracy into Hull and environs. The significance of these attitudes for your Study, it seems to me, is that consideration should be given not only to a gradual approach to institutional change but that any change must recognize the need to provide for the different needs and aspirations of various groups.

4. Another prevalent concern on both sides of the river is the power in the hands of the Federal Government as represented by its land holdings. This concern is expressed mainly by elected representatives in the area and is symptomatic of a deep concern about the division of the "power pie". To put it another way, there appears to be a growing resentment on the part of those who must attempt to exercise their legislative and political responsibilities at the local level towards another power (the Federal Government) which is not visibly represented at the Council table. This situation gives rise not only to feelings of impotence but, on the positive side, to feelings that a democratic framework ought to be so arranged that the exercise of Federal power should be in the form of a tangible and accountable role within the context of the local and regional political structure.

5. Another common attitude is lack of unanimity on goals and objectives coupled with a lack of communication which might hopefully lead to a more harmonious achievement of commonly perceived ends. It is ironic, for instance, that one of the most respected "governments" of the area is the N.C.C., providing as it does a number of popular and praiseworthy projects, but which is at the same time considered by many local politicians to be the most unaccountable and withdrawn group in terms of relating to the aims of other governments. As many have said, it is remarkable that the area has been able to provide the degree of satisfaction that it has, under the circumstances of a myriad of local, regional, provincial, and many (conflicting) Federal departments and agencies.

6. Finally, there is an attitude which would accommodate change in the political structure but there is less willingness to accept a dramatic kind and rate of change. While some persist in the view that Ottawa is the Capital and that no part of Quebec should be included, most people agree with an extension of the Federal presence in the Hull area. There is related support for the establishment of some form of government organization with, in most cases, a newly defined role for the Federal and Provincial Governments.

It goes without saying that hardly any two opinions were identical but I believe I have not overstated or inaccurately stated the major attitudes affecting the Study.

Assertions

When Donald Patterson and I conducted the Ottawa-Carleton local government review in 1965 for the Province of Ontario, I found a settlement pattern which I described as an embryonic metropolitan area. In 1973 the embryo has developed and matured, and plans for the future proposed by the regional governments clearly show the move toward maturation of that form of settlement. It is both possible and necessary, I suggest, to give political recognition to this physical, social and economic reality. With this in mind, and having regard to other considerations noted previously, I make the following assertions as the basis for later discussing alternative forms of organization:

1. The increasing degree of interdependence in the area requires some form of area government(s) somewhat similar perhaps to the two regional governments now in existence.

2. Provision should be made for the Federal Government to play a more responsive and responsible role in the governmental structure of the Capital Area.

3. In the long run, the role of the Provinces of Ontario and Quebec should be reduced by way of transfer or delegation of most present responsibilities to the area or regional governments in each province.

4. Whatever form of government is established, it should be subject to effective democratic control with as few functions as possible remaining in the jurisdiction of appointed boards, commissions, etc.

5. The government organization should be so structured, organized and financed that needs can be assessed on a common basis and resources can be equitably shared.

6. The government structure should be highly accessible to the people of the area specifically and more generally to the people of Canada, and at the same time be responsive and responsible.

7. While simplicity of structure may be difficult in otherwise complex circumstances, the main objective should be to create the simplest possible form of government organization so that most people can understand the system and influence its policies and programs.

8. Any effective structure must recognize the dual reality of the interests of the parts of the metropolitan area as well as the interests of the whole. A prime requirement will be to provide for self-evolution of the institutional arrangement.

There are obviously a myriad of other detailed objectives which could be asserted but these seem to me to provide the essential framework for discussing alternative courses of action.

Alternatives

As indicated earlier, the nature of my involvement in the Study could not result in my suggesting proposals based on a comprehensive research and analysis. In addition to the views I expressed during the Study, I feel it is appropriate to sketch out some broad alternatives knowing that much deeper analysis is proposed to be undertaken subsequently, including public participation through public hearings. A further merit of suggesting alternatives, as I indicated previously, is that the people of the area are willing and able to analyze the implications of alternative suggestions and conversely are not receptive to a "take-it-or-leave-it" approach associated with a single proposal.

There are obviously many alternatives that could be suggested as well as a myriad of variations within a single theme. I have chosen, however, to consider three approaches, each so different in character that confusion can be avoided in public debate. They have been deliberately constructed in part to aid those who see the political process as one of polarization. At the same time, the supporters of the consensus process will be able to select the parts of each alternative which they feel are desirable. It would be most unlikely therefore, if any one of the three alternatives will be considered as absolutes; they are really not intended to be.

1. *Retain the Status Quo*

This is always an attractive choice in that it does not ask anyone to do anything. While attractive, it is also unrealistic in that change does occur bit by bit over a long period of time. At the local government level for instance, two regional governments have recently been formed and already change has either occurred in the second tier municipal organization or is being proposed (a consolidation of the 12 urban municipalities in the Outaouais region). What is meant therefore by status quo in this context is not to propose any radical change but rather to see the structure and organization of government in the area evolve in much the same way as it has in the past. Some of the arguments for this alternative are:

- (*a*) It raises no constitutional issues and does not disturb the division of the present "power pie".
- (*b*) There is a lack of evidence of any deep or urgent concern for a drastic change on the part of the Federal Government.
- (*c*) There is little or no evidence that the provinces would be willing to reconsider their basic position in a constitutional sense.
- (*d*) There is lukewarm to cool reaction from municipal leaders to become seriously involved in any new set of municipal institutions which would recognize the horizontality of problems within an increasingly interdependent area.
- (*e*) The only popular movement is the emergence of so-called reform groups advocating a decrease in the rate of change and a limit on growth—a very status quo approach.
- (*f*) It is always easier "to let sleeping dogs lie"—provided of course that they really are asleep.

In essence, therefore, this alternative is most attractive if the traditional growth ethic can be significantly altered. But since changes in attitudes (or the presumed lack of change) is much more significant to the attainment of this objective than institutional change, I have serious doubts about the realism of this alternative. Major changes have occurred—others will be made and many are needed; status quo is therefore both unreal and undesirable.

2. *A New Structure*

I think of this alternative as a radical one in that it calls for a significant degree of change in the present structure. Some of the principal elements of this alternative would be:

- (*a*) The appointment of a Federal Minister with a possible title of Secretary of State for National Capital Affairs.
- (*b*) Giving the Minister the responsibility for determining and exercising the total Federal interest in the Nation's capital.
- (*c*) The dissolution of the N.C.C. and the transfer of its functions to the Ministry.
- (*d*) A reduction of the role of the Provinces through agreement to delegate certain powers either to the Federal Government or to the Regional Government(s).

(e) The maintenance of a local (regional) government on each side of the river, preferably of the one-tier variety with the characteristics similar to those I recommended in 1965.

(f) The establishment of a Parliamentary Committee which would relate to the Minister and the Government in a similar manner as existing Committees do, with a specific mandate to hold periodic public hearings.

(g) The establishment of a continuing consultative organization formed by agreement, consisting of the Minister, the Provincial Ministers of Urban (local, municipal) Affairs of the Provinces of Ontario and Quebec and the Chairmen of the two regions. This organization would not have a budget except for secretariat purposes and have no powers other than those of consultation and recommendation. It would, however, be highly visible by reason of conducting regular meetings in public and receiving submissions from the public.

It could be argued that the role of yet another Minister in a large Cabinet, regardless of the powers conferred on him by legislation, would be ineffective since all of Cabinet would have to be convinced on major policy matters. It has been argued by many, and with force, that it would be symbolically correct and politically more effective if this Ministry were headed by the Prime Minister who could appoint a parliamentary assistant to aid him.

There are several ways in which the Parliamentary Committee could be organized: on straight party lines and regardless of the geographic location of the constituencies of its members; all of the MP's from the National Capital Area plus at least one from each province; etc.

I do not propose in this alternative to place Federal representatives, elected or appointed, on the regional councils. While some have suggested this, I do not believe it would result in any better coordination of policies and programs and would probably confuse the distinct roles that the Federal and local governments have to play.

I do not think that the area is ready for one local (regional) government for the whole National Capital Area. It may be desirable and acceptable at some later time but proposing it now would only serve to prevent the establishment of those aspects of reorganization which are most necessary now. I have suggested an informal bridge which may overlap somewhat with the role of the proposed Parliamentary Committee but I am not concerned with this potential flaw due to the necessarily high degree of integration required between the development and implementation of National Capital Area policies and programs, and the specific interests of the Federal Government.

It could be argued that the above is not a particularly radical alternative since the only institutional change called for on the part of the Federal Government is probably already within its statutory authority. Two major weaknesses of this alternative are that there is no guarantee of a unity of Federal interests in the area—far from it!—and unity of objectives between any of the parties would still depend upon voluntary cooperation.

3. *An Institution for Organized Change*

Another name I had for this alternative was institutional incrementalism, but although I understand what I am trying to say, I doubt if anyone else would. This sounds like status quo with a difference and perhaps it is, but the difference is so distinctive that I feel that it is quite a separate alternative. The scenario for this alternative goes something like this: Even though it is admitted that the area is undergoing rapid change, even though there is a growing awareness of the potential effects of present policies, and even though there is a growing sense of interdependence, what is needed is not a radical change in the institutional arrangements but rather a mechanism through which all kinds of desirable changes can be identified, and legislative, administrative, political and social adjustment made to carry out the desired changes over time. To put it another way, the evolution of democratic institutions requires continuous hard work on an organized basis and, since political institutions are established to reflect value systems and reconcile conflicts, it is important to consider this as a process rather than a product. Because power is not voluntarily given up, it is unrealistic to think that existing political institutions are capable of sponsoring a political process designed to take it away from some in favour of others. What is suggested here is a sort of free theatre (and perhaps guerrilla at times) in the form of an on-going constitutional-institutional Conference where governments and various interest groups would set themselves the prime objective of identifying those matters requiring the most urgent change and which would provide a forum in which a monitoring process would seek to assess the effect of each change both in the short and the long run.

This may sound like a useless notion but I was impressed in some of the interviews with a recurring expression of people wanting to find a vehicle for continuing dialogue and mutual understanding. I am aware that such an organization would be wholly lacking in statutory power, but in the complexity of the existing governmental structure in the National Capital Area, it may be a more acceptable process than any proposal for direct structural change.

Conclusion

While the Study is being conducted for the Federal Government, I have found it necessary to approach the issues without regard to matters of jurisdiction. Anything I have said affecting Provincial jurisdiction did not result from any consultation with Provincial officials and will not, I hope, be construed by them as interference in matters of Provincial authority.

These brief notes are my impressions resulting from discussions with other Study group members, interviews and submissions. They are intended primarily as an aide-memoir rather than as a full-fledged report and I trust they will be of some assistance.

Appendix B-4

Local Government and the National Capital

A Proposal

R.G. Poulin, A.M.C.T., C.M.C.

Introduction

During these last nine years, as Clerk-Administrator for the City of Vanier, I have been closely associated with local government in the National Capital Region. This association and the experience it has given me has forced me to conclude that there is a need for a critical re-examination of the whole concept of government in the National Capital Region, especially with respect to the number of local governments.

There are in my opinion, three particular areas where there are difficulties in operations and communications:

(*a*) City Hall and the Community

(*b*) Ontario and Quebec (referring only to those areas or each province within the National Capital Region).

(*c*) Ontario and Quebec and the Federal Government (as their interdependance and relationship is affected by the National Capital dimension).

The existence of over 40 municipalities not only creates excessive and costly duplication of services, but encourages political conflicts, increases overlapping authorities and jurisdictions, and dissipates valuable time in endless and often unfruitful talks and negotiations. So many governments operate in the National Capital Region it is almost impossible for the average person to know who does what. Indeed, one has to be amazed at the devotion and determination of those public spirited citizens, who in spite of these odds, are determined to still, somehow, try and make the thing work.

Local Government is that government which is closest to the people, or at least it should be. Identified with "City Hall" or the "Township Offices", local government was originally designed "for the purpose of carrying out the wishes of the inhabitants of the area within their jurisdiction, within the scope and to the extent permitted by law"... Crawford.

It is essential therefore that if local government is to fullfil this role, there must be communications between the elected and the electors who have put these people in office. However, because of the multiplicity of municipal government structures, councils are often too busy talking with each other and do not have the time to talk with the people of their own community, who after all deserve priority since it is they who are footing the bill.

One example of duplicating jurisdictions is policing. There are over 14 central police administration systems in the National Capital Region. Is police protection any better because of this? Is protection more economical...are communications between departments facilitated... is it more difficult for crime to operate? Obviously the answer is no... yet the situation is allowed to persist. Indeed the contrary is probably closer to the truth. Crime knows no boundaries, respects no authority, recognizes no person. Yet this is typical of the duplication of service and cost of local government in the National Capital Region. We are at a point therefore where alternatives must be considered and implemented in order to control the escalating costs of municipal taxes and increase the yield of municipal services.

There are undoubtedly alternatives, many of which will be covered adequately elsewhere in this report. Indeed an effort is being made to gradually reduce the number of municipal government units in the National Capital Region. However, removing this duplication, on a do-it-when-we-can attitude, without any other criteria will only result with the problem of co-ordinating so many small units of government being replaced with the problem of co-ordinating too many large units, with the cure quite likely being worse than the disease.

The Proposal

I personally favour two area councils, one on each side of the Ottawa River, each taking in all of their provincial territory within the National Capital Region, at the same time, retaining and enhancing their provincial characteristics under their respective provincial jurisdictions.

This alternative appears almost too simple, yet it would appear to provide the means necessary to bring about meaningful change. Firstly, all of the existing local government units in the Ontario territory of the National Capital Region should be dissolved in favour of one municipal government taking in all of the same area. All of the existing local government units in the Quebec territory of the National Capital Region should be disolved in favour of one municipal government taking in all of the same area on the Quebec side; for the purposes of this document, I will identify these two area councils as "The Corporation of the National Capital Council of Ontario" and the "Corporation of the National Capital Council of Quebec". Each area would be divided into boroughs of approximately 50,000 persons each.

Such an alternative would end needless differences and discrepancies in licensing, housing standards, store closing hours, building standards, recreation facilities, water and sewer services, police and fire protection, public health services, social and welfare services to name but a few areas of impact. Of importance as well, is the fact that all business and commercial assessment in a provincial area, would provide additional taxes for the whole area, one of the very serious shortcomings of the present system.

With only one municipal government for each provincial sector, would mean vastly simplified municipal-provincial relations... each province would only have to deal with one municipal government, and vice-versa.

Matters that touch the National Capital Region as a whole would be dealt with by the National Capital Council, which would be made up of the membership of both the Ontario area Council and the Quebec area Council. For example, the National Capital Council would undoubtedly be the local authority to have the final word on inter-provincial bridges, connecting highways etc.

Representation

Each provincial area municipality would have council membership from three sources;

(1) members elected at large

(2) members elected as Borough Chairmen

(3) members of Parliament (perhaps one from each party) appointed by the Parliament of Canada.

With nine boroughs in the Ontario area, the Corporation of the National Capital Council of Ontario would have 9 borough chairmen on it's Council; I suggest that four members be elected at large, and there are the four members from Parliament. This gives a council for Ontario of seventeen members plus the chairman. If Quebec has three boroughs, the Corporation of the National Capital Council of Quebec would have three borough chairmen on it's Council; I suggest that Quebec as well have four members elected at large, and add to this the four members from Parliament, this gives the initial council for Quebec eleven members, plus the chairman.

The Chairman

There are two avenues open for the position of chairman. I would favour one chairman for the three Councils, elected to office by both Councils at a joint meeting of the National Capital Council. The vice-chairmen could assist in the chairing of provincial area Councils; the whole of the National Capital Region would have a head that would be representative for all concerned.

The alternative is to have the Ontario area Council chairman elected by it's members, and the Quebec area Council chairman elected by it's members, but alternating as Chairman of the joint National Capital Council.

Permit me to digress for a moment to touch on another reason for having members of Parliament on the National Capital Council. The Capital of Canada is not "the Hill", nor the "changing of the Guard", nor "the driveways and parkways", but every street, every shopping area, every neighbourhood, every park, these too must be in accordance with it's national significance. It is appropriate, then, that the Parliament of Canada participate in the decision-making process for the development of the National Capital Region. Indeed, the capital of this country is as worthy of it's place on the order paper of Parliament as is any other piece of business that the representatives of Canada must see to. I have made reference to Parliament, and not to the Government. The National Capital of this great country must be free from the ups and downs associated with political forces, but rather it must grow and blossom as the institution of Parliament will grow and blossom. It is for this reason that I prefer Parliamentarians rather than government officials, appointed to sit on these National Capital Councils.

The Provincial area representatives would be elected at large in order to assure a "regional" dimension to area council decisions. The chairman's term of office should be four years, i.e. extending over two two year terms of council or one four year term; needless to say agreement is desirable from both provincial governments as to similarity of terms of office to assist in continuity and consistency at the National Council level.

The members of Parliament chosen to sit on the National Capital Council would be subject to an agreement drawn up by the House of Commons and all political parties concerned.

Executive committees or a similar mechanism should of course be provided for as well in the operation of the area councils. I would suggest that the Chairman or his representative, two of the Parliamentary members, two borough members, and two members elected at large (all on a rotating basis) make up the membership of such a body.

The Boroughs

From the outset, boroughs in the context of this paper take on a special definition when used in the proposed structure. Essentially the borough is not a separate unit of government but rather a vehicle for people liaison which the larger cities of to-morrow require if government is not to become a blind force. The boroughs and their enabling legislation should be integrated in the area municipality act as a mechanism for the area city to develop as and when required, as well as borough boundary adjustments etc.

Boroughs could be about 50,000 population in size, giving consideration to tradition, geography, ethnic composition, etc. in considering territorial area. Boroughs could elect 3 or 5 members, one chairman and 2 or 4 others; the borough chairman would sit on the area council and the National Capital Council.

Each borough would have a "Town Hall" facility, where borough meetings would be held, secretariat services provided but only for the borough council, possibly branch facilities of the central municipal unit. Borough activities would centre on dialogue between the elected and the electors, meeting facilities for community groups, public information meetings etc.

No formal legislation for implementation at the borough level would be permissible, otherwise the whole costly area of duplication opens up again.

All borough requests would be dealt with by the area city, if they do not conflict with area statutes. If extra costs are involved, the borough should be prepared to pay for their extra services. The area city should levy on the whole of the provincial area a special borough rate, making available to each borough a specific amount of dollars, to be spent by the area council as dictated by the borough community; these amounts would be uniform, say $100,000 for each borough, and could be accumulated by the borough or used to pay for special services of their choice. This would ensure that all boroughs enjoy the revenues of commercial and business taxes throughout the entire provincial area. Otherwise all boroughs are billed equally, for their common services.

The two "provincial" cities

These two area governments, the Corporation of the National Capital Council of Ontario and the Corporation of the National Capital Council of Quebec, would now operate as self-contained single-tier governments. For each of these area cities, there would be one clerk's office and executive services; one set of municipal by-laws; one municipal election; one treasury function; one legal department; one property department; one personnel department (with a formidable decrease in the amounts of agreements to be negotiated); one fire department; one police department; one building code; one roads department; one garbage collection and disposal system; one planning department etc. In all cases, services immediate and deferred benefit, would be paid by those receiving the benefit only, charging garbage collection to someone in the country who never sees a garbage truck lacks common sense to say the least. Each Council would be it's own Planning Board.

Tax base

Property assessment would remain as separate provincial functions. Too much time and effort has gone into the re-assessment scene to consider any changes there, at least until the conversion to market value is completed and operative for a few years; the major difference in the tax base for each provincial area city, is that *ALL* assessment, business, commercial, residential and government grants-in-lieu of taxes would be revenues to reduce the tax requirements for all properties in the Ontario area, which is of course all properties in the National Capital Region; for the Quebec area, again the same would apply, all assessment, business, commercial, residential and grants-in-lieu of taxes would be available to all properties in the Quebec territory of the National Capital Region.

The National Capital Council

The National Capital Council is that body, composed of both the Ontario and Quebec area City councils, which would have jurisdiction on all matters of an inter-provincial nature as related to the National Capital dimension. In other words, the Council would provide the co-ordination necessary for the development of the National Capital Region, in accordance with National Capital Planning objectives established by it. The National Capital Council would be essentially a planning and co-ordinating body, with implementation carried out by either the Ontario or Quebec area Cities, as it relates to their requirements. All decisions of the National Capital Council on matters within it's jurisdiction would be binding on the two area cities; the planning objectives of the National Capital Council as would be established in the Official Plan for the National Capital, would be binding on all construction and development activities.

The National Capital Council should not be understood as another level of government, but rather as a tool for both cities to assist and co-ordinate each others efforts; this point is emphasized by the fact that both councils make up the National Capital Council and no one else. The National Capital Council would be the designated planning board for the National Capital Region, and the area city councils would be subsiduary planning areas, meaning of course that all planning matters at the "local" level, must mesh with the National Capital Council planning objectives. The National Capital Council should be directed by a highly competent and efficient planning, engineering, and architectural team, to direct and administer planning activities, as well as their co-ordination with the area cities.

Costs of operation for the National Capital Council should be borne by the three senior levels of government, Ontario 12.5%, Quebec 12.5%, and Canada 75%. Considering the reduced costs of operations for these governments, brought about by the reduction of municipal units, and savings brought about through inter-provincial co-ordination, it would be difficult to understand why such participation could be refused.

Role of the National Capital Commission

If something works well, there is little reason to change it, except perhaps to improve again on it. In my opinion the biggest single obstacle to receiving the best that the National Capital Commission has to offer, has been the communication between it and the area municipalities. Granted that these communications were seriously hampered through the multiplicity of municipal governments that had to be co-ordinated, but with one National Capital Council, there is no reason why the right and left hands of the NCR officials (on the Commission and the Council) do not know what each other is doing. The Federal Government needs such an organization to project its presence in the Capital area. What becomes important, then, is that this projection be in harmony and not at the expense of everything else in the National Capital

Region. This will be achieved through it's relationship with the National Capital Council which in effect will represent Local Government for the entire National Capital Region.

Voting—National Capital Council

Both the Corporation of the National Capital of Ontario and the Corporation of the National Capital of Quebec, have real stakes in the future of the National Capital Region, it is essential therefore, that at National Capital Council meetings, there be an equality of votes for both Cities. If either City requires weighted votes at any time to assure this equality, then their right to this is justified.

Name

I suppose that one of the most emotional areas in re-structuring is the name for both cities; many of the present communities will undoubtedly retain their name at the borough level. This would seem to permit all of the Ontario area to be called Ottawa, and all of the Quebec area to be called Hull, with of course the National Capital being called Ottawa-Hull.

Headquarters

The National Capital Council headquarters should be strategically located, away from the Hill... not in Ontario nor in Quebec, but preferably mid-way between the two provinces on one of the islands of the Ottawa River. I would recommend as well that for convenience purposes, these buildings house as well, the administrative and technical staff of the National Capital Commission; since the efforts of both will be so closely linked to their common goals, it would seem rather foolish to have one work far away from the other.

Appeal procedures

Any democratic structure requires appeal procedures to assure healthy and responsible operations. Any appeal at the "City" level of activity, would use existing provincial mechanisms; with the province assigning appeal and discretionary powers more and more to the larger municipal units, this means many of these appeals could be coped with in each provincial area.

There will undoubtedly be appeals against decisions of the National Capital Council, and these should be made to a special appeal board. This Board (Capital Appeal Board) would have one member appointed by each Province and one member appointed by the Federal Government. Their decisions would be final and binding and subject to appeal only through the courts.

Implementation

The final proposal of the task force should be presented to a joint meeting of, the Minister of Treasury, Economics and Intergovernmental Affairs of the Province of Ontario, the Minister of Municipal Affairs for the Province of Quebec, the Chairman of the National Capital Commission, the Chairmen of the Regional Municipalities of Ottawa-Carleton and the Outaouais Regional Community, the Mayors and Reeves of all the municipalities in the National Capital Region, at a special conference held for this purpose. At the same time, the proposal should be made public, for input from that important sector.

A steering committee, representing the two provinces and the federal governments should be set up to liaison, correct and modify where necessary, re-convene the parties for up-date, and ultimately present the appropriate legislation to the governments concerned for implementation.

Conclusion

Changes are needed to the present arrangement regarding the operations of Local Government in the National Capital Region; if these changes are not brought about now, it may be a long time before the opportunity is right again. In the meantime, there are simply too many man hours and dollars being absorbed by an unproductive, costly, disheartening and frustrating structure, that prevents Local Government, the National Capital and the Twentieth Century from coming to terms with each other.

Various charts, summarizing my proposal, are attached.

Respectfully yours,
R. G. Poulin, A.M.C.T., C.M.C.

THE CORPORATION OF THE NATIONAL CAPITAL COUNCIL OF QUEBEC

(One City taking in all of the territory of the Province of Quebec within the boundaries of the National Capital Region)

12 Members on Council

CHAIRMAN

- 4 members of Parliament agreed to and chosen by the political parties
- 4 members elected at large from the Quebec territory of the National Capital Region
- 3 members who are Chairmen of the City Boroughs and ex-officio members of the City Council

THE CORPORATION OF THE NATIONAL CAPITAL COUNCIL OF ONTARIO

(One City taking in all of the territory of the Province of Ontario within the boundaries of the National Capital Region)

18 Members on Council

CHAIRMAN

- 4 members of Parliament agreed to and chosen by the political parties
- 4 members elected at large from the Ontario territory of the National Capital Region
- 9 members who are Chairmen of the City Boroughs and ex-officio members of the City Council

THE NATIONAL CAPITAL COUNCIL

(One Planning co-ordinating body, taking in all of the territory of the National Capital Region)

25 Members on Council

CHAIRMAN   1 Vote

4 Votes	13 Votes	13 Votes
4 Members of Parliament	13 Members of the Ontario City Council	7 Members of the Quebec City Council

Appendix C

The Proposal For a Federal Capital Territory For Canada's Capital

Donald C. Rowat

Professor of Political Science
Carleton University

Prepared for the
Ontario Committee on Confederation, 1966

The approval of the Government of Ontario to reprint the attached study by Professor Rowat is gratefully acknowledged.

Many of the briefs to the Royal Commission on Bilingualism and Biculturalism advocated the creation of a federal district in which the bilingual-bicultural character of Canada would be symbolically reflected. As a result, the Advisory Committee decided to commission Professor D. C. Rowat of Carleton University to prepare a study for them on this question. Professor Rowat submitted his report to the Committee in September, 1966. The knowledge of the existence of such a report stimulated a great deal of further discussion and research on the problems of a capital district by the federal and Quebec governments and by citizens' groups in the Ottawa-Hull area.

Professor Rowat's report is a broadly based study in which the question of a federal district is approached from the point of view of three objectives:

1. *The effective implementation of the national capital plan; that is, a desirable development of the community through such means as a comprehensive zoning law and the establishment of a so-called Greenbelt and reform of local administration.*
2. *The development of Ottawa and Hull as an area symbolic of the nation rather than as mere regional centres in Ontario and Quebec.*
3. *The creation of a truly bilingual environment in the Ottawa area which would make the capital an attractive place for French Canadians to work.*

The report concludes that these objectives could be met by means of greater co-operation among the Ontario, Quebec, and federal governments. Since this co-operation cannot be assured, Professor Rowat thinks that these objectives would more likely be achieved by the creation of a federal capital territory.

Preface

Ever since Confederation there have been proposals that the area surrounding Ottawa should be turned into a federal capital territory, like those that have been created for other federal capitals such as Washington and Canberra. It has been argued that, as a matter of principle, the national seat of government of a federal country should not come under the control and laws of a single municipality in a single province. However, the case for a federal territory did not become really strong until after the Second World War, when Canada's rise to a middle power on the world stage gave her people a greater interest in developing a capital city as a symbol of the nation.

The wartime growth of the civil service and the expansion of population in the whole Ottawa-Hull metropolitan area made it clear that the problems of the future development of the capital could not be solved simply by arrangements worked out between the federal government and the city of Ottawa. The federal government therefore decided to have a Master Plan prepared for the future development of the national capital, and since then has devoted considerable effort and money, through its agent the National Capital Commission (formerly the Federal District Commission), to the implementation of the Plan. Because the federal government has no direct governmental control over the capital area, however, numerous difficulties have been encountered in completing the Plan. It has become clear that the Plan cannot be fulfilled under existing arrangements because it depends for its implementation on the agreement and co-operation not only of the Governments of Ontario and Quebec but also of the numerous municipalities in the Ottawa-Hull metropolitan area. Their interests often do not coincide with those of the federal government, and their financial resources and administrative capabilities are often inadequate to meet the tasks of executing the Plan. There has therefore been a continuing interest in the proposal for a federal capital territory as a solution to this problem.

Recently, the proposal has been given additional support from another source. It is argued that a federally governed capital territory could be made genuinely bilingual and bicultural, and would become a model in this respect for the rest of Canada.

Since no adequate history or analysis of the proposal has as yet been written, the Ontario Advisory Committee on Confederation has asked me to prepare this brief study.

Because of the confusion in the use of terms applied to the national capital area, it may be useful to clarify at the beginning what the proposal means. Because of the division of powers between the central government and the provinces in the *British North America Act*, the former has no control over the federal capital or its surrounding area regarding any matter which comes under provincial or municipal jurisdiction. For any such matter Ottawa and its adjacent municipalities are governed by the laws of the province of Ontario, while Hull and its adjacent municipalities are governed by Quebec law. This means that the central government has no direct power to impose its will on the capital district, or to implement any plan it may have for it, without the agreement and co-operation of the provincial and municipal governments that may be affected. The proposal for a federal territory, on the other hand, would require the ceding of land on the Ottawa and Hull sides of the Ottawa river by the governments of Ontario and Quebec to the federal government, and the whole area would come directly under the jurisdiction of the federal parliament. It is important to note, however — because of the frequent assumption to the contrary — that the proposal does *not* necessarily imply the abolition of all municipalities in the area, the loss of voting rights, or *direct* administration by the federal government, as in Washington.

Provincial laws and court systems would no longer apply to the federal territory, except by agreement between the federal government and the provinces concerned, and all normal provincial and municipal services and taxes would have to be provided for under federal law. The proposal usually assumes that the boundaries of the new federal territory would approximate those of the present National Capital Region, as defined for the purposes of the National Capital Plan and for the activities of the National Capital Commission.

Because the District of Columbia is often referred to as the federal district, the terms "federal district" and "national capital district" are often used in Canada to describe this proposal. Unfortunately, however, the terms "federal district" and "national capital district" were also adopted to describe the area of interest and planning for the old Federal District Commission. In order to avoid confusion I have therefore chosen to use the term "federal territory" in reference to the proposal for a capital area coming exclusively under the jurisdiction of the federal government.

The proposal is similar to but not as far-reaching as another one made recently: that the National Capital Region should be turned into an eleventh province. This idea will also be considered briefly in the present study, because of its similarity to the proposal for a federal territory.

For information on the history of the capital, I have relied heavily on Wilfrid Eggleston's invaluable *The Queen's Choice.* I should like to thank officials of the National Capital Commission and the Cities of Ottawa, Hull and Eastview for their help in providing information on recent developments in the National Capital Region.

I hope that this study will help to solve the problem of reconciling the interests of the local residents and those of the people of Canada, in the government and in the future development of the nation's capital.

D.C.R.
Ottawa,
September, 1966

The Proposal For a Federal Capital Territory For Canada's Capital

I. The Origin of the Problem

It was mainly an accident of history that the federal government's present area of interest for the development of the national capital covers two cities in two different provinces as well as territory beyond the cities in both provinces. When Ottawa was chosen as the capital city, scant attention was paid to the fact that part of the urban population lived across the river in a different province. It was not at that time realized that building bridges across the Ottawa river would to a large extent remove the river as a barrier between the two populations on each side, and that the whole area would develop into one vast interdependent urban complex. Nor was it thought that the relationships between the central government and the City of Ottawa would be at all complicated. Those were the days before the age of the welfare state, when the civil service was extremely small. It was therefore expected that the federal land on "Barracks Hill" would be sufficient to contain the Parliament buildings of all federal administrative offices for the foreseeable future. Perhaps for this reason no one at the time of Confederation seems to have seriously proposed a federal territory for the capital, despite the precedent established by the creation of the District of Columbia long before this in the United States.

The difference between the choice of Washington and Ottawa as capitals is that Washington had been created as a new capital after the formation of the United States, whereas Ottawa was a thriving lumber town and had already been chosen as the capital of the Province of Canada before Confederation. Since Toronto and Quebec were the obvious choices for the newly created provinces of Ontario and Quebec, it seemed logical to leave Ottawa as the capital of the new Dominion, and simply to place the new federal parliament and its administration in the buildings that had been constructed for the parliament of the former Province of Canada.

There was an inherent flaw and source of future friction in this arrangement, however, though it seems to have aroused little or no apprehension at the time. "The point is", as Wilfrid Eggleston has pointed out, "that the constitutional position of Ottawa as the capital was materially altered by the decision of 1864-67; and the change in that particular respect was a retrograde step. As capital of the *Province* of

Canada, no serious jurisdictional problems could possibly arise between the Crown and the Town in Ottawa, for the municipality of Ottawa would have continued to be under the direct control of the provincial government on Parliament Hill. Nor would any problems arise if government activities spread into adjoining municipalities or even across the Ottawa river into Canada East, since between 1840 and 1867 the Ottawa river merely separated two geographical divisions of one province.

"But Confederation changed all that. Now Ontario and Quebec were autonomous states within their defined powers, and these powers included the exclusive control of municipal and local matters. Now Ottawa, by the *B.N.A. Act*, was a federal capital located *within a provincial municipality*, and the latter took its orders not from Parliament Hill, but from Queen's Park, 275 miles away, and from a jurisdiction separate and autonomous and independent in broad respects from the central federal government. And the Ottawa river had once again become a boundary between two autonomous governments."[1]

Hence any extension of the federal government's interest beyond the immediate boundaries of Parliament Hill was bound to cause differences of interest and delicate relations with the City of Ottawa, and ultimately with the City of Hull, the municipalities surrounding these cities and the provincial governments of Ontario and Quebec, under whose control they came for all provincial and municipal purposes. Moreover, the Ontario side of the river was mainly English-speaking, Protestant, and governed under the English common law, while the Quebec side was soon to become mainly French-speaking and Roman Catholic, and was governed under the radically different Quebec civil code, which had been inherited from French law.

As long as the interests of the federal government in the capital city remained largely confined to Parliament Hill or even mainly to the City of Ottawa, the difficulties inherent in this situation did not become acute. In fact, they were not revealed for many years, because the majority of the people and of Parliament remained unimpressed by the early declaration of one of the Fathers of Confederation, John Hamilton Gray, that the capital city "might fairly rest its claim for support upon the people of the Dominion."[2]

The reason for this lack of interest by the people of the Dominion in their responsibility for the capital city, least of all in Gray's proposal of a federal territory for Ottawa, is explained by Wilfred Eggleston (p. 147) in this way:

> When a capital city is created from the ground up, in hitherto unoccupied territory, as at Canberra and Brasilia, the national or federal government must perforce proceed to establish a new community from scratch. There are no taxpayers yet to levy upon for municipal services, and the central government must construct and operate and pay for its own. In such circumstances, a "federal district" comes into being almost automatically.
>
> But such was not the case with Ottawa. It was already a city of 18,000 persons by 1867. The rudiments, at least, of essential municipal services were already in existence. There was a well-established tradition of self-government in municipal matters, long predating Confederation. The Government of the Province of Canada in 1859 never proposed to set up a

separate or rival municipality, when it began erecting the Parliament Buildings. Nor did the Government of the Dominion of Canada in 1867. It is true that pending the strengthening of Ottawa's municipal services the Canadian Government undertook to provide some utilities of its own. In 1859, the City of Ottawa still had no water supply except that provided by private carriers freighting water from the river. The Provincial Commissioner of Public Works put in a small plant down below the Library, to pump water for the buildings. A separate sewage system was built by the Provincial Government when the buildings were under construction. Some elementary fire protection was also provided, and the policing of the Hill was under provincial and then federal control.

The early government buildings were physically confined to Parliament Hill, which from the beginning had been Ordnance Land, and which had never been taxed for municipal purposes. Since at first the government buildings even provided their own utilities, the people and Parliament of Canada felt no great responsibility for the welfare of the city. Nor was the City Corporation very conscious of the costs or inconveniences arising out of the presence of a seat of government. In fact, the activities of the federal government did not impinge very much on the municipality for the first fifteen years.

But the existing arrangements contained an incipient conflict of interests between Crown and Town. "In several respects," Eggleston has observed (p. 147), "the effect of the planting of the Canadian capital within the munipical limits of Ottawa was not unlike that of the location of a large private corporation. Both operations require massive new construction, create new jobs, and, before long, additional municipal burdens. But in two vital elements there is a sharp contrast. Government properties are given permanent exemption from municipal taxation by the terms of the *British North America Act*, and governments possess contingent powers no private company ever enjoyed. One is the power of expropriation." Before long the federal government would find it necessary to expand beyond the limits of Parliament Hill into the heart of the business section of Ottawa. Then the municipal services needed for the new government buildings would begin to lay heavy new burdens on the City and the difficulties inherent in placing the federal capital within the confines of a municipality controlled by a single province would begin to be revealed.

II. Early Attempts To Meet the Problem

The problem created by the location of the federal capital within the boundaries of a municipality governed by provincial law, and immediately adjacent to another municipality governed by the laws of a different province, did not become fully apparent until the federal government began taking an interest in the beautification and future development of the capital.

It was almost the turn of the century before the government began to recognize its special responsibilities for developing the area in which its seat of government was situated. The 1890's had seen a great quickening of interest throughout North America in city architecture and planning. In June of 1893, while leader of the Opposition, Wilfred Laurier had stated that Ottawa should become the "Washington of the North", and this idea had begun to fire people's imaginations toward the future development of a great capital city. But until after 1895 — the end of the "Great Depression" — the federal government was chronically hard up. Just before Laurier's accession to power in 1896, two city councillors, Fred Cook and Robert Stewart, succeeded in getting Ottawa's Council to appoint a committee to make a study of the principal capitals in the British Empire, in order to demonstrate to the federal government both its opportunities and its obligations for the development of the federal capital. In 1897, the City made use of this information in a petition to the Laurier Government. The petition pointed out that the United Kingdom Government paid municipal rates to London on all its properties, including the Houses of Parliament, and noted that the tax-exempt properties owned by the Crown within the City of Ottawa in 1897 were valued at $14 million. Also the City had received no compensation from the federal government for the City's large outlay on public works, in contrast with the practice in other parts of the world. This petition no doubt had considerable influence upon the government, for in 1899, it initiated an annual grant to Ottawa of $60,000 to meet these claims. It also created the Ottawa Improvement Commission, which consisted of four commissioners, three chosen by the federal government and one by the City of Ottawa, and which began its work with an annual grant of $60,000.

In the early years of this century the Ottawa Improvement Commission did much good work in beautifying Ottawa's parks and driveways. But, as Eggleston has noted (p. 166), it was "handicapped by insufficient funds, restricted powers, and possibly, by lack of imagination. As it was not created as a town planning body, and in any event lacked authority in that field, its remedies were bound to be superficial rather than basic." Although it had hired an architect, F. G. Todd, who had submitted a plan for the future development of the Ottawa area as early as 1903, architects and others began to realize that the Ottawa Improvement Commission was incapable of meeting the problem. In 1911, for example, a deputation of members of the Royal Architectural Institute of Canada presented a brief to the new Prime Minister, Robert Borden, complaining about the lack of planned development of the capital, pointing to the difficulties of finding a satisfactory site for new government buildings, and to the still-existing need for relocating the railways and amending the street system of the city. As a result, in 1913 the Borden Government appointed a Federal Plan Commission, chaired by Herbert S. (later Sir Herbert) Holt of Montreal, with five other members, including the mayors of Ottawa and Hull. The terms of reference instructed the Commission to "draw up and perfect a comprehensive scheme or plan, looking to the future growth and development of the City of Ottawa and the City of Hull, and their environs. . . ." This was the first time that the federal government had officially recognized any responsibility for the development of the Hull side of the river or even of the environs of Ottawa. The Holt Commission, which reported in 1915, developed a comprehensive and impressive plan for the future development of Ottawa, Hull, and the surrounding area. It recognized that the power to implement the far-reaching proposals it had made (which included the reconstruction of a good deal of Ottawa) came constitutionally under the jurisdiction of the Governments of Ontario and Quebec and of the municipalities in the area. Foreseeing the difficulties of divided jurisdiction, the Commission proposed the outright creation of a federal district and federal control over local government.

Unfortunately, the report of the Holt Commission was badly timed, coming as it did in the midst of the First World War, and just at the time that the Parliament Buildings burned down. The building, which burned on February 3, 1916, required ten years and $12 million to rebuild, to enlarge and to furnish. As a result, except for raising the annual grant to the Ottawa Improvement Commission in 1917 from $100,000 to $150,000 a year, for ten years nothing much was done about the recommendations in the report, even though Noulan Cauchon, planning consultant to the City of Ottawa, had in 1922 produced an updated revision of the plan.

Cauchon had proposed, as his administrative solution to the problem, a federal commission which would have authority over the physical features and public utilities of a "federal district", but which would preserve provincial and municipal autonomy in other respects. Being essentially an architect and planner, he did not seem to realize that, constitutionally, even the federal Parliament did not possess this authority and so could not delegate it to a commission. Hence the commission would not have the power to carry out the far-reaching plans for redevelopment that he and the Holt Commission had proposed. Those who read his report may have been led to believe that all that was needed to complete the plans was for the federal government to establish a more powerful body with jurisdiction over an enlarged "federal district", and that therefore the creation of a federally governed territory would be unnecessary. At any rate, in 1927 the Ottawa Improvement Commission was reconstituted as the Federal District Commission, with broadened powers and the extension of its interests into Quebec. The (by then) eight members of the older Commission were increased to ten, of which one was to be a resident of Hull. Thus, for the first time, Hull was officially recognized as being part of the federal capital.

The next year a situation arose in the heart of Ottawa which forced the federal government to intervene. It led to a reduction in the new annual grant from $250,000 to $200,000, and the provision of the capital sum of $3 million to create the open space now known as Confederation Square. The old Russell House Hotel at that time was being demolished, and the owners were proposing to erect a new modern hotel on the site. In order to preserve the site as an open space, the federal government had to act quickly to enable the Commission to expropriate it and other properties needed to open up the area. However, aside from this major expropriation to create a vista of the Parliament buildings from the south-east, the Commission acted essentially as a parks and driveway development commission. In the twelve years from 1927 to 1939 the F.D.C. parks area was enlarged to 900 acres, and the length of the federally-owned and maintained driveway was increased to 22 miles, including an extension across the Champlain Bridge into Quebec. But the constitutional limits to the F.D.C.'s powers, the long depression of the 1930's, and the outbreak of war discouraged any more ambitious attempts to carry out the Holt Report of 1915.

Meanwhile, the growth of the welfare state in the 20's and 30's had caused a gradual encroachment by the federal government into the heart of Ottawa, for buildings to house its administrative personnel. The great influx of military and civilian personnel connected with the Second World War greatly accelerated this encroachment. The total space in the city rapidly being occupied by the federal government through construction, purchase or rental could not help but create tensions and difficulties between Crown and Town. Eggleston (p. 177) lists a total of 23 permanent buildings that had been erected between 1918 and 1945 and notes that no fewer than 14 wartime so-called "temporary" buildings had been built in assorted locations throughout Ottawa. These properties of course were all tax-exempt, and often occupied the space of former businesses that had been paying property and business taxes to the City. At the same time they required the continuing provision of all normal municipal services. The growing number of foreign embassies and headquarters of Crown corporations, which were similarly tax-exempt, increased the problem.

This was a problem which could be largely solved by larger grants to the City. But the problem created by the constitutionally restricted powers of the Federal District Commission to redevelop the cities of Ottawa and Hull and their surrounding area, could not be so easily solved.

III. The Evolution of the National Capital Region, 1944-58

The federal government responded to Ottawa's claim for "better fiscal terms" by setting up a special Joint Committee of the Senate and House in 1944. Although the Committee did not accept the City's contention that an annual payment of nearly $1,600,000 was needed to offset the loss of taxes from government tax-exempt property, it did recommend that for a period of five years the annual grant to Ottawa should be raised from $100,000 to $300,000, and the government accepted this recommendation. Part of the government's difficulty was that it could not pay adequate compensation to Ottawa without recognizing a similar responsibility for its tax-exempt properties in other cities of Canada. In 1949, however, it recognized these responsibilities by passing the *Municipal Grants Act*, and by 1955 Ottawa was receiving under this Act an amount substantially larger than that requested by the City in 1944. The government also agreed to pay grants in lieu of taxes on embassy properties and required Crown corporations to pay similar grants (though the City still complains that some Crown corporations refuse to pay normal business taxes).

Although the Committee of 1944 devoted most of its attention to the City's financial problem, it could not avoid recognizing the larger problem of how to redevelop the national capital under divided jurisdiction. In its final report it recommended "that the powers of the Federal District Commission be increased, and its personnel be enlarged to include, not only representation from the Ottawa area, but of the people of Canada as a whole. The name Federal District Commission might even be changed to include the idea of a National Capital."[3] But the Committee felt that the only permanent solution to the problem might lie in the creation of a federal territory, as shown by these words from its report:

> From the observations made by this Committee during its investigations, it is clear that with the growth of Canada and the corresponding expansion of its governmental activities, the administrative problems arising between the City of Ottawa and the Federal Government will become more complex and more difficult of settlement than they are now. As an indication of that prospect we would merely stress the inevitable difficulty that will arise in connection with the present reckless system of sewage disposal in the Ottawa river, the both banks of which within the most directly affected area, are the property of the Dominion of Canada.
>
> It is not the purpose of this Committee to make definite recommendations to the Government regarding the future character of a Federal District to embrace the park area and the municipalities on either side of the Ottawa river . . . We are of the opinion, however, that this long-term project should be committed by the Government to a special commission of experts for investigation and report, involving as it would the possession of expert professional knowledge and the need for extended travel to study the plans and workings of federal capital districts in other countries.[4]

In 1928, at the time of the debate in the House of Commons over the expropriation of the site of the old Russell House Hotel, Mackenzie King had expressed his conviction that the creation of a federal territory was the eventual solution to the problems of the national capital. Hence it is curious that his Government did not take up this recommendation of the Committee of 1944. It may be that his view was changed in this respect by the opinion of M. Jacques Greber, the French town planner whom he had invited to Ottawa in 1937 to prepare plans for the development of Confederation Square. Eggleston reveals (p. 184) that at that time they had some discussions on the desirability of a federal territory and the French adviser said his own studies of such authorities in other parts of the world led him to believe that this was not the answer. M. Greber, of course, had not lived under a federal system of government and was not fully conversant with the difficulties of divided jurisdiction.

In any case, nothing was done about the Committee's proposal for a thorough study of the constitutional and administrative problems and the idea of a federal territory, even though the Prime Minister had by then become convinced that the redevelopment of the entire national capital area should be undertaken as a national memorial of the Second World

War. Apparently he had been persuaded that this project could be brought to fruition without the creation of a federal territory. Instead, he brought M. Greber to Ottawa at the end of the war to prepare a new plan for the capital, and an Order-in-Council was passed in 1945 defining some 900 square miles as the National Capital District for purposes of this plan.

The proposals for redevelopment contained in the resulting National Capital Plan, completed in 1950, were much more far-reaching than those of the earlier Holt Report. Since in the meantime Ottawa and Hull had developed without a plan and the National Capital District now took in many municipalities surrounding Ottawa and Hull, the problem of correcting the errors and implementing the Plan would be that much more difficult.

Perhaps because of his lack of knowledge of constitutional law and political realities, M. Greber seems to have fallen into the trap into which many other purely technically trained town planners have fallen, of not distinguishing clearly between the preparation and the fulfilling of a plan. In 1939, in a preliminary report to the Prime Minister he had pointed out his lack of qualifications for discussing the administrative problem, but at the same time had left the inference that a comprehensive plan could be fully implemented through co-operation and co-ordination between the many interested jurisdictions:

> I understand that the question may be considered of eventually creating a District Capital for the Dominion of Canada, along the principle of the District of Columbia in the United States.
>
> As I have no qualification for discussing the need for a Federal District Capital from the political or general administration viewpoint, I beg to submit to you the following remarks, limited to the *purely city planning problem*.
>
> Several examples of regional planning and comprehensive by-laws on city development, in Europe and in America, show that this particular problem, even when it affects a large number of municipalities, may be *successfully studied and solved without deeply changing their respective administrations*, but by organizing, only for the purpose of their *better co-ordinated planning and common zoning and building legislation, a central Planning Board*, specially appointed to elaborate and to control the execution of the plans and the enforcement of the by-laws.[5]

In these words, M. Greber reveals that he failed to make the vital distinction between the elaboration of plans and the control of their execution. Further on in this report, he drew encouragement from the experience of France and the United States with regional planning, but in doing so ignored the fact that France did not have a federal government, and that the regional plans in the United States to which he referred (The New York Regional Plan and the Philadelphia Tri-State Planning Corporation) did not include the federal government. By stating that these regional authorities were "entrusted with a *purely technical work, without interfering with the exising Town or State administrations*,"[6] he was again failing to make a distinction between their success at preparing a plan and the governmental problem of ensuring its completion.

ADMINISTRATIVE BOUNDARIES
WITHIN THE NATIONAL CAPITAL REGION
1948

LEGEND
— INTERPROVINCIAL BOUNDARIES
—·— COUNTY BOUNDARIES
····· TOWNSHIP BOUNDARIES
----- MUNICIPAL BOUNDARIES

THE NATIONAL CAPITAL
PLANNING SERVICE

J GRÉBER — CONSULTANT

399

It seems clear that the federal government was greatly influenced by these views. The only significant administrative change it made in preparation for the capital's redevelopment was to arrange for the kind of planning body M. Greber had recommended. This was a National Capital Planning Committee, with local and national representation. It was created merely by a by-law of the Federal District Commission. In 1946 the latter's membership was increased from ten to nineteen, to include a representative from each province, and it was given additional powers, including authority over the site and architecture of federal buildings. But basically its status remained unchanged.

Both the Master Plan preliminary and final reports of 1948 and 1950, which were prepared by the National Capital Planning Service under M. Greber's direction and approved by the National Capital Planning Committee, reprinted M. Greber's preliminary report of 1939. The final report recommended no change in the status and powers of the Federal District Commission, and in its section on "legal matters" clearly indicated that it was depending upon the co-operation of the Governments of Ontario and Quebec and of all the municipalities in the new National Capital District for the successful implementation of the Plan. But the problem of what would happen if these governments did not co-operate was never squarely faced. The fact is that the National Capital Committee was purely an unofficial body so far as these governments were concerned, and neither it nor the Federal District Commission had power to enforce any part of the Plan which did not lie on federally owned territory.

Because the City of Ottawa co-operated whole-heartedly in taking the initial action necessary to control the development of its urban fringes and to preserve the Plan's proposed Greenbelt around Ottawa, this difficulty did not become revealed for some time. After the appointment of the National Capital Planning Committee, Ottawa took steps under the *Ontario Planning Act* of 1946 to establish in 1947 the Ottawa Planning Area Board, whose planning area included not only the City of Ottawa, but also the Town of Eastview, the Village of Rockcliffe Park and the Townships of Gloucester, Nepean, March, Torbolton and Fitzroy — all the municipalities that were within the boundaries of the Ottawa side of the National Capital District. Membership on the Board was weighted in favour of the City, with usually five from Ottawa, one from the Federal District Commission, one from the Central Mortgage and Housing Corporation, and only two from the surrounding municipalities (Gloucester and Nepean). The City also applied to the Ontario Municipal Board to annex those parts of the Townships of Nepean and Gloucester which lay within the inner ring of the proposed Greenbelt. But it met opposition from Nepean and also from the County of Carleton. Because of this, and perhaps also because the boundaries of the Greenbelt had not been definitely established at this time, the size of the original area asked for was reduced by the Ontario Board. As a result, a considerable gap was left between the new southern boundary of the

City and the inner ring of the Greenbelt in Nepean. Gaps were also left at the western boundary of the City, and at the eastern boundary in Gloucester. Other effects of the annexation, which became effective on January 1, 1950 were to enclose Rockcliffe Park and Eastview completely within the boundaries of the City, and to multiply the City's area by five times.

The effective completion of a city plan requires a comprehensive zoning by-law, or at least zoning by-laws for those parts of a municipality which are undergoing rapid subdivision and urban development The older City had had no Master Plan, no detailed plan of land use, and no comprehensive zoning by-law. Although Ottawa was now at least in a position to begin work on these matters within its own territory, none of the other municipalities in the area had zoning by-laws or any facilities for implementing the National Capital Plan. The Ottawa Planning Area Board was staffed by the City's Planning Department, and tended to ignore the planning needs of the surrounding municipalities. Although the Board had approved in principle the proposals of the National Capital Plan for the Ottawa side of the river, it did not have adequate facilities to control urban development, especially beyond the boudaries of the City and in particular in the area designated as the Greenbelt. Nor at that time did it have any facilities to plan and carry out redevelopment. On the Hull side of the river, no adequate planning machinery existed for implementing that side's share of the Plan, nor was any created. As Eggleston has pointed out (p. 200), "When work began on the Master Plan not a single one of the municipalities in the capital region had 'land use plans' or effective zoning plans. *Vis-a-vis* the local authorities, the Federal District Commission possessed only the power to advise and persuade. Lacking direct control, the Commission had to seek to attain its objectives by oblique and indirect means."

Yet when the Plan was presented in 1950, the Ottawa metropolitan area was on the verge of one of the most dramatic periods of urban expansion that it had ever seen. Since there existed no adequate machinery to control this development, the result was urban sprawl on both sides of the Ottawa river, and inevitably, developments that went contrary to the Plan. The most striking example of this was in the Township of Nepean. For financial reasons developers tended to jump beyond the new boundaries of the City and even into the proposed Greenbelt. Nepean had a population approaching 25,000 in 1949. When the annexation was complete Nepean was left with an almost exclusively rural population of only 2,500. Yet in the next five years the outflow from the city again raised the population to 8,000, largely urban. The Township of Gloucester showed a similar pattern. Its population was cut from 10,000 to 5,000 by the annexation, but by 1956 its population had again jumped back to 11,500. Indeed the pace of urban subdivision in the proposed Greenbelt proceeded so fast that it forced the federal authorities to redefine the Greenbelt and to extend its inner boundary, making it in places even farther from the boundaries of the City. The fact was that the Greenbelt was nothing more than an attractive dream drawn on a map, and it would never be realized unless something were done quickly.

The difficulty, inherent from the beginning, was a genuine conflict of interest between the federal and local governments in the area. While the federal government was interested in developing a national capital worthy of Canada, the local governments were, individually, incapable of meeting this challenge, especially since the financial burdens fell upon them unequally. There was a similar but lesser conflict of interest between the federal and provincial governments. So long as the provincial governments remained responsible to their electors in the national capital area, they could not be expected to turn a deaf ear to representations from local citizens desiring action contrary to the Plan. Nor could they be expected to have any very positive incentive to create the governmental and planning machinery that would be necessary to enforce the Plan.

As a result of these difficulties another parliamentary Joint Committee was appointed in 1956, and the evidence given before that Committee well illustrates this conflict of interests, especially regarding the preservation of the Greenbelt. "Unlike a zoning by-law, which is for the general benefit of persons within the zoned area, a Greenbelt, if it has any benefit, is for the benefit of those outside the zoned area, is for purposes wholly dissociated with the enhancement of the value of the ratepayers' property," the Reeve of Nepean told the Joint Committee. "A municipal council is only the instrument of its ratepayers and it is wholly beyond the realm of practicability to expect any municipal council so to act in direct opposition to the interests of its ratepayers. If some national policy requires a Greenbelt, with which suggestion Nepean does not agree, then the national government must adequately compensate the Nepean ratepayers. Certainly, it must not expect the Nepean Council under the phony excuse of 'zoning', to deprive its ratepayers of the present values of lands which they and their forefathers have held for generations."[7] Reeve Moodie might also have admitted, had he been pressed, that neither did it wish to deprive its ratepayers of *future* values which might result from subdivision.

In her evidence to the Committee, Mayor Charlotte Whitton of Ottawa explained the failure of the Ottawa Planning Area Board to prevent undesirable development:

> In cases where subdivisions are proposed far in advance of normal development the Ottawa Planning Area Board has refused to recommend approval. In these cases, an appeal to the Ontario Municipal Board is open to the developer, and, unfortunately, most of the appeals which have been taken have succeeded and the Ontario Municipal Board has recommended to the Minister of Planning and Development the approval of the plan of subdivision, notwithstanding the opposition of the Ottawa Planning Board. This is a result which the City deplores, but which it is powerless to prevent . . .
>
> The Ottawa Planning Area Board has, with four exceptions, three of which were insignificant, consistently refused to approve of urban-type subdivisions in the area designated as a rural-urban zone (Greenbelt) by the Ottawa Planning Area Board. Here again, appeals have been taken by developers

to the Ontario Municipal Board, and that Board, refusing to recognize the rural-urban zone as having any special character, has on several occasions approved of large urban-type subdivisions in this transition area.[8]

While there was a special conflict of interests between the federal government and Ottawa on the one hand, and the outlying municipalities and the Government of Ontario on the other, there was also a normal and natural conflict of interest between the federal government and all of the municipalities in the area, as explained by Mayor Whitton. She pointed out that the National Capital Plan meant changing the actual physical setting and development of the community but that this could not be done to the disregard of the overriding responsibility of the municipal authority to the people of the community:

> The fact of Ottawa, the city, a community, almost half a century older than Confederation and fully a century older than the "National Capital Plan", cannot be set aside. The zones of its business and commerce, its residential areas — luxury, average, mediocre and sub-standard — cannot be ruthlessly dealt with on the lines of a blueprint or an overall plan or sudden sweeping zoning and rezoning.
>
> The reality of living, the rights of ownership, the relationship of the homes, the churches, the schools, the stores and services, the community's recreation resources, both commercial and otherwise, their eating places, in short all of the pattern of their living must be seen through the "overlay" as it were of what the planners may dream, may desire, may work towards, but only in justice and consideration of what is, as well as what may be. It can all be very frustrating, but it is important to distinguish whether it is the slower, surer, safer processes of a self-governing democracy at the level of its people's local government, or a culpable indifference or non-co-operation which explains the gradualness of development and change among the municipalities which are practically all no less anxious than any especially constituted mechanism of the national government, to justify and realize their dignity as part of the national capital area.[9]

The Committee of 1956 devoted a good deal of its report to the problems of divided jurisdiction and conflict of interest, but it did not think, as did the Committee of 1944, that the proposal for a federal territory should be studied. It probably thought that the federal government was already too heavily committed to a program of voluntary co-operation with the provincial and municipal governments concerned. It considered that there was still a reasonable hope of achieving the objectives of the Plan through such co-operation, especially if the federal government were prepared to spend enough money in a program of assistance to the local municipalities and of control over the use of land through purchase or expropriation.

The pertinent paragraphs from the final report regarding the problems of divided jurisdiction are as follows:

> The proposed National Capital area includes portions of the Provinces of Ontario and Quebec. It is superimposed upon certain municipal organization within each Province. As the Plan is brought to fruition works must be undertaken which affect the sphere of provincial or municipal responsibility. But because they are conceived as part of a scheme for the creation of a national rather than provincial or municipal development, these works may be more elaborate than would be required for provincial or municipal purposes. Again, since they are to be installed within populous municipalities, they have a bearing upon the works required by these municipalities for their own development. Sometimes, as in the case of driveways and parkways, they add improvements which the municipality would not install, or

if they were installed, would be installed upon a more modest scale. At other times the creation of the work of the National Capital imposes upon the municipality concerned the burden of additional services or the building of works of greater magnitude than the municipality alone might undertake. For the resolution of these conflicts, co-operation between the three levels of jurisdiction is essential. Hitherto, the emphasis is upon co-operation between the Federal District Commission and the municipalities concerned. A greater measure of integration of planning with the provincial authorities should emerge ...

It seems not too much to say that Ontario municipalities have an onus cast upon them to avail themselves of the provisions of the *Ontario Planning Act*, and to establish long-range and far-reaching plans for their future development thereunder. Even if Ottawa were not a Federal Capital it might still be expected that the municipal corporations in the area should invoke the provisions of the Act.

But for the Ottawa area more is available, namely the National Capital Plan. It is not imposed on the area by any Statute which superimposes upon the City and its environs an additional plan for beautification over and above any municipal plan. As we see it, this National Capital Plan should be developed as far as possible without assuming obligations proper to the province or the municipalities concerned. Sometimes it is difficult to draw the line ...

We think that the realization of the National Capital Plan must imply the co-operation of federal, provincial and municipal authorities. In many respects such co-operation is not wanting; in others there is much to be desired. We believe that a series of local demands by individual municipalities or groups of municipalities is no substitute for the reasoned provisions of the National Capital Plan.

The Committee is of the opinion that the over-all plan of the national capital should be submitted to both the Ontario Minister of Planning and Development and the Quebec Minister of Municipal Affairs. This, if agreement is possible, should be regarded as the background against which all individual cases should be dealt with as they arise. At the same time, we think that an appropriate representative of the Government of Canada should consult with the above provincial authorities in view of determining ways and means of implementing the Plan, and we feel that this could be achieved in such a way that it would be fair to all concerned.[10]

Regarding the problem of preserving the Greenbelt, the Committee stated:

> Evidence given to the Committee warrants our hope that some workable arrangement could be made with the municipalities concerned. The Federal District Commission is willing to try to work out a compromise. We urge that an attempt be made to solve the differences. However, should these negotiations fail, resort might be had to the Minister of Planning and Development for Ontario. It might be possible to invoke the provisions of the *Planning Act* of Ontario, either as drawn or under suitable amendments, to provide for the special circumstances arising in the National Capital area and arising particularly out of the recommendations contained in the National Capital Plan of 1950. We would suggest that this avenue be explored before an expropriation program proceeds.[11]

This plea for co-operation from the provincial and municipal governments was apparently unsuccessful, and if any further time had been lost in trying to secure co-operation the battle to preserve the Greenbelt would have been lost. In 1958, therefore, the federal government decided to proceed with a program for the Federal District Commission to purchase or appropriate all the land necessary to preserve the Greenbelt. It also implemented two other recommendations of the 1956 report. A new *National Capital Act* was passed changing the name of the Federal District Commission to National Capital Commission, and the National Capital District was officially renamed the National Capital Region and doubled in size (from 900 square miles to 1,800 square miles, most of the increase being on the Ottawa side of the river). The Region now took in all or part of 66 municipalities in Quebec and Ontario. This of course further complicated the problem of divided jurisdiction.

At the same time, the new Act removed the mayors of Ottawa and Hull from the Commission. Instead it specified that, of the twenty commissioners, the Governor-in-Council must appoint one from each of the provinces and a minimum of two local residents from Ottawa, one from Hull, and two others—from the other municipalities on each side of the Ottawa river. Since 1958, local representation on the Commission has customarily consisted of four residents of Ottawa, two others from the Ottawa side of the river, one from Hull and one from the Hull side of the river. Also, the National Capital Committee was discontinued and the Commission was given the direct power "to prepare plans for and assist in the development, conservation and improvement of the National Capital Region in order that the nature and character of the seat of the Government of Canada may be in accordance with its national significance."

The financial resources of the Commission were greatly enlarged. From now on the federal government would attempt to solve with money the problem of divided jurisdiction—through massive purchase and expropriation of property, by paying the full cost of many projects vital to the success of the Plan, by sharing a large proportion of the cost of many others, and by providing free technical help and advice on planning and other matters to the municipalities in the Region.

IV. Recent Progress and Future Difficulties

Since the federal government's decision in 1958 to provide a massive increase in its financial support for the National Capital Plan, great progress has been made in fulfilling the main provisions of the Plan. The annual report of the National Capital Commission for 1965-66 shows that between April 1, 1947, and March 31, 1966, it spent a total of $156 million for development and improvement within the National Capital Region (see chart). Of this total it spent $87.8 million on property acquisitions, including $34.4 million for the Greenbelt, $16.7 million for LeBreton Flats, $5.5 million for Gatineau Park, $4.9 million for Sussex Drive, $4.3 million for the Queensway, and $4.3 million for the Ottawa River Parkway. On other projects of its own it spent $19.8 million, of which $7.1 million was for Gatineau Park, $4.6 million for the Ottawa River Parkway, and $4.9 million for other parks and parkway projects. It also spent $20.2 million on the relocation of the railway facilities and $1.4 million on the construction of the Mackenzie King bridge.

On projects requiring the sharing of expenditures with Ottawa or other

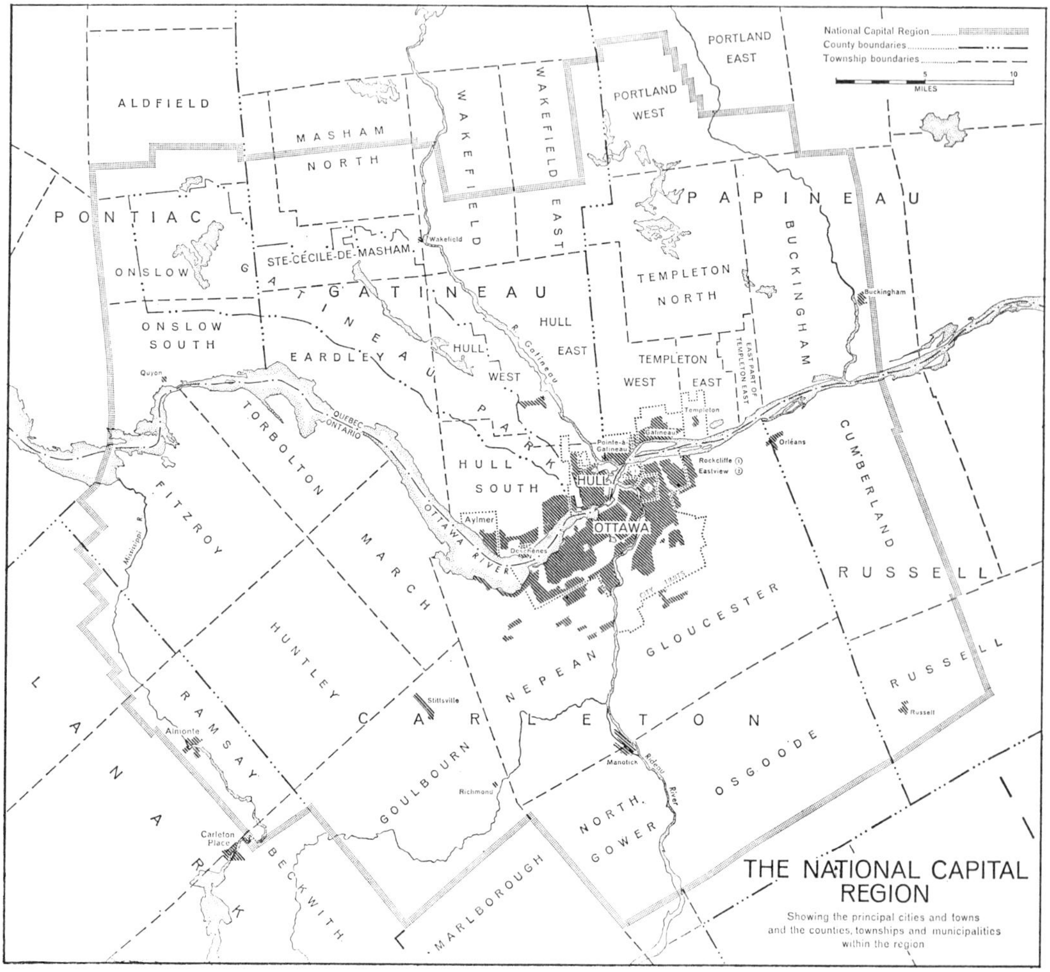

THE NATIONAL CAPITAL REGION

Showing the principal cities and towns and the counties, townships and municipalities within the region

NATIONAL CAPITAL COMMISSION

EXPENDITURES FOR DEVELOPMENT AND IMPROVEMENT
WITHIN THE NATIONAL CAPITAL REGION
APRIL 1, 1947 TO MARCH 31, 1966

Fiscal Year	Expenditure
1947-48	370,638
48-49	936,833
49-50	1,146,200
50-51	1,634,074
51-52	1,832,964
52-53	1,911,536
53-54	2,678,623
54-55	5,508,955
55-56	4,612,787
56-57	3,422,380
57-58	4,533,857
58-59	7,740,285
59-60	13,758,703
60-61	11,862,201
61-62	11,484,739
62-63	16,933,984
63-64	21,852,600
64-65	18,582,674
65-	25,297,115

FISCAL YEARS

Source:
National Capital Commission, *Sixty-Sixth Annual Report, 1965-1966*, Part Two.
(Reproduced by permission of the National Capital Commission)

local municipalities and in some cases also with the provincial governments, the Commission spent $13.4 million or about 9% of its total expenditures. This amount included grants of $2.8 million to Ottawa for the construction of sewers and water mains in advance of need, $5 million to Ottawa for the construction of a sewer to the new sewage disposal plant at Green Creek, $1.2 million for the reconstruction of Riverside Drive, $1 million for the construction of the Bytown bridges and improvements to Sussex Drive, $1.7 million for construction and approaches of other bridges, $160,000 to Nepean Township for a new sewer and sewage disposal plant, and $312,000 for research, studies and other types of assistance.

There is little doubt that contributions to local governments for research and other technical assistance was money well spent, for it has stimulated the local municipalities and the two provinces to take some of the action necessary to carry out their share of the Plan. The staff of the Commission, which now numbers about 750, including professional engineers, architects and planners, have also been generous in their provision of technical assistance and advice. Thus, the Commission has tried to follow the recommendation of the Committee of 1956 that the municipalities and the provinces should be brought more closely into the arrangements for completing the Plan.

Examples illustrative of the Commission's assistance, advice and co-operation are given in its annual report for 1964-65. On the Ottawa side of the river, it was represented on the Ottawa Planning Area Board and on the City and County technical advisory committees of the Board. In Ottawa it was represented on the Building Appearance Committee and the Joint Staff Committee for the Urban Renewal Study. Statistical data were provided to Eastview for official studies, and representatives of the Commission attended preliminary discussions for the preparation of an urban renewal study for Eastview. In Gloucester, representatives of the Commission, acting as advisers to the Township Planning Board, assisted in the preparation of a proposed Official Plan for the northwestern part of the Township that lies within the Greenbelt. Representatives of the Commission discussed with the Council and Planning Board of Cumberland Township the need for a planning program, and assistance was given in the preparation of a proposed Official Plan for part of the Township near Orleans, which is likely to undergo urban development. For the Township of March, the Commission agreed to prepare a plan of land use as a guide for the revision of the existing zoning by-law. Officials of the Commission had discussions with the Planning Board of the Village of Stittsville on the need for an Official Plan for the community, and the Commission agreed to assist in its preparation. On the north side of the river, the Commission was represented on the General Planning Committee for the City of Hull and its Environs, and on its sub-committees. The Commission was also represented on the planning committee engaged in the preparation of a Master Plan for the Towns of Gatineau and Pointe Gatineau and their adjacent six municipalities. The

Commission prepared a brief outlining the projected growth in that area and also made a financial grant to assist in the work.

The Commission has tried also to bring the local municipalities and the provinces more directly into the planning process for revising the National Capital Plan. A notable achievement in this respect was the Ottawa-Hull Area Transportation Study of 1965. Although it was prepared by two private joint-venture firms for the City of Ottawa, these firms were assisted by a technical co-ordinating committee chaired by the City's Director of Planning and Works, but with representation from — besides Ottawa and its transit commission and parking authority — Hull, Eastview, Ontario, Quebec, the National Capital Commission, the Ottawa Suburban Roads Commission, the County of Carleton, and the Canadian National and Canadian Pacific Railways. The Study made proposals for a major thoroughfare pattern for Ottawa-Hull and the rest of the National Capital Region over the next twenty years. It is significant that all of the municipalities affected by the proposals have adopted them in principle.

There is no doubt that the federal government has managed to overcome many of the difficulties of divided jurisdiction through its program of massive land acquisition and co-operation with and assistance to the provincial and local governments. By 1966, the major projects contained in the Greber Plan of 1950 had been successfully completed or were well on the way to completion. The Greenbelt had been saved, the Queensway had been built, the railways were being relocated, opening the way for many improvements in the downtown area of Ottawa, the parkway system and the development of Gatineau Park were almost complete, and many of the key bridges had been built.

This has not been accomplished, however, without considerable dissatisfaction and complaint on all sides — from the local municipalities, from groups of local citizens, and from the federal government. The removal in 1958 of the representatives named by the Cities of Ottawa and Hull to the Federal District Commission meant that the local municipalities in the area had no direct representation on the National Capital Commission. Formerly they had also had representation on the National Capital Planning Committee, but under the new arrangement they are not represented at the federal level for purposes of either implementing or revising the National Capital Plan. Not surprisingly, there were some rather bitter comments from the local municipalities regarding this change, especially since the National Capital Commission was still represented on the Ottawa Area Planning Board. Similarly, the expropriation program led to a good deal of opposition, especially in the Greenbelt. The *Expropriation Act* had not been revised, as recommended by the 1956 Committee, to ensure that procedures were scrupulously fair, and complaints were made that the National Capital Commission was acting arbitrarily and without regard to the rights of local citizens. In fact, one of the land owners in the Greenbelt even brought an important test case before the Exchequer Court questioning the constitutional right of the federal government to expropriate land for the purpose of preserving a Greenbelt, on the ground that this interfered with provincial powers over property, civil rights and, in particular, zoning. This case was appealed to the Supreme Court of Canada, and was recently decided in favour of the federal government because expropriation for the purpose of implementing the National Capital Plan comes under its general power to make laws for the "peace, order and good government of Canada."[12]

On the other hand, the federal government is now pouring millions of dollars into the centre of the Region in the form of development projects, joint sharing of development, and grants in lieu of taxation to the Cities of Ottawa and Hull; yet it has no direct control over or representation on any of the local councils which would give it a chance to help to determine how this money will be spent. As already noted, the National Capital Commission had spent $156 million in the Region by April of 1966. Also, by 1964 the municipalities in the Region were receiving about $6.6 million annually from federal grants in lieu of taxation. The largest recipients were Ottawa ($5.7 million), Hull and its school commission ($500,000), Gloucester ($90,000) and Nepean ($80,-000).[13] Ottawa got by far the largest grant in Canada, the next largest being Halifax ($1.7 million), Toronto ($1.6 million), North York ($1.6 million) and Montreal ($1.4 million). In 1966 Ottawa will receive for its current budget $8.4 million in federal grants, about 23% of its own City budget (but only about 9% of the City's current gross expenditure requirements, including schools, compared with 19% from provincial grants, 42% from taxes, and 30% from other sources). In addition, between 1966 and 1970 the City expects to receive $15 million in federal grants toward its capital budget.[14] Impressed by these contributions to the City, Hon. George McIlraith, President of the Privy Council and M.P. for an Ottawa constituency, proposed in 1964 that the federal government should be represented on Ottawa's City Council. Paul Tardif, M.P. for Russell and for many years a member of Ottawa's Council, endorsed this suggestion. The reaction of the Council was to reject the idea vigorously and to demand City representation on the National Capital Commission instead.[15]

That the difficulties of divided jurisdiction have by no means been overcome may be illustrated by three examples. The parliamentary Committee of 1944 had stressed that the pollution of the Ottawa river was already serious, and the Committee of 1956 had placed this as the number one priority on its list of problems to be solved. Yet in 1966, over twenty years later, some ten million gallons of raw sanitary sewage are dumped into the Ottawa river in the capital area every day.[16] The municipalities on the Quebec side are the worst offenders, since most of them have no sewage treatment whatsoever. In addition, tons of industrial wastes are discharged into the river daily from the pulp and paper mills of the E. B. Eddy Company and the Canadian International Paper Company. Since Hull has had to give priority to a water filtration plant, it has no immediate plans for sewage treatment. Yet it dumps six million or more gallons of raw sewage daily. But even on the Ontario side the first sewage disposal plant was not installed until 1962. With help from the National Capital Commission, Nepean installed a treatment plant in 1962, and Ottawa did likewise in 1963. However, the Nepean plant is now overloaded and periodically discharges an overflow of raw sewage into the river, and the City's plant does not remove all of the pollutants from the sewage. About 35% of solid matter and 65% of biochemical pollutants remain in the estimated 36 million gallons of sewage treated daily.

The second example is a minor but typical one arising out of the relocation of Ottawa's Union Station to the east side of the city, beyond Hurdman's Bridge. When the new station opened in August, 1966, no provision had been made for bus service. The Ottawa Transportation Commission and Mayor Reid took the view that, since the new bus service would mean a heavy loss for the O. T. C. and since the station had been moved at the insistence of the National Capital Commission, "that makes it their responsibility to make sure there is public transportation to the new site."[17] In this case, divided jurisdiction had left visitors and residents with no bus service closer than the three blocks to the Union Station, and this distance was across a rough construction site.

The third example, a more serious one, is the fulfilment of a freeway and street plan proposed in the Ottawa-Hull Area Transportation Study. This plan, which included the technical co-operation of all three governments, was prepared by private firms under a contract with the City of Ottawa. It was not produced by the National Capital Commission as part of the National Capital Plan. Yet it is revolutionary in its proposals for the construction of a new freeway system and the reconstruction of a good deal of downtown Ottawa, calling for fundamental revisions of municipal Master Plans and of the National Capital Plan. The fragmentation of municipal responsibility in the area is such that, although the main municipalities concerned approved the plan in broad principle, what assurance is there that they will adhere to the plan? "In terms of transportation needs," as the Study notes, "the Study Area (which included 13 municipalities in Ontario and 15 in Quebec) function as an entity. . . . Should one body wish to alter the detail of the plan in any way, all the other participants must be given the opportunity of assessing the consequences, both in terms of their own repsonsibilities and in terms of effectuating the total plan for the benefit of the entire Study Area."[18] Moreover, the cost will be tremendous, requiring $435 million over the next twenty years. Of this, $103 million will be needed in Quebec and $332 million in Ontario, with expenditures in Ottawa alone accounting for $226 million, or over half the total. The second question, then, is: who is going to pay for this redevelopment? Since the federal government did not produce the plan, the temptation for it to disclaim financial responsibility will be great.

Despite the impressiveness of the national capital projects completed to date, and despite considerable private rebuilding of Ottawa's business core in recent years, parts of the centres of Ottawa and Hull still remain a disgrace to the nation. "To apply cosmetics to the decayed body of a disorganized city," as Wilfred Eggleston notes (p. 280), "will not achieve the purpose for which the (National Capital) Commission exists." Nor has the existing planning machinery prevented a great deal of uncontrolled and undesirable urban sprawl, which still continues beyond the boundaries of Ottawa and Hull. Unfortunately, the plain facts are that, constitutionally, the National Capital Commission cannot control development or redevelopment on land that it does not own; that the planning, land use and zoning controls by the local municipalities in the area are in many ways still unsatisfactory; and that the Provinces of Ontario and Quebec and the Cities of Ottawa and Hull are not prepared to pour the amount of money into urban and road redevelopment that would be necessary to create a capital worthy of Canada's growing stature as a nation.

It is now more than fifteen years since the National Capital Plan was published; yet only bits and pieces of it are fully in effect in the form of legally enforceable official Plans. It is true that Ottawa now has a comprehensive zoning by-law, approved in 1965, and that the Ottawa Planning Area Board now has a Master Plan for procedures, roads, parks and land use, approved in 1963. But the parks and land use sections apply only within the boundaries of Ottawa. The other municipalities in the Region either have no plan, bits and pieces of a plan, or a general plan which may or may not be officially approved by or conform with the National Capital Plan.

The accompanying chart, prepared by the Ontario Department of Municipal Affairs, reveals that at the end of 1964—fourteen years after the approval of the National Capital Plan—of the twenty-one Ontario municipalities in the National Capital Region, Ottawa was the only one that had a Master Plan officially approved by the Ontario Government. Although Ottawa also had a complete zoning by-law, it had only partial subdivision control. The four others in the Ottawa urban area (Rockcliffe, Eastview, Gloucester and Nepean) had complete zoning by-laws but only partial Official Plans, and only Gloucester and Nepean had complete subdivision control. The other three townships that come under the Ottawa Planning Area Board (Fitzroy, March and Torbolton) had neither Official Plans nor complete zoning by-laws. Of the thirteen municipalities not under the Ottawa Planning Area Board, none had Official Plans and only the Village of Richmond and Stittsville had complete zoning by-laws.

The situation is much the same on the Quebec side of the river. With help from Central Mortgage and Housing Corporation, Hull had a general plan for urban renewal prepared in 1962. And with help from the federal and provincial governments, Hull plus the four other municipalities west of the Gatineau river co-operated to have a Master Plan produced in 1964. But under Quebec law no provision exists for provin-

A SUMMARY OF PLANNING STATISTICS FOR THE NATIONAL CAPITAL REGION

(including 21 Municipalities in the Counties of Carleton and Prescott-Russell)

Municipality	Planning Area		Zoning By-law		Committee of Adjustment	Subdivision Control	
	Planning Board	Official Plan	Complete	Partial		Complete	Partial
Town of Rockland	—	—	—	—	—	X	
Village of Casselman	—	—	—	—	—	—	—
Twp. of Cumberland	S.I.	—		X	—	X	
Twp. of Clarence	—	—	—	—	—	—	—
Twp. of Cambridge	—	—	—	—	—	—	—
Twp. of Russell	—	—	—	—	—	—	—
Village of Richmond	—	—	X		—	—	—
Village of Rockcliffe Park	J.	partial	X		—		X
Village of Stittsville	S.I.	—	X		X	X	
Twp. of Fitzroy	J.	—		X	—	—	—
Twp. of Gloucester	(J)Sub.	partial	X		X	X	
Twp. of Goulburn	—	—	X		—	X	
Twp. of N. Gower	S.I.	—	X		—	X	
Twp. of Huntley	—	—	—	—	—	—	—
Twp. of March	J.	—	X		—	X	
Twp. of Marlborough	—	—	X		—	—	—
Twp. of Nepean	J.	partial	X		—	X	
Twp. of Osgoode	S.I.	—	X		—	X	
Twp. of Torbolton	J.	—	X		—	X	
City of Ottawa	J.	X	X		—		X
City of Eastview	(J)Sub.	partial	X		X	—	—

J. — Joint Ottawa Planning Area Board
S.I. — Single, independent Planning Board
Sub. — Subsidiary Planning Board

Source: *What's New in Planning* (Bulletin of the National Capital Region Branch, Community Planning Association of Canada), No. 7 (May, 1965), p. 19.

cial approval of a town, city or regional plan, so these plans have no official status. The Master Plan has not even been approved by the cooperating municipalities. It is regarded as nothing more than a guide. None of these municipalities has adequate zoning by-laws. A Master Plan study is now being prepared, with help from the federal and provincial governments, for the eight municipalities east of the Gatineau river, but when it is completed it similarly will have no official status.

The successful completion of the major projects contained in the 1950 Plan means that planning in the area is now entering a new phase of redeveloping the urban cores of Ottawa and Hull — a process which will touch the lives of businesses and citizens of Ottawa and Hull much more closely and is likely to lead to renewed friction. Moreover, the unexpectedly rapid expansion of population in the metropolitan area since the war has made the Plan of 1950 in many ways out of date. Since this rapid expansion is likely to continue indefinitely into the future, the Plan must be continuously revised. This raises the difficulty — in addition to the old problem of how to carry out the Plan — of how to revise it so that it will be acceptable to the local authorities and citizens. They have no direct representation on the National Capital Commission, the federal body now charged with revising the Plan.

Recent urban growth in the area has been so great that it will require a change of Greber's original concept of an urban centre surrounded by a Greenbelt with only small satellite towns beyond it. The Greber Plan had projected that the urban population of the national capital area would reach 500,000 by 1980, but this population figure was reached in 1963. The growth has been so marked that between 1956 and 1961 Ottawa-Hull was the fastest growing metropolitan area in eastern Canada and third in Canada, exceeding even Toronto. The most recent prediction is that the National Capital Region will have a population of over 800,000 by 1980, and possibly a million by the year 2000. It will soon contain as big a population as any of the Atlantic provinces.

Studies of the future urban growth pattern made by the technical co-ordinating committee for the Ottawa-Hull Area Transportation Study indicate that this growth will take place in three specific areas to the west, south and east of the Greenbelt on the south side of Ottawa, and in two large areas north of Ottawa on the west and east sides of the Gatineau river. By the year 2000 Ottawa's population may reach 540,000 and the present Aylmer-Hull urban area will be about 160,000. The populations of the four new satellite cities will also be large. Indeed, the one to the west of the Greenbelt may be larger than Aylmer-Hull, with an estimated 180,000, while the ones east of Hull and south of the Greenbelt are likely to have about 120,000 each. The percentage distribution of the population is likely to be about as follows: 38% within the Greenbelt, 40% beyond the Greenbelt on the Ontario side of the river, and 22% on the Quebec side.[19] Since the residents of the whole metropolitan area will depend for their employment mainly upon the federal government, a large proportion of them will travel to work in the urban core on high-speed traffic arteries. This situation will be considerably different from Greber's vision of small self-contained satellite towns far beyond the Greenbelt.

The projected speed and pattern of this urban development will soon require, for its effective control, a reorganization of local governments in the Region more fundamental than that which took place in 1950 through Ottawa's multiplication of its area by five times in an attempt to control urban development within the proposed Greenbelt. The present existence of the Greenbelt, and the expectation that the new urban areas in the south will be established along widely separated traffic arteries and that urban Hull will grow rapidly and split into two big urban areas separated by the Gatineau river, means that simple annexation and integration of governmental services will no longer be the answer. It is clear, as it was before 1950, that a comprehensive plan for a metropolitan area requires a governmental authority over the area which has control over all the services of local government that have relevance to planning and development. Except for Ottawa, the existing local governments cannot provide the finances, the experts or the control necessary to make them viable units of a national capital plan or even of a desirable metropolitan plan.

For this reason, the idea of a basic reorganization of the local governments on the Ontario side of the Ottawa river has been gaining ground. The local municipalities no doubt have been influenced in this respect by the successful creation of second-tier metropolitan authorities in Toronto and Winnipeg, which govern the whole metropolitan area for certain purposes but have not destroyed the existing municipalities in the area. In 1964, the Government of Ontario, which has been initiating studies of urban regions upon local request, appointed Murray Jones to study the problems of local government in the Ottawa region over an area somewhat smaller than the Ontario side of the National Capital Region (sixteen versus twenty-one municipalities). One wonders why the boundaries of the study area and Region could not have been made to correspond. Mr. Jones had formerly been Director of Planning for the Toronto metropolitan authority and was now a consultant on municipal problems. Most of the municipalities in the study area and a number of individuals presented briefs at his hearings, and most of them agreed that a reorganization of local government was necessary. Many thought that some new form of metropolitan government was the answer, but there was not much agreement on what shape this new structure of government should take.

One of the main findings of the Jones Commission Report, published in 1965, was that the municipalities in the study area show a great variation in their standard of services and in their ability to raise revenue for these services. In order to provide a more uniform standard of services and revenues and to control future urban development, he therefore recommended the abolition of all existing municipalities, boards, and commissions, except school and hospital boards, and the creation instead of a centralized regional council which would control beneath it a system of urban and rural nine-member district councils to administer purely local affairs. The urban districts would each have about 30,000 population. There would also be several development districts on the urban fringe which would later become urban districts. The boundaries of the districts would not correspond with existing municipalities. Although the Jones proposal may have been ideally desirable from the point of view of efficient administration, it would have been too great a break with the past, meaning as it did the abolition of the existing local authorities. Their reaction was one of almost universal opposition. Eastview feared that its French-speaking majority would be swallowed by the plan. And since the proposal would have required carving up Ottawa into districts, Ottawa's Council also rejected the scheme. Instead it supported a counter-proposal which it had presented to the Commission: that the City should annex Rockcliffe Park, Eastview and the parts of Nepean and Gloucester that lay within the inner boundary of the Greenbelt, and that Carleton County should be strengthened, perhaps by being incorporated as a city. Ottawa and the County would have over them either a general planning body or a weak metropolitan authority which might control a few metropolitan-wide services.

Constitutionally, the reorganization of local government in the Ottawa metropolitan area requires action by the Government of Ontario. Since it is unlikely to take action without the agreement either of the City of Ottawa or of most of the other municipalities in the area, the Jones proposal is not likely to be adopted. Since no other proposal has been made which appears to be both viable and acceptable, a reorganization is not likely to take place for some years.

A basic flaw in the Jones investigation, because of the constitutional and political limitation upon its terms of reference, was its failure to include the Hull metropolitan area. Even if reorganization should occur on the Ottawa side, the problems of a unified governing authority for the Hull side and for the whole Ottawa-Hull area still would not be solved. On the Hull side, the same need for reorganization exists. The present and potential Hull urban area is split up among four municipalities west of the Gatineau river (Hull, Lucerne, Deschênes and Aylmer), and at least four east of it (Gatineau Point, Templeton-West, Gatineau and Templeton). Among these municipalities the usual problems of lack of co-operation arise. Lucerne, for example, fears that part of it will be swallowed by Hull, or that Hull will gobble up the whole potentially urban area west of the river. To avoid too intimate association with Hull, Lucerne recently had its name changed from Hull South to its present name, and has made overtures to Aylmer and Deschênes for an amalgamation with them as a sort of counter-balance against Hull.[20] But no move has been made yet by either the local governments in the Hull area or the Quebec Government to create any sort of metropolitan authority.

The conclusion seems to be inescapable that a fundamental reorganization of the municipalities on both sides of the river that are slated for future development will soon be desirable. Yet this is not likely to be achieved effectively by the independent action of two different provincial governments and two different sets of municipalities on each side of the river. It could be achieved by the federal government if it had undisputed jurisdiction over the National Capital Region. The federal government could achieve this without even abolishing the existing municipalities, by creating a superior governing authority for the whole Region. From the point of view of effectively developing and governing the national capital of the future, therefore, the time appears to be more opportune than in any period since Confederation to reconsider the proposal for a federal territory.

V. The Bilingual-Bicultural Issue

Until recent years the National Capital was thought of mainly in terms of physical development—as an efficient place for members of Parliament and civil servants to work and live, and as an impressive place worthy of a capital city for Canadians and foreigners, such as heads of national organizations, journalists, and representatives of foreign governments, to visit, to conduct their business and to reside. Not much attention was paid to the development of the National Capital as a symbol of the successful uniting of Canada's two main ethnic groups into a single nation. Ottawa remained predominantly an Anglo-Saxon city in an English-speaking province.

From this point of view, Montreal might have been a better choice as the federal capital. It is interesting to recall that for a short period before Confederation, from 1844 to 1849, Montreal was the capital of United Canada. Though Montreal was in Canada East, it had a slight English-speaking majority at this time. The later growth of the federal civil service would have maintained a much larger English-speaking minority. This, combined with the predominance of the English-speaking majority in Parliament, might have turned Montreal into a genuinely bilingual-bicultural capital. Its much greater size would have made it a more cosmopolitan centre for the mingling of the two cultures. Moreover, the existence of the National Capital within the territory of Quebec would have made it much more difficult for the "separatists" to think of Quebec's withdrawal from the federation.

It is difficult, however, to predict the extent to which the capital's location in Montreal would have cemented English-French relations. Would it instead have exacerbated them? Since complaints have been made that Montreal is even now dominated in its business world by the English-speaking minority, would not the presence of Parliament and the growth of the federal civil service there merely have increased the power and predominance of this minority? Also, one thinks of the close and delicate relations that would have been created between the federal government and the governments of Quebec and Montreal by the existence of the federal Parliament and other buildings within the boundaries of Montreal. Yet the prospects of turning Montreal Island into a federal territory would have been slim, and in any case the urban population would have overflowed the boundaries of the territory as it has done in the District of Columbia.

At any rate, because of the riot in Montreal aroused by the *Rebellion Losses Bill*, the burning of the Parliament Buildings and the physical attack on Lord Elgin in the streets, the capital was moved from Montreal in 1849. From then until the choice of Ottawa in 1857, the capital oscillated dizzily every four years between Toronto and Quebec, but Montreal was never considered seriously again. During this period, because of the intense rivalry between Upper and Lower Canada over the location of the capital, Ottawa was chosen as the least of evils. "Ottawa is in fact, neither in Upper nor Lower Canada," Sir Edmund Head noted in a confidential memorandum to the Queen in 1857. "Literally it is in the former; but a bridge alone divides it from the latter. Consequently its selection would fulfill the letter of any pledge given or supposed to be given, to Upper Canada at the time of the union."[21]

Although the rivalry between Upper and Lower Canada had been so intense that they were willing to put up with the inconveniences of shifting the capital back and forth, and although this rivalry continued even after the Queen's choice of Ottawa in 1857, no one before or at the time of Confederation seems to have thought of or proposed the creation of a capital which would be located in *both* Upper and Lower Canada. Yet this could have been done before Confederation (since Upper and Lower Canada were then united) by turning Ottawa and Hull into a single city, or after Confederation by carving out the area around Ottawa and Hull as a federal territory. Ottawa already had a French-speaking minority and the addition of Hull would have added strength to this minority. Also it would have partly satisfied Lower Canada's desire to have the capital located in French-speaking territory. Downtown Hull is close to Parliament Hill; the existence of the Union bridge and the early construction of another bridge would have made quite possible the extension of federal buildings to that side of the river.

As it turned out, however, the relevance of Hull to the national capital was ignored for sixty years after Confederation. Since Hull had been cut off more definitely from Ottawa by Confederation and was from then on governed by a different legislature in a new province, this is perhaps not surprising. In any case, it was not officially included in the federal government's concept of the National Capital until the creation of the Federal District Commission in 1927, when Hull was specifically named as part of the capital district to be improved. Even then, little was done to recognize Hull as part of the National Capital. It is true that the Champlain bridge was completed, the federal driveway was extended to the Quebec side, and a beginning was made at acquiring the land north of Hull necessary to form Gatineau Park, which is now an important recreation area for Ottawa. But it was not until after the Second World

War that the first important federal building, the Printing Bureau, was constructed in Hull.

Even the Master Plan of 1950 did not envision Hull as an integral part of the National Capital. Although proposals were made for beautifying Hull, no large-scale migration of administrative buildings or national cultural or research centres, such as the National Library, Museum, Gallery, Performing Arts Centre, Research Council, or Central Experimental Farm, was projected. Among other things, such a migration would have reduced Hull's dependence for employment upon the E. B. Eddy Company and would probably have made possible the removal of its manufacturing plant, which mars the north shore directly across from Parliament Hill, flaunts a large neon sign advertising its toilet tissues, and periodically blankets downtown Ottawa in sulphurous fumes.

In the process of fulfilling the Master Plan the federal government tended to under-emphasize Hull. Although the municipality was obviously too poor to pay for its share of the Plan, and lost considerable tax revenue through the expropriation of land for federal parkways, parks and other purposes, it received no special grants as Ottawa did before 1949, and the parliamentary Committee of 1944 had made no recommendation for such grants. True, Hull began to receive small grants in lieu of taxation under the general Act of 1949, but the Act does not include tax grants for federal park or parkway land. It was not until the federal government began its massive financial support of the Plan in 1958 that Hull began to receive substantial aid in the form of joint sharing of the cost of projects such as the new interprovincial bridge. And it was not until after 1962 that much was done about assisting Hull and its surrounding municipalities to draw up detailed plans for the future development of the Hull side of the river. Although the National Capital Plan had included a proposal for a Greenbelt surrounding Hull, this idea was abandoned, and the decision in 1958 to purchase land to preserve the Greenbelt did not include the Hull side. Today only one federal capital building, the Printing Bureau, stands as evidence that Hull is considered a functional part of the federal capital. Hull residents feel strongly about this neglect, and fear that the Government's increasing practice of contracting out its printing will reduce the Printing Bureau to little more than a warehouse for government documents.

Why was Hull's claim that it should be regarded as part of the national capital ignored for so long and then so grudgingly admitted? From an employment point of view it had always been closely tied to the national capital. At the hearings of the parliamentary Committee in 1956, the Mayor of Hull pointed out that by then between 5,000 and 6,000 residents of Hull were working in the federal civil service, and that half of the population depended upon the presence of the federal government for their employment. "If the Ottawa river had not stood there as an effective barrier," suggests Eggleston (p. 211), "had the bridge connections between the cities of Ottawa and Hull been more numerous and satisfactory, had the political relations between Quebec City and federal Ottawa been at times more cordial . . . I suspect that governmental Ottawa would have overflowed Parliament Hill to the north (as well as to the south-west and east)." His first reason may have been true of the first sixty years, but it has not been sufficient since. It is more likely that his second reason has been the predominant one, especially in this century. One can argue that if the federal government had been more forthright in its recognition of the Hull side of the river as part of the national capital by placing federal buildings there, and more generous in its financial support and in the representation of the Hull side on successive federal capital commissions, co-operation from the Hull-side municipalities and from the Government of Quebec would have been much better.

From Quebec's point of view, the difficulty has always been that the National Capital is in a sense an alien capital in alien territory. The culture and language of Ottawa are predominantly Anglo-Saxon and English-speaking, and it is governed under a different system of judicial and provincial law. French-speaking Canadians who come to live in Ottawa as members of Parliament or as federal civil servants find that they are cut off from their cultural roots and are forced to speak, read and write English most of the time. They dislike living in Hull because it is only a run-down lumber town and a poor cultural home for educated French Canadians. On the other hand, if they live in Ottawa, they become part of an alien minority who lack equal linguistic and educational rights under Ontario law. And in the city government there has always been a strong majority of English-speaking Canadians. As a result, they tend to congregate in a separate French-speaking section of the city known as Lower Town, or migrate to Eastview.

These circumstances no doubt explain Eastview's continuing existence as a separate municipality even though it is now an island within the boundaries of Ottawa. The annexations of 1950 tended to overwhelm the French-speaking minority in Ottawa, and Eastview became a kind of French-speaking bastion through its majority control of that municipality's Council and other local institutions. Eastview, for example, is one of the few municipalities in Ontario which conduts its council business in both languages and which has bilingual by-laws, tax bills and traffic signs, and a bilingual public high school where several subjects are taught in French. French is the mother tongue of about half the teachers and over two-thirds of the students.

Ottawa has no bilingual public elementary or secondary schools. In 1965 the Public School Board refused the request of a group of French-speaking parents for a bilingual elementary school on the grounds that the children were too scattered and the classes would be too small. Nor are there any purely French-speaking separate schools in Ottawa or Eastview. Historically, under Ontario's educational system French-speaking children, like the children of immigrants, were expected to learn English as soon as possible. The curriculum required certain subjects, such as science and mathematics, to be taught in English, with progressively more English expected in the upper grades. In recent years a concession to this policy, in areas where the parents are predominantly French-speaking, has been to allow the first three grades to be taught almost entirely in French and several subjects to continue in French even into high school. About half of the separate schools in Ottawa and most in Eastview are bilingual schools of this kind.

Moreover, in the separate school system the standard of facilities and instruction is lower than that of the public schools, and separate school supporters must pay higher taxes. There are several reasons for these discrepancies. First, the number of school children in relation to the number of taxpayers is greater. Also, under Ontario law a corporation may split its school tax and pay the separate school tax in the proportion in which its shareholders are Roman Catholic, but most corporations elect to pay the lower public school tax. Similarly, a Roman Catholic may elect to pay the public school tax, and many do, particularly businessmen who wish to keep down competitive costs. On the other hand, non-Catholics (including non-Catholic fathers in a mixed marriage) must pay the public school tax even if they send their children to separate school. Although provincial grants have increased markedly in recent years, they do not make up for these costs and tax deficiencies. For 1966 the separate school tax rate is still about 12% higher than the public school rate.

Local tax and provincial support for separate schools does not go beyond grade 10. While a few Roman Catholic bilingual high schools exist, they are costly to the parents and provide a much lower standard of instruction than the public high schools. Similarly, the bilingual University of Ottawa was not provided with adequate financial support by the provincial government until it was reorganized as a non-sectarian university in 1965.

As a result of these educational difficulties and of the overwhelming predominance of the English language in business, in the federal and local public services, and in everyday living, French Canadians in Ottawa are threatened with the gradual loss of their language and culture. The 1961 statistics for the Ottawa census metropolitan area (which includes the Hull side) reveal that this loss has already taken place to some extent. I have assembled the relevant figures on the population's ethnic group, mother tongue, official language and religion in Tables I-IIA. These tables show that, of Ottawa's total population of 268,000 in 1961, nearly 70,000, or about one-quarter, gave their ethnic origin as French. On the other hand, only 57,000, about one-fifth, gave their mother tongue as French, indicating some loss of the French language from one generation to the next. The whole metropolitan area on the south side, except for Eastview, shows a similar loss. Hull, on the other hand, actually shows a slight gain, indicating that some children of English-speaking parents have adopted French as their mother tongue. Out of Hull's population of 57,000 in 1961, only 5,500, or under 10%, did not give their mother tongue as French. Because of the existence of some English-speaking communities in the Hull metropolitan area, however, this area as a whole shows no gain for the French language. Exactly the same proportion, 85%, gave French as their ethnic group and mother tongue.

The figures on official language show a similar predominance of English and French, respectively, on the south and north sides of the river, and also indicate the extent to which the metropolitan area is bilingual. In the Ottawa area south of the river, whereas nearly 70% of the total population stated that of the two official languages they could speak English only, a mere 15,000, or under 5%, stated that they could speak French only. The Hull metropolitan area, and in particular the city of Hull, shows almost the reverse situation. Of Hull's total population of 57,000, a mere 3,200 spoke English only, while over 25,000, or nearly half, spoke French only. In the city of Ottawa, only about one quarter spoke both English and French, while in Hull and in its whole metropolitan area, there were more people who spoke both English and French than who spoke French only, indicating the much greater degree of bilingualism north of the river. In Hull almost exactly half of the population is bilingual. The reason, of course, is the predominant influence of English-speaking Ottawa. Much of the French-speaking population has been required to learn English in order to work in Ottawa, whereas in Ottawa the English have not had to learn French.

The comparative figures on religion show that, as might be expected, the number of people in the Hull metropolitan area who give their

TABLE I
ETHNIC GROUP, MOTHER TONGUE, OFFICIAL LANGUAGE AND RELIGION OF POPULATION IN CENSUS METROPOLITAN AREA OF OTTAWA, 1961
(Population in thousands)

	Ottawa	Rest of Ottawa Area	East-view	Total Ottawa Metro.	Hull	Rest of Hull Area	Total Hull Metro.	Total Whole Area
Ethnic Group								
British Isles	148.1	23.0	6.5	177.6	4.5	7.1	11.6	189.2
French	68.5	9.4	15.6	93.5	50.9	31.0	81.9	175.4
Other	51.6	7.8	2.5	61.9	1.5	1.8	3.3	65.2
Mother Tongue								
English	188.1	29.3	8.4	225.8	4.6	8.8	13.4	239.3
French	56.9	8.2	15.0	80.1	51.4	30.5	81.9	162.0
Other	23.2	2.6	1.2	27.0	.9	.6	1.5	28.5
Official Language								
English only	188.8	29.4	7.8	226.0	3.2	7.1	10.3	236.3
French only	9.0	2.3	3.6	14.9	25.5	16.4	41.9	56.8
English and French	67.0	8.3	12.9	88.2	27.9	16.4	44.3	132.5
Neither	3.4	.2	.3	3.9	.3	.0	.3	4.2
Religion								
Rom. Catholic	127.4	16.7	19.4	163.5	54.8	35.3	90.1	253.6
Other	140.8	23.4	5.2	169.4	2.1	4.6	6.7	176.2
TOTAL, 1961	268.2	40.1	24.6	332.9	56.9	39.9	96.8	429.8
TOTAL, 1956	222.1	24.9	19.3	266.3	50.9	28.3	79.2	345.5

Source: Based on *1961 Census of Canada, Series 1.2: Population* (Canada, Dominion Bureau of Statistics), Tables 39, 70 and 46, in Bulletins 1.2-5, 1.2-9 1.2-6.

TABLE IA
PERCENTAGE DISTRIBUTION OF POPULATION
BY ETHNIC GROUP, MOTHER TONGUE OFFICIAL LANGUAGE, AND
RELIGION IN CENSUS METROPOLITAN AREA OF OTTAWA, 1961*

	Ottawa	Ottawa Metro.	Hull	Hull Metro.	Whole Area
Ethnic Group					
British Isles	55.2	53.3	7.9	11.9	44.0
French	25.5	28.0	89.4	84.6	40.8
Other	19.2	18.5	2.6	3.4	15.1
Total	100.	100.	100.	100.	100.
Mother Tongue					
English	70.1	67.8	8.0	13.8	55.6
French	21.2	24.0	90.3	84.6	37.6
Other	8.6	8.1	1.5	1.5	6.6
Total	100.	100.	100.	100.	100.
Official Language					
English only	70.3	67.8	5.6	10.6	54.9
French only	3.3	4.4	44.8	43.2	13.2
English and French	24.9	26.4	49.0	45.7	30.8
Neither	1.2	1.1	.5	.3	.9
Total	100.	100.	100.	100.	100.
Religion					
Roman Catholic	47.5	49.1	96.3	93.0	59.0
Other	52.4	50.8	3.6	6.9	40.9
Total	100.	100.	100.	100.	100.

Source: Table I.
*Totals do not add to exactly 100.0, due to rounding of figures.

TABLE II
COMPARISON OF FRENCH AS ETHNIC GROUP, MOTHER TONGUE
AND OFFICIAL LANGUAGE, AND WITH ROMAN CATHOLIC RELIGION
IN OTTAWA, HULL, AND CENSUS METROPOLITAN AREA, 1961
(Population in thousands)

	Ottawa	Ottawa Metro.	Hull	Hull Metro.	Whole Area
Ethnic Group	68.5	95.5	50.9	81.9	175.4
Mother Tongue	56.9	80.1	51.4	81.9	162.0
Official Language					
(French only and Both)	76.0	103.1	53.4	86.2	189.3
Roman Catholic	127.4	163.5	54.8	90.1	253.6
Total Population	268.2	332.9	56.9	96.8	429.8

Source: Table I.

TABLE IIA
PERCENTAGE COMPARISON
OF FRENCH AS MOTHER TONGUE, ETHNIC GROUP AND OFFICIAL
LANGUAGE, AND WITH ROMAN CATHOLIC RELIGION
IN OTTAWA, HULL AND CENSUS METROPOLITAN AREA, 1961

	Ottawa	Ottawa Metro.	Hull	Hull Metro.	Whole Area
Ethnic Group	25.5	28.0	89.4	84.6	40.8
Mother Tongue	21.2	24.0	90.3	84.6	37.6
Official Language					
(French and Both)	28.2	30.8	93.8	88.9	44.0
Roman Catholic	47.5	49.1	96.3	93.0	59.0

Source: Table II.

religion as Roman Catholic is about the same as those who give their ethnic group as French. The Ottawa metropolitan area, however, and Ottawa in particular, indicates a surprisingly larger number of people who are Roman Catholic than are of French origin; in Ottawa in 1961 about 128,000 were Catholic, nearly half the total population. This is because of the presence of a considerable number of Irish Catholics in the area.

In view of the disadvantageous situation of the French minority in Ottawa, it is not surprising that the federal Civil Service Commission has found it difficult to attract French-speaking civil servants to Ottawa and to keep them there. Coming from a French-speaking culture in Quebec, they find living in Ottawa an unpleasant shock. As a result, many of them resign and return to their home province. After the reform government of Jean Lesage came into power in Quebec and began hiring well-qualified provincial civil servants, some of the best French-speaking federal civil servants left for Quebec. In recent years, the federal government has been making valiant efforts to meet one of the chief sources of French-Canadian dissatisfaction: the neglect of the French language in the civil service. A massive program has been launched to teach French to English-speaking civil servants, and the federal service is gradually becoming more bilingual. A new spirit is now developing among English-speaking civil servants. Many of them want their children to become fluently bilingual by taking their schooling in French, and also would like to see the position of the French-speaking minority in Ottawa improved.

The city government in Ottawa, however, has remained relatively untouched by these developments. True, the Council recently decided to introduce bilingual traffic signs in one French-speaking ward, and to print its future tax bills in both languages. But it decided that bilingual letterheads and by-laws would be too costly. And when the Royal Commission on Bilingualism and Biculturalism began looking into the use of the French language by the civic administration and the relative proportions of English and French-speaking civil servants, it received a singular lack of co-operation from the City, which at first objected to any inquiry being conducted and later refused to allow a questionnaire on language practices to be distributed.

In April, 1966, the new Minister of Citizenship, Jean Marchand, in a speech to the Ottawa Board of Trade, criticized the general resistance to the use of French in Ottawa. Commenting on the cold reception this speech received from English-speaking Ottawans, Gérard Pelletier, newspaper columnist and new member of Parliament, gaves this graphic description of the French Canadian's reaction to Ottawa:

> The capital city of a supposedly and officially bicultural country is about as bilingual as Kitchener, Ontario, or Edmonton, Alberta . . . It seems **rather ludicrous to me that in order to represent a French-speaking riding** of a French-speaking province in the Parliament of my country, I am forced to live in a unilingual city where I get unilingual summonses when I disobey unilingual traffic signs; where I would have to appear before an English-speaking court if I were to plead not guilty; where there is not

> a single public school in which my teen-age son and daughter could pursue their studies in their own language. All day long, one is reminded by a thousand details that the so-called "national capital" of Canada is an English-speaking city.[22]

The attitude of French Canadians to the capital city, then, is not hard to understand. They—and also many fair-minded English-speaking Canadians—are beginning to ask questions such as these: is it right that the national capital, which is necessarily the home of many French-speaking M.P.'s and civil servants, should provide an atmosphere which to many of them is hostile? Is it right that they should be deprived of their own cultural environment, especially the use of their own language? Is it fair that they should not have equal educational services and linguistic rights? Isn't Ottawa as the National Capital a special case—shouldn't it be a symbol of the two founding peoples and cultures, and shouldn't it become a model of bilingualism and biculturalism for the rest of Canada?

The real problem, however—as with the physical planning and development of the National Capital—is that the federal government has no control over Ottawa. A number of people have recently come to believe, therefore, that the problem can only be solved by cutting the Ottawa area adrift from the overwhelming English-speaking majority and Anglo-Saxon culture and laws of Ontario, and combining it with the Hull area as a separate territory or province. This, then, explains the origin of the recent proposals to this effect made to the Royal Commission on Bilingualism and Biculturalism and elsewhere.

VI. The Case for a Federal Territory

1. History of Proposals for a Federal District

Because of the basic problem created by the location of the capital of a federal state within a city governed by the laws of a single province, proposals for a federally governed capital district have been made ever since Confederation. The proposals made in the early period were at various times given serious consideration until about 1939.

The first of these early proposals was made almost incidentally by John Hamilton Gray in his *Confederation*, published in 1872. His case for a Federal District was so well stated that it is worth quoting at some length (p. 108):

> At the time of the Convention, one mistake occurred: no provision was made for creating a Federal District for the capital, and withdrawing it from the exclusive control of the local legislature of one of the Provinces. That which was designed to be the capital of the Confederation, might fairly rest its claim for support upon the people of the Dominion. Its order, well-being, sanitary arrangements, police regulations, adornments and improvements are essential to the comfort and security, not only of the representatives who attend Parliament, but of all those who are compelled to resort to it as the capital of the country in the discharge of the various duties attendant upon the administration of public affairs. Its reputation should be national, not provincial. It belongs no more to Ontario than it does to New Brunswick, Nova Scotia, Quebec or any of the provinces constituting the Confederation. The expenses incident to its civic control must

necessarily be far greater than would devolve upon it if merely an ordinary municipality. It is no answer to say that increased value in property is sufficient consideration for the increased burden put upon its inhabitants. That does not meet the question. They may not choose to accept the responsibility; and the Dominion Parliament, under Confederation, has no power to legislate upon the matter.

The legislation for the capital in all civil matters is entirely under the control of one province, differing in its laws from the others. The employees and officials of the Dominion Government, residing at Ottawa, numbering almost two thousand men, in every respect competent as voters, and under other circumstances, capable of enjoying and exercising their franchise, are wisely interdicted, by the policy of the Government of the Dominion, from interfering in the local Provincial politics, or taking part in the elections for the Provincial Legislature. Yet they are subject to the taxation imposed upon them by that Legislature; and bluff old Harry the Eighth never unfrocked a bishop with more satisfaction than the Ontario Legislature, for local purposes, taxes a body of men whom they do not pay, and who are debarred from exercising any influence upon the selection of their body.

Gray then goes on to describe favourably the experience of the United States with the District of Columbia, and concludes (p. 110):

Thus we see that the character of a national capital, the security of those who attend it, the elimination of sectional and provincial interests in its government, the preservation of the national public property, the protection of the public interests, and the maintenance of the national reputation in its status, are too important to be left to local councils, however good they may be.

Americans have their capital, Canadians have no capital for their country, They borrow a municipality from Ontario, and whether they come from the Provinces of the Atlantic or the Pacific, whether from Quebec or Manitoba, their representatives in the Dominion Parliament have no power to legislate on any matter touching the property or civil rights of the so-called capital of the Dominion, however great the wrong to be redressed or the evil to be remedied. This should not be.

The city of Ottawa, with a certain area around it, should be created a Federal District; the laws for its future government (not interfering with private rights, or the city's present municipal privileges without adequate consideration), should be passed by the Dominion Parliament, and carried out by officers responsible to the Dominion Government, and through it to the people of the whole Dominion; or by a territorial arrangement, as in the District of Columbia, the legislatures of Ontario and Quebec ceding such portion of territory on both sides of the river as would make the District thoroughly unprovincial, and stipulating such terms in the cession as would preserve existing rights and interests.

By "a territorial arrangement", Gray probably meant a territorial government such as that which had just been set up for the District of Columbia and which lasted for a short time. A territorial government for Canada's Federal District would not have been necessary at that time, of course, if the District were confined to a small area on the Ottawa side of the river and the city's government were to continue. In other words, Gray seemed to be proposing either that the city government should come under the direct control of Parliament, or that a larger district should be created including part of the Hull side of the river and governed by a territorial council. He does not make clear whether under the second arrangement the local governments would disappear.

By the turn of the century the idea of a federal territory was gaining ground. Eggleston mentions (p. 156) that in 1898 Laurier's Minister of Finance, W. S. Fielding, prepared a memorandum expressing the hope that while Laurier was in Washington he would make some inquiries about the system of government for the District of Columbia, and stating that Fielding "would not be disposed to object to moderate contributions from the Dominion treasury" to develop the capital under a proper system of government. An extract from Lady Aberdeen's diary, written a few days later, implies that by a "proper system" Fielding had in mind something like a federal district on the Washington model:

> Mr. Fielding says "Get Ottawa under a Commission like Washington and I am with you." Probably he is right for the Ottawa authorities have not been very wonderful up to now.[23]

By 1906 the idea had gained such favour in Ottawa that a plebiscite was actually held on the issue. Out of a total vote of about 8,000, the proposal was defeated by only about 800 votes.[24] In other words, 45% of those who voted approved of a federally governed district.

The first and only official proposal for a federal territory was that made by the Holt Commission in 1915. Although this six-man Commission included the Mayors of Ottawa and Hull, and its cost was shared by these municipalities, the Commissioners stated flatly as their first recommendation that "the future improvements in the area about the Capital at Ottawa and Hull should not be attempted without first establishing a Federal District and securing for the federal authority some control of local government."[25]

"At the outset," says their report (p. 23), "the Commissioners were confronted by the problem of control of the capital, and they formed the opinion that an indispensable requisite to the success of their plans would be the creation of a Federal District with federal control of the area composed of Ottawa, Hull and the surrounding suburbs. It is not certain that it would be necessary or wise to adopt for Ottawa in all respects the same kind of federal control that is applied to Washington. But it is certain that federal control alone will ensure the carrying out of really adequate plans. It is also certain that the dignity and beauty of the capital of Canada are not more the business of the people of Ottawa than of the people of Canada as a whole. It could not be expected that a municipality would be able to perform such a task on an adequate scale. It would require more money than they could afford, and a steady continuous policy which does not exist under municipal government. For the future of the national capital, control of the left bank of the Ottawa river and the City of Hull is vital. The two cities look at each other across a beautiful stretch of flowing water. Nature has made them part of one whole, and they can come under one control only by union in a federal district."

Other than this statement and a favourable description of the development of Washington under federal administration, the Commission provided no further justification or analysis of the implications of this proposal, and made no comment or proposal of any kind about the kind of governmental machinery that should be set up in the proposed federal territory. It is perhaps for these reasons that the proposal was not given more serious consideration by the federal government. Although in 1928 Prime Minister Mackenzie King stated that a federal territory would eventually be necessary, nothing was done about the Holt proposal.

In 1938 Fred Cook, a former Mayor of Ottawa and member of the old Ottawa Improvement Commission, who had favoured the proposal for forty years, tried to revive it in a long series of articles in an Ottawa newspaper, but unfortunately proposed direct federal administration and the abolition of the local governments. In 1939 Carleton J. Ketchum, a journalist, published a short book, *Federal District Capital*, which reviewed the still unrealized Todd and Holt plan for redeveloping the Ottawa area, gave some information about federal capital districts elsewhere, and again proposed a federal territory for Ottawa, but without stating the nature or implications of the proposal in any detail. No extensive discussion of the problem has appeared since. A few influential individuals have publicly stated their support for the proposal, notably F. E. Bronson, former chairman of the Federal District Commission, before the Joint Committee of 1944, and Senator Connolly and M. J. Coldwell before the Joint Committee of 1956 (see Eggleston, pp. 182, 213). But public discussion of the issue was not revived until the appointment of the Royal Commisson on Bilingualism and Biculturalism in 1963.

In view of the "mistake" made in 1867, as explained by Gray, the Holt recommendation of 1915, and the Prime Minister's favourable view in 1928, why has the proposal not been taken more seriously since Confederation, and especially since 1915? The main reasons in the early period seem to have been the strong tradition of local self-government in Ottawa, the small size of the federal service, the lack of federal interest in, and unwillingness to pay for building up an impressive national capital and the consequent early absence of the difficulties of divided jurisdiction inherent in the Confederation arrangement. Later, the fact that no full-scale study of the problem or of federal capitals elsewhere had been made, the constant reference to Washington as a model and the consequent identification of federal jurisdiction with authoritarian control, the fear that Ontario and particularly Quebec would be unwilling to cede the necessary territory, the onset of the Depression and the War, and Mackenzie King's apparent persuasion by Jacques Greber in 1937 that the planning problem could be solved without creating a federal territory—all seem to have been important factors.

In any case, the proposal has been revived by the Royal Commission, with a new justification. One of the complaints made by French Canadians has been that the French language and French-Canadian interests have not been given sufficient recognition outside Quebec and particularly that the federal civil service under-represents French Canada and is not sufficiently bilingual. At the first public meeting of the Commission in November, 1963, one of the Associate Chairmen, Mr. Davidson Dunton, had suggested the following question for consideration by persons or groups who proposed to appear before the Commission: "Do you think that Canada should have a federal capital district in which the two main cultures and the two official languages would be equitably represented?"

As a result, out of about 375 briefs submitted to the Commission about 60 of them dealt with this question—some much more fully than others, of course. About 50 of these briefs were in favour of a federal district, a few were non-committal, and only four were directly opposed. The majority of those in favour were from New Brunswick or Quebec. The ones that were non-committal or directly opposed came mainly from western Canada or the Ottawa area. Only seven were from the Ottawa area, with none from the Hull side. Of these, five favoured the proposal—a faculty group from Carleton University, the University of Ottawa (conditionally), and three personal briefs. The other two—from the Civil Service Association of Ottawa and the Union of Saint Jean-Baptiste Societies of Eastview—were non-committal.

One cannot, of course, take the opinions expressed in these briefs as in any way representative of Canadian opinion as a whole, since it is likely that only those most in favour of the proposal took the trouble to discuss it. Most of the discussions were less than two pages in length and contained little analysis of the problem. For the most part they complained about the lack of bilingualism in the capital, often objected to the statement of the former Mayor of Ottawa, Charlotte Whitton, that the City could not officially use the French language or bilingual signs because this use was not provided for by Ontario law, and concluded simply that federal control was desirable because the capital should become a model of bilingualism and biculturalism. The longest presentations were from the Conseil de la Vie française, Québec (7 pages), the Association des Educateurs de langue française, Québec (7 pages), the Chambre de Notaires, Québec (4 pages), the New Democratic Party of Ontario (4 pages), and three individuals: John H. McDonald, Ottawa (9 pages), Frank Flaherty, Ottawa (6 pages), and A. R. Kear, Fredericton (16 pages).

Only the briefs from these three individuals presented specific proposals. Mr. McDonald's brief was also presented in much the same form to the Murray Jones Commission, the Ontario Advisory Committee on Confederation, and the Committee on the Constitution of the Quebec Legislature. It proposed that the federal territory should have two Senators and should elect three or four members to the House of Commons, and that these might form a joint committee of Parliament, under the chairmanship of the Secretary of State or the President of the Privy Council, to consider the national capital budget. The Flaherty and Kear briefs proposed that the National Capital Region should become an independent eleventh province. Mr. Flaherty's proposal was also published in *Weekend Magazine* on June 29, 1963. Both had picked up a semi-serious proposal I had made the year before in *Macleans* magazine, that the metropolitan areas of Toronto and Montreal should be provinces, and had applied it to the Capital Region. Both also used as precedents the existence in other federal countries of capital "city states", such as Vienna, Mexico City, and Berlin under the Weimar Republic.

The hearings before the Commission stimulated considerable public discussion of the idea of a bilingual federal territory.[26] In the fall of 1965 Dr. Seraphin Marion, a retired professor from the University of Ottawa, published an article in *La Vie Franco-Ontarienne,* the bulletin of the French-Canadian Educational Association of Ontario, supporting the idea. He pointed out the favourable effect a federal territory would have on the Roman Catholic and French-speaking minorities in the Ottawa area, despite its unfavourable effect of reducing the French-Canadian minority in the rest of Ontario. Dr. Marion mistakenly claimed that there were 200,000 Franco-Ontarians in the Ottawa area. Table I shows that there were only 94,000 of French origin in 1961. However, he was nearly correct in his contention that the addition of the Hull side of the river to a federal territory would make it 42% French-speaking, 58% English-speaking and 60% Roman Catholic, so that the Roman Catholic majority would help to counterbalance the French-speaking minority. This article was summarized in Ottawa's *Le Droit* (Nov. 30, 1965) and also in English by the Canadian Press.[27]

In the hearings before the Jones Commission on local government, of the forty-five submissions proposing changes, only one, that by Mr. John McDonald, recommended a federal district, and one, by the Greenbelt Property Owners' Association, proposed a province, suggesting that provincial status is required effectively to represent and safeguard local interests against federal authority. On the other hand, several of the other briefs indicated strong opposition to a federal district, usually on the ground that they thought it would be the antithesis of democratic local self-government.

In March, 1966, the Quebec wing of the federal Liberal party adopted a resolution in favour of a bilingual capital district, and Horace Racine, M.L.A. for Ottawa East, having decided that the Jones Commission's recommendation for a regional government on the Ottawa side of the river was unacceptable, gave his support to the proposal for an eleventh capital province. The typical local press reaction was one of opposition, again based on the assumption that municipal governments would be abolished.[28]

2. Summary and Analysis of the Arguments

Much of the case in favour of a federal territory has been presented in the earlier chapters describing the difficulties of divided jurisdiction, and in the preceding history of the proposal. It remains only to summarize the arguments here and to analyze them briefly. They may be reduced to four main arguments, all of which are closely related: (1) on grounds of principle the capital of a federal country should belong to the people of the whole nation and should not be located within the boundaries of any one province or city of that province; (2) precedents elsewhere demonstrate the superiority of a federal capital territory;

(3) the physical redevelopment of the capital would be much easier under a federal territory; and (4) the bilingual-bicultural nature of the National Capital would be greatly improved.

The Principle of a Federal Capital

John Hamilton Gray's eloquent exposition of this principle has already been quoted in full. His arguments as to why federal members of Parliament and civil servants resident in the capital city should not come under the laws of any one province are very convincing. To these may be added the argument that the far-away provincial capitals of Toronto and Quebec tend to neglect the interests of the Capital Region, especially since such a large proportion of its residents are non-political civil servants. Two opposing points, however, should be noted. Nine-tenths of federal civil servants are located outside Ottawa, and are subject to the laws of the provinces in which they live. Also, Ottawa and Hull have histories which pre-date Confederation, and a large proportion of their residents are not federal civil servants. In this respect, the Capital Region is a sort of "Siamese-twins" area—being at one and the same time the location of the National Capital and an old population centre with its own traditions of self-government and its own industrial, commercial and agricultural interests. Gray's arguments would have been truer of a newly created capital such as Washington or Canberra where from the beginning the overwhelming proportion of its residents were federal civil servants or their dependents. Nevertheless, since Ottawa is not a great industrial or commercial centre, well over one third of its residents are federal employees or their dependents. Throughout this century the federal government has become increasingly important as a source of employment in the area and is by now by far the largest employer.[29] A comparison of labour force distribution by major industry group in 1961 shows 33.2% in "public administration and defence" in the Ottawa metro area as compared with, for example, 5.5% in the Toronto area. This figure does not include the employees of a number of large federal Crown corporations in Ottawa, which would considerably increase the percentage. Nor does it include embassy staff, headquarters of national organizations, political lobbies or parliamentary newsmen. Probably three-quarters of the labour force in the area directly or indirectly are dependent for their employment upon the fact that Ottawa is the National Capital.

Precedents Elsewhere

Throughout the history of the argument over a federal district, reference has always been made to the existence of precedents elsewhere. Since the United States, as the original federal system, was regarded as a model for the rest of the world, and was close at hand, the example of the District of Columbia was constantly used. Gray devoted a considerable proportion of his argument to praising the American example, and every proposal since then seems to have done likewise, adding to it the example of Canberra after its successful creation into a federal territory by the Government of Australia after 1909. Because of the constant reference to these two examples, they came to be regarded as the standard and only possible models. Unfortunately, both of them provided for direct administration by the federal government and allowed literally no self-government or voting rights for the local citizens. As a result, these facts became standard arguments against a federal territory for Canada. The facts that other arrangements were possible and that other federal capital territories existed with different arrangements, were ignored. For example, in an article entitled "We Don't Want a Federal District for Ottawa" (*Canadian Business,* Feb., 1958), J. Harvey Perry, a former senior civil servant, constantly identified the proposal with the existing arrangements in Washington and Canberra and used them as a *main reason* for opposing the idea.

Opponents often fail to note that Washington had a locally elected government until 1871, and that one of the main reasons for its failure and abolition was the lack of sufficient financial support from the federal government. Nor do they note that in recent years there has been a rising criticism of the lack of self-government and voting rights in Washington and Canberra. Self-government has not been granted to Washington because of the opposition of Southern representatives in Congress to giving political power to the majority negro population. The grant of voting rights in federal elections to the residents of the District of Columbia requires a cumbersome constitutional amendment procedure. Nevertheless, as a result of the growing criticism, the Constitution was amended recently to allow them to vote in presidential elections, and proposals are now being made for an amendment to give them representatives in Congress. In the Australian Capital Territory, until now the one member elected to the House of Representatives has had only the right to vote on matters affecting the Territory, but in future he will have full voting rights on all matters. The Australian Government also is considering proposals for replacing the present partly elected Advisory Council for the Territory with a fully elected governing council.

Those who favour a federal territory often fail to note that the main provisions for it must be placed in the Constitution and so cannot be adapted easily to social and economic change. The difficulty of obtaining voting rights in the District of Columbia is a case in point. Also, urban Washington long ago overflowed the boundaries of the constitutionally created District into the two surrounding states, and this has created frightful problems of governing and controlling the development of the whole metropolitan area. The lesson to be learned is that if a federally governed district is to be created, the provinces must cede enough territory to accommodate any conceivable future expansion of the built-up area. Projections indicate that the present National Capital Region will comfortably contain the urban population until the year 2000. But will it do so in the year 2050, or 2100?

No thorough study of other federal capital districts has been made in Canada, the relevant information is not easily available, and not much is known about them. Many of them—such as Mexico City, Buenos Aires in Argentina, Caracas in Venezuela, Rio de Janeiro and later Brasilia in Brazil—are in South American countries which are not regarded as models of democratic government. But others do or did exist in countries having a stronger democratic tradition, such as Vienna in Austria, New Delhi in India, and Berlin under the Weimar Republic. In any case, some of them seem to provide for some form of local self-government, with varying degrees of local independence and voting rights, so that a study of their experience in this respect, and of their forms of territorial government, would be valuable.

The Physical Development of the Capital

From the beginning, one of the main arguments has been that the physical and aesthetic development of the Ottawa area into a capital worthy of a great country would be much more easily and fully achieved under a federal territory. The lack of a planned development of the area in the early years seemed to prove this contention, and the federal government was faced with the much more difficult and costly problem of re-development, especially in the urban core. Earlier chapters have described fully the difficulties of divided jurisdiction that were involved. Chapters III and IV described how these problems had been partly solved since the war, but pointed to new difficulties that were developing for the future.

The argument has always been that if the federal government had control over the physical development and government of the area, the plans for the capital could be much more ambitious and impressive in concept, and much more successful in execution. Experience elsewhere has demonstrated that a metropolitan plan cannot be successfully and completely carried out unless a corresponding metropolitan government exists or is created with authority to complete the plan.[30] On the other hand, the history of planning in the National Capital shows that generous federal financial support is able to overcome many of the present difficulties of divided jurisdiction. From a democratic point of view the participation of the local residents in both the formulation and execution of the National Capital Plan is desirable. Yet even under a federal territory this problem would still remain, and there would be inevitable conflicts of interest between the federal government and the local residents.

The Desire for a Bilingual-Bicultural Capital

The gist of this argument has already been given. There is no doubt that federal control of a capital territory, with proper guarantees for equal minority rights—linguistic, religious, educational and cultural—would make it possible for the National Capital to become a symbol and model of bilingualism and biculturalism for the rest of the country. Ottawa is already the most bilingual of the large cities outside Quebec.

Eastview is the only city outside Quebec that has a French-speaking majority. Except for one small city in Quebec (Sillery, population 14,000 in 1961), Eastview and Hull are the only cities in Canada whose population is half bilingual (see Table III). The addition of these cities to the capital would therefore greatly strengthen its bilingual-bicultural character.

The formation of a federal territory corresponding with the boundaries of the National Capital Region would greatly improve the whole ethnic, linguistic and religious balance of the capital's population. In 1961, 91% of the population of the Region resided within the Ottawa-Hull urban area. By 1986 it is predicted that the urban population will be 96.6% of the total.[31] The 1961 census figures for the urban metropolitan area may therefore safely be taken as representative of the whole Region. The ethnic and linguistic proportions have not changed very much by 1966, nor are they likely to be altered significantly in the near future. The 1961 figures reveal that turning the whole Region into the federal capital would increase French Canadians as an ethnic group from one quarter to about 40% of the total population (see Tables IA, IIA). It would also increase those whose mother tongue is French from under one quarter to nearly 40%, and the number of people who could speak both English and French would increase from one quarter to over 30%. The ethnic distribution of the population would then be: Anglo-Saxon, 44%; French 41%; and other, 15%. Those whose mother tongue is English would be 56%; French 38%; and other, 6%. Although English would predominate as a language, Anglo-Saxons and French would be about equally balanced as ethnic groups, and Roman Catholics would be in a comfortable majority (59%).

Since elsewhere in Canada the population tends to be either overwhelmingly English-speaking and Protestant or overwhelmingly French-speaking and Roman Catholic, the Capital Region would have the best-balanced ethnic, linguistic and religious population of any large metropolitan area or province in Canada (Tables IV and IVA). Its balance would, for example, be far superior to that of the provincial capitals of Ontario and Quebec. The only serious competitors would be New Brunswick and metropolitan Montreal. New Bruswick's ethnic and linguistic proportions are much like those of the Capital Region. Of the total population, 39% are of French origin and 35% have French as their mother tongue. However, only 6% are of other than Anglo-Saxon or French origin (compared with the Region's 15%), and fewer than one-fifth are bilingual (compared with the Region's nearly one-third). Just over half of them are Roman Catholic.

On most counts a federal Region would compare favourably with the Montreal area. Whereas about 40% of the Region's population would be of French origin, and 38% of French tongue, in metropolitan Montreal only 18% are of Anglo-Saxon origin, and only 23% are of English mother tongue. Whereas Roman Catholics are an overwhelming majority in metropolitan Montreal (78%), they would constitute only 60%

TABLE III

BILINGUAL AND FRENCH-SPEAKING POPULATION
OF SELECTED CITIES, 1961

(Population in thousands)

	Total	Bilingual	French Tongue	Percent Bilingual	Percent French
Ottawa	268.2	67.0	56.9	25	21
Eastview	24.6	12.9	15.0	52	61
Hull	56.9	27.9	51.4	49	90
Cornwall	43.6	19.0	18.5	44	42
Moncton	43.8	14.7	14.1	34	32
Lachine	38.6	15.3	20.7	40	54
Montreal	1,191.1	462.8	806.1	39	68
Outremont	30.8	14.2	15.3	46	50
Quebec	172.0	46.0	164.2	27	95
St. Boniface	37.6	13.5	13.4	36	36
St. Laurent	49.5	19.0	20.4	38	41
Sherbrooke	66.6	23.0	58.7	35	88
Sillery	14.1	7.1	11.7	50	83
Sudbury	80.1	23.2	23.3	29	29
Timmins	29.3	11.4	12.0	39	41
Verdun	78.3	30.9	44.7	39	57
Westmount	25.0	10.2	5.1	41	20

Source: Based on *1961 Census of Canada, Series 1.2: Population,* Table 67.

of the population in the Region. Montreal has a slightly higher proportion (18%) whose ethnic origin is other than Anglo-Saxon or French. Also, its population is somewhat more bilingual than the region's population would be at the beginning (37%, compared with 30%).

In this respect it is interesting to compare what proportion of the English- and French-speaking populations can speak the other language. In the Capital Region only about 10% of those whose ethnic origin is from the British Isles and who speak English can also speak French, while in metropolitan Montreal nearly 30% of them can speak French. On the other hand, in the Region almost exactly two-thirds of those who are of French origin and who speak French can also speak English, whereas in the Montreal area only 42% of these can speak English.[32] It is not surprising that in Montreal, where French is the majority language, a higher proportion of English-speaking people learn French than in Ottawa; or that in Ottawa, where English is the majority language, a higher proportion of French-speaking people learn English. But it is interesting that the proportion of the minority who have learned the majority language is much higher in Ottawa than in Montreal, while the proportion of the majority who have learned the minority language is very much higher in Montreal than in Ottawa.

Certainly, the number of English-speaking people in the proposed federal territory who would be able to speak French would at first be disappointingly small. However, since Ottawa's civil service is now becoming more bilingual, and since one of the main objectives of creating a federal territory would be to promote bilingualism, one could expect the proportion of people who can speak both English and French fluently,

TABLE IV
COMPARISON OF ETHNIC AND RELIGIOUS
CHARACTERISTICS OF POPULATION IN SELECTED
METROPOLITAN AREAS AND PROVINCES, 1961
(Population in thousands)

	Ontario	Toronto Metro	Quebec Province	Quebec Metro	Montreal Metro	Ottawa Metro	New Brunswick
Ethnic Group							
British Isles	3,711.5	1,107.2	567.1	14.2	377.6	189.2	329.9
French	647.9	61.4	4,241.4	336.8	1,353.5	175.4	232.1
Other	1,876.7	655.9	450.7	6.6	378.4	65.2	35.9
Mother Tongue							
English	4,834.6	1,398.3	697.4	13.4	494.7	239.3	378.6
French	425.3	26.0	4,269.7	341.2	1,366.3	162.0	210.5
Other	976.2	400.2	292.1	3.0	248.5	28.5	8.8
Official Language							
English Only	5,548.8	1,690.6	608.6	5.1	462.3	236.3	370.9
French Only	95.2	3.1	3,254.9	265.2	826.3	56.8	112.1
Both	493.3	78.3	1,338.9	86.7	776.6	132.5	113.4
Neither	98.8	52.5	56.8	.6	44.3	4.2	1.5
Religion							
Roman Catholic	1,873.1	478.6	4,635.6	350.5	1,641.7	253.6	310.6
Other	4,363.0	1,345.9	623.6	7.1	467.8	176.2	287.3
Total Population in Thousands	6,236.1	1,824.5	5,259.2	357.6	2,109.5	429.8	597.9

Source: Based on Table I and *1961 Census of Canada, Series 1.2: Population,* Tables 35, 39, 42, 46, 64, 70.

TABLE IVA
PERCENTAGE COMPARISON OF ETHNIC AND RELIGIOUS
CHARACTERISTICS OF POPULATION IN SELECTED
METROPOLITAN AREAS AND PROVINCES, 1941

	Ontario	Toronto Metro	Quebec Province	Quebec Metro	Montreal Metro	Ottawa Metro	New Brunswick
Ethnic Group							
British Isles	59.5	60.6	10.7	3.9	17.8	44.0	55.1
French	10.3	3.3	80.6	94.1	64.1	40.8	38.8
Other	30.0	35.9	8.5	1.8	17.9	15.1	6.0
Total*	100.	100.	100.	100.	100.	100.	100.
Mother Tongue							
English	77.5	76.6	13.2	3.7	23.4	55.6	63.3
French	6.8	1.4	81.1	95.4	64.7	37.6	35.2
Other	15.6	21.9	5.5	.8	11.7	6.6	1.4
Total*	100.	100.	100.	100.	100.	100.	100.
Official Language							
English Only	88.9	92.6	11.5	1.4	21.9	54.9	62.0
French Only	1.5	.1	61.8	74.1	39.1	13.2	18.7
Both	7.9	4.2	25.4	24.2	36.8	30.8	18.9
Neither	1.5	2.8	1.0	.1	2.1	.9	.2
Total*	100.	100.	100.	100.	100.	100.	100.
Religion							
Roman Catholic	30.0	26.2	88.1	98.0	77.8	59.0	51.9
Other	69.9	73.7	11.8	1.9	22.1	40.9	48.0
Total*	100.	100.	100.	100.	100.	100.	100.

Source: Table III
*Totals do not add exactly to 100.0, due to rounding of figures.

and in particular the number of English-speaking people who can speak French, to rise rapidly.

These comparisons show that though the ethnic and linguistic balance in the federal territory would be good, it would be far from perfect. For this reason the political difficulties of creating and governing the territory would not easily be solved. Although the addition of the Hull side of the river would certainly add strength to the French minority on the Ottawa side, French Canadians would still be slightly in the minority. Yet one could expect their position to improve further if the proportion of French-speaking civil servants were increased, as may be expected. Moreover, linguistic and educational guarantees in the constitution of the new territory could further protect their position, even though the Parliament of Canada, which would be the ultimate governing authority, has an English-speaking majority. As Dr. Marion has pointed out, the position of the Franco-Ontarians in the Ottawa area would be greatly improved, compared with their present position under the laws of Ontario. Even if they did not consider it an ideal arrangement, from their point of view it would certainly be by far "the best of evils."

The Hull side of the river, however, would have far less to gain. At first glance their position would appear to be considerably worsened. The reaction of Gatineau's M.L.A. to Mr. Flaherty's proposal for a capital province was to object to it for this reason.[33] Yet with suitable guarantees for minority rights, and especially if a considerable measure of local self-government were granted to the Hull side, this may be a false fear. By becoming constitutionally *part* of the national capital, Hull could expect to participate much more fully in, and to benefit much more financially from, the beautification of the capital and the redevelopment of its urban core. For example, many more federal buildings would be located on the Hull side of the river. Although the effect of this might be to increase the English-speaking population, one could also expect many more French-speaking civil servants to live on the Hull side. These would include educated senior officials, some of whom would become leaders in the local community. The position of French Canadians on the Hull side of the river might therefore be improved by becoming part of a federal territory.

The creation of a federal territory would itself be very likely to stimulate a rapid growth of bilingualism, especially if the educational system in the territory were reorganized so as to provide genuinely bilingual public and separate schools with instruction given in both languages. On the Ottawa side of the river the difficulty at present is that in most areas there are not enough non-Catholic French-speaking families in any one area to justify the creation of a bilingual public school. This is true even of separate schools in a predominantly English-speaking area. The Separate School Board of Nepean, for example, recently refused the request of an organized group of French-speaking families for such a school because only the first grade would have a large enough class. As a result, some of these families are moving from the township because they fear that their children will lose the ability to speak French. The answer to the problem lies in direct encouragement and financial subsidies from a higher level of government to support small, uneconomic schools of this kind, or to transport the pupils to larger schools. At the same time, there are now a number of English-speaking parents who would like their children to become bilingual by attending bilingual public or separate schools. If the schools were easily available, and with proper encouragement, many more English-speaking parents would desire their children to attend. This attendance would increase the size of the schools and make them a much more economically feasible proposition.

There is also a need for bilingual schools on the Hull side of the river. But there the need is not as great because the English-speaking minority is not in as much danger of losing its mother tongue and the French Canadians tend to become bilingual in any case. Nevertheless, somewhat the same need exists for establishing bilingual Catholic schools where part of the instruction is given in English, and bilingual Protestant schools where part of the instruction is given in French.

3. The Proposal for a Capital Province

The proposal made by Mr. Flaherty and Mr. Kear that the National Capital Region should be carved out as Canada's "eleventh province" is much like the proposal for a federal territory with an elected territorial government. The use of the term "province" in the proposal has many attractions. It avoids the confusion that has arisen over the term "Federal District" because of its former use to describe the area of jurisdiction of the former Federal District Commission, and it avoids the stigma that has become attached to this term by constant association with the Federal District of Columbia and the absence there of self-government and voting rights. The term "province" in the proposal is arresting and dramatic, and as an added attraction for the local residents, implies a high degree of local autonomy and self-government. For these reasons, there is much to be said in favour of using this term in public discussion to describe the proposal for a separate capital territory.

At the same time, it should be realized that the National Capital Territory could not be given the same constitutional independence and power as a province. For then the federal government would have no direct control over its own seat of government. To make the National Capital Region into a province with virtually the same constitutional independence and autonomy as the existing provinces would place the federal government in much the same powerless position as it is now in relation to the National Capital: the capital would again be under the control and laws of a single province. There would no doubt be advantages to this new arrangement. The metropolitan area would come under the unified control of a single provincial legislature, which would, unlike the governments of Ontario and Quebec, single-mindedly concentrate its attention upon solving the problems of this area alone. But the position of the federal government in relation to the new province would be the same as it is now in relation to the two provinces of Ontario and Quebec regarding control of the National Capital Region. Constitutionally, its control over the area would be left unchanged, and the same difficulties of divided jurisdiction would remain.

Moreover, the proposal assumes that political parties would continue to operate in the new province. This would raise the problem of the exclusion of federal civil servants from participation in "provincial" political activities. They and their families would almost constitute a majority of the population in the new province. It would also raise the even more difficult problem of federal-"capital province" political relations, as demonstrated by the experience of Austria. In Austria—where the capital city, Vienna, has the status of a state in the federation—between the wars a Christian Democratic federal government was constantly faced with an unco-operative Socialist government in control of the national capital. Once the government of the new province came into power there would be no guarantee that the objectives of those who had created the province would be achieved. For example, the English-speaking majority in the area might decide *not* to promote the objectives of bilingualism and biculturalism.

The examples of other "city-states" used by Mr. Flaherty and Mr. Kear are not strictly relevant because some are not federal capitals and because the states in their federations are not as autonomous as Canada's provinces. Moreover, the capital city-states cited, Vienna and Berlin, are huge industrial and commercial centres with a wide range of interests and a long tradition of independence. There the federal government's interest in the urban area as a seat of government would not predominate as it does in Ottawa, and the case for full status as a state would be stronger.

It would therefore seem that in any new arrangement for the government of the National Capital Region, the federal Parliament must have ultimate authority, subject to any superior constitutional guarantees that would be placed in the *British North America Act* by agreement between the federal government and the provinces. These guarantees could be placed in the Constitution just as easily for a federal territory as for a province.

However, the concept of a "capital province" is useful as an analogy. It highlights what fundamental constitutional, legal and political changes would be needed in the creation of a federal territory. All of the powers now possessed by the two provincial governments in the National Capital Region would have to be taken over by the federal government and a new territorial government. And the services now provided in the Region by the two provinces would similarly have to be taken over except that at first they might continue to be provided by agreement with these provinces. Similarly, what are now provincial taxes would have to be decided upon, levied and collected by either the federal or territorial government. Also, the present federal-provincial tax-sharing agreements and the system and level of federal grants to the provinces would have to be used as a guide for the financial arrangements between the federal government and the new territorial government.

VII. The Arguments Against a Federal Territory

The case against a federal territory may be summed up under these four broad arguments: it would be both constitutionally and politically difficult to create such a territory, especially because of local opposition and Quebec's reluctance to cede territory to the federal government; the problem of governing it as a unit would be insoluble because of the double-splitting of interest—federal versus local, and French law, language and culture on one side of the river versus Anglo-Saxon on the other; other alternatives are available; in any case, a federal territory is not needed. Let us consider each of these in turn.

1. Difficulty of Creating a Federal Territory

From a constitutional point of view the creation of a federal territory does not appear to present any great difficulty. As John H. McDonald has pointed out in his brief, (p. 18), the *British North America Act* was amended in 1871 to provide that the Parliament of Canada may alter the boundaries of a province with the consent of that province. The relevant provisions are as follows:

> 3. The Parliament of Canada may from time to time, with the consent of the Legislature of any Province of the said Dominion, increase, diminish, or otherwise alter the limits of such Province, upon such terms and conditions as may be agreed to by the said Legislature, and may, with the like consent, make provision respecting the effect and operation of any such increase or diminution or alteration of territory in relation to any Province affected thereby.
> 4. The Parliament of Canada may from time to time make provision for the administration, peace, order and good government of any territory not for the time being included in any Province.

It would therefore be possible for the federal government to arrange for the provinces to cede the necessary lands without a constitutional amendment.

Politically, however, the creation of a federal territory would no doubt require such an amendment, because it would affect the rights and interests of a large number of the residents of Ontario and Quebec. The power of the federal government to amend the Constitution is at present governed by the provisions of the 1949 amendment to the *B.N.A. Act*, which provides that the federal Parliament has power over "the amendment from time to time of the Constitution of Canada, except as regards matters coming within the classes of subjects by this Act assigned exclusively to the Legislatures of the Provinces, or as regards rights or privileges by this or any other Constitutional Act granted or secured to the Legislature or the Government of a Province, or to any class of persons with respect to schools, or as regards the use of the English or the French language . . ." Since the ceding of territory by Quebec would affect the language and school rights of Quebec and of a considerable number of its present citizens, it seems clear that the instrument creating a federal territory would have to be in the form of a Statute passed by the United Kingdom amending the *B.N.A. Act*. Constitutionally it would require the consent of only Ontario and Quebec, but politically it would be wise to secure the consent of the remaining provinces.

The desirable linguistic, cultural, educational and religious guarantees for the residents of the territory could be worked out by agreement with Ontario and Quebec and placed in the Statute creating the territory, so that they could not be abrogated or changed by the federal government without the agreement of these provinces and an amendment to the Imperial Statute. If it were thought that the objectives of promoting bilingualism and biculturalism should be emphasized, these objectives could be included in the Statute. Similarly, certain essential features of the form of government for the new territory might also be placed in the Imperial Statute so that they could not be changed without the consent of the other provinces, or at least Ontario or Quebec. For example, to ensure a desirable degree of self-government for the territory, it might be specified that the local residents shall elect representatives to Parliament, to the territorial council or legislature, and to local governments in the Region. Even the main outlines of the structure of government for the territory might be specified in the Statute but with the instruction that this structure may be changed in future by a simple Act of the federal Parliament. This would be somewhat like the provision in the *British North America Act* of 1867 for the constitutions of Ontario and Quebec until such time as their legislatures might decide to amend their constitutions. It would have the advantage of allowing provincial participation and agreement in drawing up the original constitution for the territorial government but at the same time would preserve flexibility by allowing the federal Parliament to make minor changes and adjustments in future by itself.

More impressive than the constitutional difficulties of creating a federal territory are the political ones. A standard opposition argument has been that Quebec would not agree to the loss of territory and population. However, the strength of this argument may be over-estimated. Ontario would be giving up over 400,000 of its population, while Quebec would lose only about 125,000. If the federal territory is to become a model for the protection of minority rights and for the development of bilingualism and biculturalism, Quebec may easily be persuaded that it has more to gain than to lose.[34]

A second standard argument has been that the local municipalities and residents would unalterably opposed to the creation of a federal territory. This argument is an impressive one, because the fact is that local civic politicians have frequently, and in recent years almost consistently, voiced their opposition to the proposal. Examples of such statements are contained in their evidence before the parliamentary Joint Committees of 1944 and 1956. The assumption is always made, however—and this is always given as the main reason for their opposition—that local self-government would disappear and the local residents would lose their political rights. This argument would be answered by a proposal which included the preservation of local self-government and the election of representatives to a territorial government and to Parliament. It is difficult to know what the attitude of local politicians and residents would be if they were faced with this kind of proposal, but I suspect that the force of opposition would decline greatly and local opinion might even change in its favour.

This raises the interesting question of the extent to which local consent should be sought for such a proposal. It seems to me that on theoretical grounds the consent of a majority—say in the form of a plebiscite—should not be required. Indeed, one can argue that on such an issue the interests of the people of Canada in the National Capital and in the objectives sought by the creation of a federal territory should override if necessary the opposition of a small minority of the country's population residing in the territory. But this would depend, of course, upon the strength of feeling of the local opposition. As long as a significant proportion of the local population seemed to be in favour of the idea, and no significant group were strongly opposed, the federal government, with the agreement of the two provinces, could justifiably proceed. In any case, the governments of Ontario and Quebec would not be likely to agree to the proposal in the face of strong opposition from a significant proportion of their local constituents.

The strongest opposition would very likely come from the Hull side. Hull feels so strongly about its past neglect by the federal government that the latter would have to make a clear commitment to finance a large share of the redevelopment of downtown Hull and to place new federal buildings there. This commitment would make sense in any case. Many people think that federal departments are now becoming physically too decentralized. Downtown Hull is in the heart of the capital. Placing key federal departments there would improve inter-departmental and policy co-ordination. It would also promote bilingualism. The resulting increase in population on the Hull side, however, would require important changes in the National Capital Plan and in the recent Ottawa-Hull transportation plan.

2. The Problem of Government

The problem of governing a federal territory means reconciling a two-way split: the split in legal systems, laws, political traditions and interests between the two sides of the river, and the split between the interests of the federal government in its own seat of government and the desire of the local residents to govern their own affairs. Opponents of a federal territory argue that the differences between the two sides of the river are so great that they would be extremely difficult, if not impossible, to reconcile, and that the creation of a federal territory would wipe out local self-government.

Regarding the first of these arguments there is no doubt that the difference in legal systems and provincial laws now in force on the two sides of the river would create problems. It should be pointed out, however, that the courts and laws need not necessarily be integrated or unified. The constitutional instrument creating the territory simply could provide that the legal systems and laws of Ontario and Quebec shall continue to be in effect unless and until they are changed by the Parliament of Canada or the new territorial government. In the creation of new governmental authorities this type of provision is quite common. One would expect any integration of the two legal systems to be done only gradually and over a long period of time, and only if and when it seemed desirable.

As John H. McDonald has suggested in his brief, the new territory would simply take over the two court systems as they now exist on each side of the river, except that it would, of course, provide for the use of the French language in the courts on the Ontario side. The Exchequer Court of Canada could be made the Court of Appeal for the territory. Local police could continue as before, and policing formerly done by the governments of Ontario and Quebec could be provided by the R.C.M.P. in the same manner as it provides policing for the other provinces.

Some legal difficulties would arise from placing the civil code and common law under one legislative jurisdiction, such as a case involving residents on each side of the river, or where the principal in a case was resident on one side, but the transaction took place on the other. However, similar difficulties occur now in cases including both the civil code and the common law in Quebec and the other provinces. The principles applied to these cases could be used as a guide. It should be recalled that the same type of situation existed for some years before Confederation, when Upper and Lower Canada were united under one legislature.

More serious than the division of legal systems are the political problems that might arise in governing the territory. These cannot be easily predicted. Although the whole territory would show a reasonable ethnic, linguistic and religious balance, there would still be a predominant French-speaking majority on the north side of the river, and a predominant English-speaking majority on the south side. Could these two groups be successfully united under a single territorial government, or would the union be relatively unsuccessful, like the union of Upper and Lower Canada before Confederation? If so, a possible solution might be to create two territorial councils—one for each side of the river—though this would mainly defeat the purposes for which the territory was created. At any rate, the difference in traditions and political interests on the two sides argues for the continued existence of municipalities and of a large measure of local self-government on each side.

The argument that the creation of a federal territory would wipe out self-government in the area is setting up a straw man in order to knock him down. Few people would seriously propose the abolition or denial of political rights as in the District of Columbia or Canberra. But the argument does raise the difficult problem of the division between federal and local interests in the territory, and of balancing these interests through a proper system of representation. Certainly, the creation of a federal territory will bring with it no magic solution to the problem of governing a large and populous area.

Many of those who have proposed a federal territory would be quite willing to concede that a proper representation of local interests requires the continuation of local self-government, continued election of representatives to Parliament, and as a substitute for electing representatives to a provincial legislature, the election of members to a territorial council. It has also been suggested by Mr. McDonald and Mr. Kear that the territory might be allotted several Senators. Mr. Kear has suggested that one of the territory's Members of Parliament might traditionally be included in the Cabinet and that another local constituency might form the basis for electing a permanent Speaker for the House of Commons.

Except for the Kear and Flaherty proposals of a fully organized provincial government for the territory, most proposals have been rather vague about the extent of local representation in the territorial government, and even whether there would be such a government. Probably the most detailed proposal was the one made by Mr. McDonald in his briefs to the Bilingualism and Jones Commissions. He has suggested a seven-man territorial commission consisting of a mayor or chairman elected for five years, three commissioners elected at large for six-year overlapping terms, and three commissioners appointed by the Ontario, Quebec and federal governments, the latter appointee to be a senior civil servant. The commission would have a single chief administrator comparable to a city manager.[35]

It seems clear that a territorial government would be desirable, for at least two reasons. Otherwise, no special governing authority would exist to take over the powers or provide the services now handled by the two provincial governments. Transferring these powers and services directly to the federal level would very likely overburden Parliament. Secondly, the residents of the territory would lose the extra representation they enjoyed by electing members to a provincial legislature. For this reason, a territorial government should exist to which they could elect members.

The questions are, however, what should be the powers and form of this new government, and what should be the division of representation in it between the central government and the local residents, in order to give a proper balance of national and local interests?

As already pointed out, a territorial government could not have the same status and independence as a province because of the special nature of the federal government's interest in the control and development of its own seat of government. Its constitutional position should be more like that of the governments of the Yukon and the Northwest Territories. Hence the constitution and organization of their territorial and municipal governments might provide some useful precedents. Because of the size, complexity and large future population of the area, and the fact that a territorial government would eventually be taking over services formerly held by the provincial governments, its responsibilities would no doubt be great. One would expect it to possess most of the powers of a provincial government as outlined in Section 92 of the *British North America Act*. Yet these powers should be granted by delegation from the federal Parliament, rather than exercised exclusively by the territorial government. Similarly, even if the powers and structure of the territorial government are spelled out in the Imperial Act creating the territory, these should be made mainly amendable by the Federal Parliament acting alone, rather than by either requiring provincial consent or allowing the territorial government to amend its own constitution. Otherwise, the territorial government would become too independent of the federal Parliament. So that it will not be regarded as having the same degree of independence as a province, the territory's representative body should be called a "council" rather than a "legislature", and it should pass "ordinances" rather than "laws."

For the same reason, and also because of the high proportion of federal civil servants in the area, the territorial government should not be controlled by political parties. Nor should it have a cabinet form of responsible government, which encourages the formation of parties. Yet, unlike Mr. McDonald, I think the territory's council should be fairly large in order to represent the great variety of interests in the territory, and to deal with the important "provincial" matters that will come under its jurisdiction. Since it should not have a cabinet as its executive body, provision could be made for an executive committee chosen from the council, as in the council of Metropolitan Toronto. The chairman of the council and its executive committee might be appointed by the federal government (just as the first chairman of the Toronto Metropolitan Council was chosen by the Ontario government). The government might even name a Cabinet minister as chairman. Or the chairman might be elected by the territorial council (as the chairman of the Toronto Metropolitan Council is chosen now).

What should be the division between federal and local representation on the territorial council? Obviously the council should not be entirely federally appointed or there would be a serious danger of disregarding local interest. On the other hand, if the council were all locally elected, there would be a danger of its disregarding the national interest, just as locally elected councils in the area have done in the past, and as the elected council in Washington seems to have done before local government was abolished there in 1871. Mr. Flaherty has suggested in his article (p. 23) that the federal and local interests might be represented by having a two-chamber legislature—a locally elected lower chamber and a federally appointed upper chamber with a veto power. While this would neatly divide the appointed and elected representatives, it might also divide federal and local interests too much. A more successful arrangement might be to have federally appointed and locally elected representatives in the same chamber and in about equal proportions. To promote a closer co-ordination of national and local interests, one or two cabinet ministers, the M.P.'s and Senators for the territory, and the members of the National Capital Commission who are not from the local area, could be appointed as federal representatives on the territorial council.

The local residents should perhaps be granted a majority of the representatives, since the federal Parliament would be legally superior to the council and would be financially predominant. It could exercise its ultimate legal control if necessary, and could exert a powerful influence through its financial support to the territory. It would therefore seem safe to provide for a locally elected majority at the beginning. If this did not work successfully, the federal government could change the arrangement by amending the constitution of the council. The local residents should, I think, be granted the right to elect their representatives *directly* to the council, in order to grant them the equivalent of their previous right to elect representatives directly to a provincial legislature, and also because of the importance and volume of the issues with which the territorial council would deal. One could not expect municipal councillors to serve double duty on the territorial council as they do on the Toronto Metropolitan Council.

Since the territory would be governed by an English-speaking majority, and would come under the ultimate control of an English-speaking majority in Parliament, it would perhaps be wise to slightly over-represent the French-speaking population on the territorial council. This could be done most easily by over-representing the population on the Hull side of the river. If it were done by constitutional provision, the likelihood of Quebec and the Hull side agreeing to the creation of the territory would be greatly increased.

What services would the territorial council provide? It would have the power to provide basically the same services as the provinces now provide in the area, plus any federal powers and services coming under Section 91 of the *B.N.A. Act* delegated to it by Parliament. One would expect the provinces to continue to provide their services, by agreement with the federal government, until such time as the council is prepared to take on their administration and to reorganize them. For example, the council might decide at an early date to reorganize education in the territory in order to provide equality of services. If the promotion of bilingualism were stated as an objective of national policy in the territory's constitution, the council might decide to increase dramatically the extent of bilingualism in the territory, especially among the English-speaking population, by providing that in English-speaking areas the instruction in elementary schools should be given partly in French, and in high schools almost wholly in French. The same approach could be taken towards English language instruction in entirely French-speaking areas. It might also make adult classes in oral French and English much more easily available, and encourage the creation of a bilingual theatre group, bilingual radio and television stations, movie theatres, etc. It might even decide, with the federal government's help and in collaboration with Carleton and Ottawa universities, to organize a great national bilingual university or graduate school in the territory, like the Australian National University.

Since the territorial council would be expected eventually to deal with the whole range of services provided and with the taxes now levied by the provincial governments, there would still be plenty of room for local governments to continue to provide municipal services. Their powers would be delegated to them by the territorial government, and it would have the power to reorganize them, perhaps subject to federal approval.

The existing municipalities on each side of the river could continue to operate under their respective provincial laws until changed by the territorial council. The council could then reorganize them and eventually adopt a comprehensive municipal code for the whole territory, picking the best features from the laws of Ontario, Quebec and elsewhere. The council might decide that the city governments of Ottawa and Hull should continue to exist but that there should be some consolidation of local government in other areas already urbanized or about to be urbanized—for example, that Hull should annex the area as far west as Aylmer and as far east as Gatineau, and that new city governments should be created for the three projected urban areas beyond Ottawa's Greenbelt. On the other hand, it might decide that the best solution to the urban problems of the area would be to leave the existing municipal boundaries relatively untouched and to take over and administer metropolitan-wide services directly. However, this would place a heavy burden on the territorial government. In view of the different traditions on the Ontario and Quebec sides of the river and of the physical splitting of the urban area by the river itself, this plan also might impose an undesirable degree of uniformity in metropolitan services without significant savings in cost and efficiency.

For these reasons, the council might decide instead to create two second-tier metropolitan councils on the Toronto model, one on each side of the river, representing the local municipalities in each area. Although this would have much to commend it from the point of view of preserving local government and at the same time solving urban metropolitan problems, it would still leave an administrative gap between the Ottawa and Hull sides of the river, and would create a four-level division of responsibility—federal, territorial, metropolitan and local. One might easily argue that this pattern would be even more complicated than the present three-level division—federal, provincial and local. But the difference would be that each level would be legally and constitutionally subordinate to the next, so that there would not be the same constitutional difficulty of divided jurisdiction. Also, there would be a cross-representation of interests at all levels. The local units would have representation on the metropolitan councils, and local residents would have representatives on the territorial council, who would meet and reach agreement with federal representatives on that council. A complex social situation, requiring both diversity and interdependence, also requires complex interlocking governmental arrangements. It would not be as complex as the four-level division that the Jones Commission proposal for an Ottawa regional government would have created. The territorial council would have the power to require joint action by the two metropolitan governments, and could control or take over any service that concerned both sides of the river, such as pollution control and public transportation.

No matter what system of local government it created, the territorial council could be the focal point for the revision, approval, and completion of the National Capital Plan. Although the National Capital Commission might continue as a manager of federal properties in the area, its planning functions could be transferred either to a committee of the territorial council, which would have both federal and local representatives, or to a new planning commission which would be an arm of the territorial council. The new commission could have representatives named by the federal, territorial and metropolitan (or local) governments. The present planning staff of the National Capital Commission could be taken over by the territorial council to work either for the planning committee or for the new planning commission, and the federal government could afford to pay for all or most of the cost of this staff because of its saving on N.C.C. staff.

The National Capital Plan and any proposed revisions to it would, of course, have to be approved by both the federal government and the territorial council. Once it was approved, the council would have the power to carry out the Plan fully and completely. The council could require all local municipalities to prepare detailed plans that are in general conformity with the Master Plan, in somewhat the same way as local municipalities in the Ottawa Planning Area are expected to prepare plans in conformity with the official plan for the Area.

With the promise of generous financial support from the federal government, the territorial council would therefore be able to call for a bold and imaginative new Federal Capital Plan, a Plan that would require the creation of a revolutionary new network of freeways and other roads (as proposed in the Ottawa-Hull Area Transportation Study), the controlled development of the projected new cities beyond the Greenbelt and on the Hull side, and the reconstruction of the cores of Ottawa and Hull into a civic centre worthy of a national capital.

This outline of the changes that could come about under a territorial government is only a vision of what *might* be achieved. As long as the decisions are left partly to locally elected representatives—and this is the way it should be in a democracy—there is no guarantee that these objectives *would* be achieved. All one can argue is that they would *more likely* be achieved under a territorial government.

3. Alternatives

There are, of course, less far-reaching alternatives to the proposal for turning the National Capital Region into a federal territory. One is the idea of restricting the federal territory to the Ontario side of the river. This idea would solve the problem of the difference in legal systems, laws and traditions between the Ontario and Quebec sides of the river, and would avoid the difficulty of gaining Quebec's agreement to ceding the necessary territory. It would also make unnecessary the creation of a second-tier metropolitan government on the Ontario side. However, it would not create as good a linguistic and cultural balance and would leave the French-speaking Canadians within the territory in a much smaller minority. Nor would it be as good a solution to the problem of implementing the National Capital Plan on the Quebec side. Nevertheless, the co-operation of the new territorial government, and the continuing co-operation of a reorganized National Capital Commission with the Quebec Government and the municipalities on the Quebec side, might go far toward solving this problem. For example, the Government of Quebec and the local municipalities might be persuaded to create a planning body and a consolidated or two-tier metropolitan government for the whole urban area on the north side, with powers to complete the National Capital Plan on that side. In order to promote co-operation, the N.C.C. could include representatives of these new authorities, and could invite them to propose revisions in their share of the Plan.

A much less far-reaching alternative was proposed to the Bilingualism Commission by the Saint Jean-Baptiste Society of Eastview: that French should be made an official language in Ontario's legislature and municipalities. Alternatively, the federal government might achieve the objective of official bilingualism in the Ottawa area by attaching appropriate conditions to its grants to local municipalities for shared national capital projects. However, neither of these proposals would go far enough toward meeting the problems of bilingualism and biculturalism in the area. They would only change the status of French in the conduct of local government. Many more educational and cultural changes would be required to make the area truly bilingual and bicultural.

Another proposal, which is restricted to an attempted solution of the purely planning problem, is that the federal government could achieve the objective of a much more imaginative redevelopment of the centres of Ottawa and Hull by a radical extension of its policy of purchasing or expropriating the land that it wishes to control. Now that its power to expropriate land for the purposes of the National Capital Plan has been constitutionally validated by the Supreme Court, it could buy or expropriate the whole of the business sections that are directly adjoining or opposite Parliament Hill. The capital cost of this move would be tremendous, but the federal government could eventually recoup a great deal of the cost through redeveloping these areas and reselling blocks of land to private interests for use or for reconstruction under appropriate regulations for conformity with its plan for redevelopment. If there were doubts about the constitutionality of the federal Parliament's power to do this, it could perhaps buttress its case by declaring the reconstruction of the core of the national capital to be a "work for the general advantage of Canada," under Section 92, subsection 10 (c) of the *B.N.A. Act*, although it is doubtful whether the Courts would accept this as being a "work or undertaking" within the meaning of the Act.

This proposal may not be as breath-taking as it seems upon first impact, because the Ottawa-Hull Area Transportation Study projects a considerable rebuilding of the business core of Ottawa by 1986. It expects, however, that a good deal of the cost will be borne by the provincial and local governments. If the federal government expropriated and redeveloped this area it would face its former difficulties of opposition from private interests, lack of co-operation from the provincial and municipal governments, and insufficient provincial and local sharing of costs.

An alternative proposal is the delegation of provincial and local planning and other powers to the National Capital Commission. This proposal has been made a number of times in the past—for example, by Mr. Cauchon in his report of 1922, and by Mr. Watson Sellar, former Auditor-General, in his evidence before the parliamentary Committee of 1956, where it generated considerable discussion. While it would be constitutionally possible for one level of government to delegate powers to the agency of another, it would be difficult in practice to co-ordinate the delegation of uniform powers from both of the provincial governments and all of the municipalities. The delegation of any extensive powers would be politically unacceptable unless the National Capital Commission were in some way made directly representative of provincial and local interests in the area. For these reasons the delegation of power would very likely be restricted to a general control over the completion of the National Capital Plan. Like the previous proposal, its adoption would provide no solution to the more general problems of bilingualism and metropolitan government in the national capital.

4. Conclusion

A more general argument against a federal territory, which sums up most of the others, is that it is not needed: most of the problems it would solve are gradually being solved anyway, and the slight benefits to be achieved would not be worth the far-reaching constitutional, legal and political disturbances that would be required. To test the validity of this argument, one must balance the time, effort, energy and cost that would have to be put into the creation of the new territory against the benefits that might be achieved; and this in turn requires a consideration of the extent to which the four main problems—revising and implementing the National Capital Plan, governing the metropolitan area, achieving a bilingual and bicultural capital, and generally overcoming the difficulties of divided jurisdiction—are now being solved or may be solved without the creation of a federal territory.

It seems clear that if a federal territory is not adopted, many changes and improvements must be brought about in order to achieve results that are in any way comparable with the results probable under a federal territory. With regard to revising and implementing the National Capital Plan, for example, the provinces and local municipalities must be brought much more intimately into the planning process. This could be done most directly by providing for locally-named representatives on the National Capital Commission and adding provincial representatives. Moreover, suitable machinery for local planning and metropolitan government must be created for the whole Ottawa-Hull area. For instance, the membership and jurisdiction of the Ottawa Planning Area Board should be extended to include all of the future urban area on the Ottawa side, or preferably to include the boundaries of the National Capital Region, and the Ontario Government should ignore the Board's decisions only for very good reasons. On the Hull side two general planning committees already exist, one each for the urban areas east and west of the Gatineau river, but they are insufficiently supported by the provincial government. The municipalities in these areas are under no compulsion to adopt the committees' plans. Although the committee for the west side prepared a Master Plan report in 1964, an official of the Quebec Department of Municipal Affairs made this significant comment: "Its final report was handed in to the municipal councils concerned, and it is now up to these to carry out (or not carry out!) as they see fit the conclusion of the above report."[36]

A revised National Capital Plan will not be carried out satisfactorily, nor the urban area governed adequately, until some form of metropolitan government is created on each side of the river. The political prospect for the creation of metropolitan governments on each side is, I would say, fairly good. Many of the municipalities on the Ottawa side have already agreed that some form of two-tier metropolitan government is desirable. A move on the Ottawa side, especially with support from the Quebec Government, would no doubt stimulate a similar move on the Hull side. If no metropolitan governments are created, especially on the Ottawa side, the prospects for controlling the future development of the capital area are not good, and the proposal for a federal territory will become more and more attractive.

Regarding the bilingual-bicultural objective, the improvement of the national capital in this respect depends largely upon changes encouraged or required by the Ontario Government. The Government is already instituting changes in the school system designed to improve and extend the teaching of French, and it may decide to encourage or to require the use of French as an official language. But it is unlikely that these changes will come fast enough or go far enough to approach what might be achieved under a federal territory. If progress in this respect is slow, the attitude of Quebec and of the French-speaking Canadians in the area may shift rapidly in favour of a federal territory.

The principle that the federal government should have ultimate and comprehensive control over its own seat of government would, of course, be impossible to satisfy without the creation of a federal territory. Under the present system the old constitutional difficulty of divided jurisdiction will inevitably continue. The creation of a federal territory is often said to be difficult, if not impossible, because the co-operation and agreement of all interested parties—federal, provincial and local—would be needed. Yet even under the existing system a proper solution to all of the capital's problems requires many and continuous co-operative arrangements between all these parties.

The problem of balancing the probable advantages obtainable under a federal territory against the improvements that may take place in future without its creation is, however, a difficult one. No full-scale study has ever been made of the proposal, of the experience of federal districts elsewhere or of a detailed consideration of the problems of creating and governing a federal territory. The Bilingualism Commission has been studying the National Capital Region and may issue a report with recommendations for it, probably late in 1967. However, it is likely to concentrate on the bilingual-bicultural aspects of the problem. For these reasons, the Government of Ontario may wish to consider putting the proposal on the agenda of a federal-provincial conference and asking that a study committee be set up. This committee might be composed of persons named by the federal government, by at least the two provinces concerned, and perhaps also by the two main cities in the area. It could be asked to consider the proposal for a federal territory and other possible solutions to the problems of divided jurisdiction, planning, metropolitan government, bilingualism and biculturalism in the National Capital Region.

Footnotes

[1] *The Queen's Choice* (Ottawa, 1961), p. 143.
[2] *Confederation of Canada* (Toronto, 1872), p. 108.
[3] As quoted in Eggleston, p. 183.
[4] *Ibid.*
[5] National Capital Planning Service, *Plan For the National Capital: General Report* (Ottawa, 1950), p. 2.
[6] *Ibid.*, p. 3.
[7] Canada, Parliament, Joint Committee of the Senate and the House of Commons on the Federal District Commission, *Proceedings* No. 13 (June 8 and 12, 1956) p. 522.
[8] As quoted in Eggleston, p. 204.
[9] *Ibid.*, pp. 205-6.
[10] *Proceedings*, No. 20 (July 26 and 30, 1956), pp. 1050-51.
[11] *Ibid.*, p. 1053.
[12] *Harold Munro v. National Capital Commission*, judgment of June 28, 1966 (Supreme Court of Canada, pp. 10, mimeo.).
[13] B. W. G. Marley-Clarke, "The Policy and Administration of the Municipal Grants Act, 1951, As Amended" (M.A. Thesis, Carleton University, 1966), Appendix.
[14] For such purposes as urban redevelopment ($9.0 million), the Civic Hospital ($2.8 million), bridges and roads ($1.4 million), and elimination of railway crossings ($1.5 million). See City of Ottawa, *1966 Current Expenditure Budget*, Part I, p. 3; and *Minutes of the City Council*, Feb. 28, 1966, pp. 690-1.
[15] Ottawa *Citizen*, July 25 and 27, 1964.
[16] See story by Donna Dilschneider, Ottawa *Citizen*, August 6, 1966.
[17] Ottawa *Citizen*, August 8, 1966.
[18] De Leuw, Cather, and Beauchemin-Beaton-Lapointe, *Ottawa-Hull Area Transportation Study* (1965), p. 152.
[19] *Statistical Review: National Capital Region*, p. 10.
[20] Ottawa *Citizen*, August 30, 1966.

[21] As quoted in Eggleston, p. 102.
[22] His column of April 28, 1966, Ottawa *Citizen*.
[23] Quoted in Eggleston, p. 157.
[24] Fred Cook, "The City of Ottawa and its Relations to the Federal Authority", Address before the Unity Club of Ottawa (March 24, 1909), p. 15.
[25] The Federal Plan Commission of Ottawa and Hull, *Report on a General Plan for the Cities of Ottawa and Hull* (Ottawa, 1915), p. 13.
[26] See, for example, proposal by E. Dandenault in Montreal *Le Devoir*, Feb. 18, 1965, and comment on this by Ottawa *Citizen*, Feb. 24 and 27; and editorial favouring the idea in Montreal *Star*, March 31, 1965.
[27] Ottawa *Citizen*, Nov. 30, 1965. Dr. Marion also published an extended version in a French-American weekly, *Le Travailleur*, Oct. 21, 1965.
[28] See stories and editorials in *Citizen*, March 5, 7, 28, 29, 1966.
[29] Larry Smith and Company, *Economic Prospects, National Capital Region*, Ottawa, Canada, National Capital Commission, 1963, pp. 35-37.
[30] D. C. Rowat, "Planning and Metropolitan Government," *Canadian Public Administration* (March, 1955).
[31] *Master Plan for Hull*, p. 14.
[32] These figures were derived from 1961 Census of Canada, Bulletin 1.3-10, Table 123-3, by totalling those from the British Isles who speak English only and both English and French and those of French origin who speak French only and both English and French. Unfortunately, one cannot get for the total number of people whose mother tongue is English the number who speak French, except by derivation from the number who speak English only. In any case, this figure would include many whose ethnic origin was from other than the British Isles, even including some of French ethnic origin.
[33] *Le Droit*, Aug. 1, 1963. On the other hand, the former mayor of Lucerne has spoken in favour of a federal territory.
[34] Mr. McDonald told me that when he presented his brief before the Constitutional Committee in Quebec, he was sympathetically received and that his brief stimulated considerable interest and discussion.
[35] Ottawa, Eastview and Carleton Local Government Review. *Summary of Submissions*, p. 57.
[36] *What's New in Planning*, No. 7 (May, 1965), p. 20.

Bibliography*

A. Books

Bond, Courtney C. J., *City on the Ottawa* (Ottawa: Queen's Printer, 1961), 146 p.
Brault, Lucien, *Hull 1800-1950* (Ottawa: Les Editions de l'Université d'Ottawa, 1950), 262 p. (in French) [Carleton]; *Ottawa Old and New* (Ottawa: Ottawa Historical Information Institute, 1946), 349 p.
Davies, Blodwen, *The Charm of Ottawa* (Toronto: McClelland & Stewart, 1932), 250 p.
Derthick, Martha, *City Politics in Washington, D.C.* (Cambridge: Harvard University Press, 1962), 239 p.
Eggleston, Wilfrid, *The Queen's Choice* (Ottawa: Queen's Printer, 1961), 325 p.
Gray, John Hamilton, *Confederation of Canada* (Toronto: Copp Clark, 1872), 432 p.
Ketchum, Carleton J., *Federal District Capital* (Ottawa: Runge, 1939), 118 p. [Carleton].
Robson, W. A., ed., *Great Cities of the World: Their Government Politics and Planning* (London: Allen & Unwin, rev. 1957), 814 p. (includes Buenos Aires and Rio de Janeiro)
Ross, A. H. D., *Ottawa Past and Present* (Toronto: Musson, 1927), 224 p.
Schmeckebier, L. F., *The District of Columbia* (Baltimore, 1928)
Schmeckebier, L. F., and W. F. Willoughby, *The Government and Administration of the District of Columbia; Suggestions for Change* (Washington, D.C., 1929)
Wigmore, Lionel, *The Long View: a History of Canberra, Australia's National Capital* (Melbourne: F. W. Cheshire, 1963), 240 p.

*For an item which may be difficult to obtain, I have shown, in square brackets, in which Ottawa library it may be found. Some relevant historical references were taken from Lucien Brault's extensive bibliography on Ottawa in 24 *Revue de l'Université d'Ottawa* (1954), pp. 345-75, and I have not seen them.

B. Reports and Documents

Australia, Department of the Interior, "Canberra—Its Origin; A Brief History of Its Government; A Survey of Some Proposals for Reform", background notes prepared by Planning Section (Canberra, 1965), 17 p. mimeo [Rowat]

Bain, H. M., *The Governing of Metropolitan Washington* (Washington: U.S.G.P.O., 1958), 98 p. [Carleton]

Beauchesne, A., "Choice of Ottawa as the Capital of Canada," Transactions (1901-1938) of Women's Canadian Historical Society of Ottawa, No. 10, 1928, p. 55 [Brault]

Canada, Department of Northern Affairs and National Resources, *The Northwest Territories Today, A Reference Paper for the Advisory Commission on the Development of Government in the Northwest Territories* (Ottawa: Queen's Printer, 1965), 136 p.

Canada, Federal District Commission, *Brief Submitted to the Joint Committee of the Senate and the House of Commons* (Ottawa: the Commission, 1956), 97 p. [Carleton]

Canada, Federal Plan Commission of Ottawa and Hull, *Report on a General Plan for the Cities of Ottawa and Hull* (Ottawa: the Commission, 1915), 155 p. [Carleton]

Canada, National Capital Commission, *Apropos of the Capital of Canada* (Ottawa: Queen's Printer, 1964), 72 p.

Canada, National Capital Commission, *Annual Reports* to 1965-66 (66th) (Ottawa: the Commission, each in 2 vols.)

Canada, National Capital Commission, *Statistical Review with Explanatory Notes: National Capital Region* (Ottawa: the Commission, 1964), 156 p.

Canada, National Capital Planning Committee, Information Committee, *Planning Canada's National Capital* (Ottawa: Federal District Commission, 1948), 48 p. [Carleton]

Canada, National Capital Planning Service, *Plan For the National Capital: General Report* (Ottawa: King's Printer, 1950), 307 p. [Carleton and N.C.C.]

Canada, National Capital Planning Service, *Plan for the National Capital Preliminary Report* (Ottawa: King's Printer, 1948), 137 p. [Rowat]

Canada, Parliament, Joint Committee of the Senate and the House of Commons on Relations Between Federal Government and Ottawa, *Proceedings* (Ottawa: King's Printer, 1944) [Carleton]

Canada, Parliament, Joint Committee of the Senate and the House of Commons on the Federal District Commission, *Minutes of Proceedings and Evidence* (Ottawa: Queen's Printer, 1956), 1056 p. [Carleton]

Canada, Parliament, *National Capital Act* (7 Elizabeth II, Chap. 27, 1958), 14 p.

Capital District Recreation Planning Survey Committee, *Capital District Planning Survey* (Ottawa, the Committee, 1951), 168 p. mimeo [Carleton]

City of Ottawa Government (Ottawa, 1919), 74 p. Pub. Arch., broch. II, 4859

Community Planning Association of Canada, Committee of the Ottawa Branch, *Intergovernmental Relations in the Ottawa Area* (Ottawa: the Committee, 1952), 9 p. mimeo

Cook, Fred, "City Government in Ottawa", 14 p. reprint from *University of Toronto Quarterly*, 1907 [Pub. Arch.]

————, "The City of Ottawa and its Relations to the Federal Authority," Address before the Unity Club of Ottawa (March 24, 1909), 16 p.

De Leuw, Cather & Co., *The Queensway Limited—Access Highway* (1955)

De Leuw, Cather & Co., and Beauchemin-Beaton-Lapointe, *Ottawa-Hull Area Transportation Study* (Ottawa: prepared for the City of Ottawa, 1965), 154 p. [Carleton and N.C.C.]

Dillon, M. M., & Co., *Southern Entrance Freeway* (1962)

Dominion Consultant Associates Ltd., *A National Centre for the Performing Arts* (Ottawa: National Capital Arts Alliance, 1963) [Carleton]

Gore & Storrie, Ltd., *Ottawa Planning Area Board Report on Water Supply and Sewage Disposal* (Toronto: prepared for the O.P.A.B., 1949), 96 p. [Rowat]

Hull City Planning Commission and General Planning Committee of the City of Hull and Its Environs, *Master Plan for Hull, Aylmer, Hull South, Deschenes, Hull West (Part)* (Hull: City Planning Commission, 1964), 94 p. [Carleton and N.C.C.]

Hull, City Planning Commission and General Planning Committee of the City of Hull and Its Environs, *Urban Renewal Report: Hull 1962* (Hull: City Planning Commission, 1963), 205 p. [Carleton and N.C.C.]

Kear, A. R., *Provincial Status for the National Capital Region,* a brief presented to the Royal Commission on Bilingualism and Biculturalism, Aug. 19, 1964 (Fredericton: the author, 1964), 16 p. mimeo. [Rowat]

Marley-Clarke, B. W. G., *The Policy and Administration of the Municipal Grants Act, 1951, As Amended* (Ottawa: M.A. Thesis, Carleton, 1966), 121 p.

McDonald, John H., *Submission to the Province of Quebec Parliamentary Committee on the Constitution,* March 31, 1965 (Ottawa: the author, 1965), 27 p. mimeo. [Rowat]

National Capital Commission v. Munro, Canada Law Reports, Exchequer Court of Canada (Part V—1965—of Vol. 2), pp. 579-645.

Ottawa, City Corporation, *Centenary of Ottawa, 1854-1954* (Ottawa: City Corporation, 1954), 76 p. [Rowat]

Ottawa, City Corporation, *Proposals for Urban Renewal Action* (Ottawa: City Corporation, 1963)

Ottawa, Eastview and Carleton County Local Government Review, *Final Report and Recommendations* (Toronto: prepared for the Department of Municipal Affairs, 1965), 66 p. [Carleton]

Ottawa, Eastview and Carleton County Local Government Review, *Report on Research Findings* (Toronto: prepared for the Department of Municipal Affairs, 1965), 212 p. [Carleton]

Ottawa, Eastview and Carleton County Local Government Review, *Summary of Submissions at Public Hearings* (Toronto: prepared for the Department of Municipal Affairs, 1965), 184 p. [Carleton]

Ottawa Improvement Commission, *Special Report of the Ottawa Improvement Commission from 1899 to 1912* [Pub. Arch.]

Ottawa Planning Area Board, *Official Plan of the Ottawa Planning Area* (Ottawa: City of Ottawa, 1963)

Ottawa Planning Area Board, *Report on the Future Development of the City of Ottawa and Its Environs* (Ottawa: the Board, 1947), 16 p. [Rowat]

Parkin, John B., Associates, *Confederation Square Development* (1962)

Pomeroy, Hugh R., *Report to the Ottawa Planning Area Board* (Ottawa: prepared for the O.P.A.B., 1948), 20 p. mimeo. [Rowat]

Putman, J. H., *City Government, Ottawa* (Ottawa, 1919) [Parl. Lib.]

Rowat, Donald C., *Ottawa's Future Development and Needs,* a brief prepared for the submission by the City of Ottawa to the Royal Commission on Canada's Economic Prospects (Ottawa: City of Ottawa, 1956), 57 p. [Rowat]

Rutherford, Geddes W., *Administrative Problems in a Metropolitan Area: the National Capital Region* (Chicago: Public Administration Service, 1952), 63 p. [Carleton]

Smith, Larry & Co., *Economic Prospects of the National Capital Region, Ottawa, Canada* (Toronto: prepared for the National Capital Commission, 1963), 107 p. [N.C.C.]

Smith, Wilbur, and Associates, *Traffic and Transportation Plan for Ottawa, Canada* (New Haven: prepared for the City of Ottawa, 1955), 245 p. [Rowat]

Statesman's Year-Book, 1965-66 (Toronto: Macmillan, 1965), for reference re federal capitals elsewhere.

Todd, F. G., *Report of F. G. Todd to the Ottawa Improvement Commission* (Ottawa, 1903), 40 p. [N.C.C. and Carleton]

United States, Congress, Joint Committee on Washington Metropolitan Problems: *Hearings,* Senate Reports and Staff Studies and Reports (Washington: U.S.G.P.O., 1958) [Rowat]

What's New in Planning (Community Planning Association of Canada, National Capital Region Branch), Nos. 1-8, 1957-66

C. Journal Articles

"A Federal District for Ottawa," *Journal of the Town Planning Institute of Canada,* (April, 1922, editorial article summarizing the Cauchon plan for Ottawa submitted to a sub-committee of the Senate), 5 p. [Rowat and N.C.C.]

Adamson, Anthony, "The Role of the Capital in Canada's National Life," an address to the Rotary "Adventure in Citizenship" Students (May 14, 1958), 12 p. mimeo. [Rowat and N.C.C.]

Cook, Fred, "The Evolution of the Federal District Idea," a series of articles in an Ottawa newspaper (1938), 17 p. [Rowat and N.C.C.]

Flaherty, Frank, "Gift Suggestion for Canada's 100th Birthday: Make Ottawa Our 11th Province," *Weekend Magazine* (June 29, 1963), pp. 1-4, 23

Fraser, Blair, "The Grave Inequalities in Our Separate Schools," *Macleans* (May 28, 1955), pp. 9-11, 58-61

Gibson, James A., "How Ottawa Became the Capital of Canada," 46 *Ontario History* (Aut., 1954), pp. 213-22

Higgins, Benjamin, "Canberra: A Garden Without a City," I *Community Planning Review* (Aug. 1951), pp. 88-102

Kopkind, Andrew and J. Ridgeway, "Washington the Lost Colony," *New Republic* (April 23, 1966), pp. 13-17

Macdonald, Bruce, "Hopes Raised for Washington Home Rule Bill," *Globe and Mail Magazine* (Dec. 12, 1964), p. 5

Marion, Seraphin, article in *La Vie Franco-Ontarienne* (Association Canadienne-française d'Education d'Ontario, Nov., 1965).

Perry, J. H., "We Don't Want a Federal District for Ottawa," 31 *Canadian Business* (Feb., 1958), pp. 84-6, 88-91

Rowat, Donald C., "Planning and Metropolitan Government," *Canadian Public Administration* (March, 1955)

—————, "Toronto and Montreal Should Be Provinces," *Macleans* (June 16, 1962), pp. 46-8

Rutherford, G. W., "Reorganization of the Government of the District of Columbia," XXXIII *American Political Science Review* (Aug. 1939), pp. 653-55

Spence-Sales, Harold, "The Preliminary Report on the Plan for the National Capital of Canada," *Layout for Living* (July, 1949)

"Why Capital District Sought—and Fought—by Ottawans," 59 *Financial Post* (May 29, 1965), p. 73 [Special issue on Ottawa]

```
352        Fullerton, Douglas H    R
.071          The capital of Canada :
384        how should it be governed?
F971
v.2
```

DATE DUE	BORROWER'S NAME	GRADE
MAY 2	Mr Steele	M5
AUG 11 1978	J D Currie	M2

```
352        Fullerton, Douglas H
.071          The capital of Canada :
384        how should it be governed?
F971
v.2
```

Wakefield Mill
Wakefield
Valley
366
Covered Bridge
Pont Couvert
Promenade
Lapêche
Wilson's Corner
Blackburn
PARC DE LA GATINEAU PARK
Beach Plage
Lac Philippe
Taylor Lake
Ramsay L
Belvédère Grandview Lookout
Picnic Field Pique-nique
Lac des Lacs
Gate Barrière
Caverne Lusk Cave
Lac Mousseau (Harrington)
Tour de garde-feu Fire Tower
Picnic Pique-nique
Farm Point
Patterson
Cascades
Chemin-des-Pins
Burnet
Larrimac
GATINEAU
Meach Bk
Meach Lake
Kirks Ferry
Gleneagle
Tenaga
Chelsea
Lac-Meach
Belvédère Champlain Lookout
Belvédère Etienne Brulé Lookout
Camp Fortune
Belvédère Huron Lookout
Kingsmere L
Kingsmere
Old Chelsea
Lariault's Hill
Moorside
Pink L
Eardley
Parker
CP
Luskville
Eardley Sta
Lusk
Heyworth
Breckenridge
OUTAOUAIS
QUEBEC
ONTARIO
Constance Bay
Kilmaurs
Woodlawn
CN
Dunrobin
Constance L
Malwood
Mud Pond
Harwood Plains
Simmons
Aylmer
Deschênes
LAC DESCHÊNES LAKE
Marchhurst
Elm
Carp
Carp River
Aérodrome Carp Airfield
South March
Strathcarn
Shirleys Bay
Crystal Bay
Kanata
Trend Village
Bells Corners
Eaglesons Corners
Glencairn
Hazeldean
Huntley
Fallowfield
Corkery
Old Stittsville
Stittsville
Manion Corners
Stanley Corners
Twin Elm
8
9
5
17
18
7
10
11
12
20
44
3
109
129
139